A

GUIDE TO HINDUSTANI

IN PERSIAN AND ROMAN CHARACTER
SPECIALLY DESIGNED FOR

THE USE OF

OFFICERS AND MEN SERVING IN INDIA

A GUIDE TO HINDUSTANI

IN PERSIAN AND ROMAN CHARACTER SPECIALLY DESIGNED FOR

THE USE OF

OFFICERS AND MEN SERVING IN INDIA

INCLUDING COLLOOUIAL PHRASES A
COLLECTION OF ARZIS, WITH TRANSLITERATION
AND ENGLISH TRANSLATIONS

G. S. A. RANKING

GYAN

Published by

GYAN

Gyan Publishing House
5, Ansari Road
Daryaganj, New Delhi-110002
Phone: 011-47034999, 9811692060
E-mail: books@gyanbooks.com

Distribution Network
gyanbooks.com
India, USA, Canada, UK, Australia

ISBN: 978-93-6780-152-9 (PB)

First Published, 1897

2nd Impression 2024

Printed at: Gyan Press, Delhi.

A GUIDE TO HINDUSTANI IN PERSIAN AND ROMAN CHARACTER
Author: G. S. A. RANKING

A GUIDE

TO

HINDUSTANI.

A

GUIDE TO HINDUSTANI

IN PERSIAN AND ROMAN CHARACTER

SPECIALLY DESIGNED FOR

THE USE OF

OFFICERS AND MEN SERVING IN INDIA,

INCLUDING COLLOQUIAL PHRASES
A COLLECTION OF ARZIS, WITH TRANSLITERATION
AND ENGLISH TRANSLATIONS.

BY

G. S. A. RANKING, M.A., M.D., CANTAB.,
SURG.-LIEUT.-COL., INDIAN MEDICAL SERVICE,
Secy. to the Board of Examiners, Fort William, Member of the Royal Asiatic Society, Member of the Asiatic Society of Bengal. Author of "Elements of Arabic and Persian Prosody," "Urdu Prose Composition," "Colloquial Urdu."

Fourth Edition, Revised and Enlarged.

CALCUTTA:
THACKER, SPINK AND CO.,
LONDON: W. THACKER AND CO., 2, CREED LANE,
1897.

PREFACE TO FOURTH EDITION.

The present Edition has been carefully revised and some additions made to the text and notes.

The system of transliteration finally adopted by the Asiatic Society of Bengal has been substituted for that given in the last edition.

I am glad to know that the book has been helpful to students of Urdu.

G. R.

CALCUTTA:
March, 1897.

PREFACE TO THIRD EDITION.

In this Edition I have endeavoured to increase the utility of the book by the addition of much that I had omitted for the sake of brevity in former editions, and it is hoped that the book will now offer far greater facilities for acquiring a knowledge of Urdu than have hitherto been available within the compass of a single volume.

G. R.

CALCUTTA:
June, 1895.

CONTENTS.

A GUIDE TO HINDUSTANI.

PART I.

A CONCISE GRAMMAR OF URDU.

The Hindustani alphabet is the Arabic alphabet with modifications, including as it does certain letters to represent sounds which do not occur in Hindi words, while on the other hand certain letters are exclusively confined to words of Hindi origin.

This composite character of the alphabet is a necessity of the language, composed as it is of three vocabularies—Sanskrit, Arabic and Persian.

Urdu is written in the Persian character, from right to left, while the Nāgri (or *Hindī* character) is written from left to right.

The following table gives the letters in the Persian character; it should be remembered that the dots are the essential part of the letters—many letters being exactly similar in form, and indistinguishable except by their dots—as will be seen from a glance at the subjoined alphabet.

Alphabet in the Persian Character.

Name.	Form.	English Transliteration.	Combined Form.		
			Final.	Medial	Initial
alif	ا	ā	ـا	ـا	ا
be	ب	b	ـب	ـبـ	بـ
pe	پ	p	ـپ	ـپـ	پـ
te	ت	t	ـت	ـتـ	تـ
ṭe	ٹ	ṭ	ـٹ	ـٹـ	ٹـ
se	ث	s̤	ـث	ـثـ	ثـ
jím	ج	j	ـج	ـجـ	جـ
che	چ	ch*	ـچ	ـچـ	چـ
ḥe	ح	ḥ	ـح	ـحـ	حـ
khe	خ	kh	ـخ	ـخـ	خـ
dál	د	d	ـد	ـد	د
ḍál	ڈ	ḍ	ـڈ	ـڈ	ڈ
zál	ذ	z̤	ـذ	ـذ	ذ
re	ر	r	ـر	ـر	ر
ṛe	ڑ	ṛ	ـڑ	ـڑ	ڑ
ze	ز	z	ـز	ـز	ز
zhe	ژ	zh	ـژ	ـژ	ژ

* See page 4.

Name.	Form.	English Transliteration.	Combined Form.		
			Final.	Medial	Initial.
sín	س	s	ـس	ـسـ	سـ
shín	ش	sh	ـش	ـشـ	شـ
ṣád	ص	ṣ	ـص	ـصـ	صـ
ẓád	ض	ẓ	ـض	ـضـ	ضـ
ṭoë	ط	ṭ	ـط	ـطـ	طـ
z̤oë	ظ	z̤	ـظ	ـظـ	ظـ
‘ain	ع	‘	ـع	ـعـ	عـ
ghain	غ	gh	ـغ	ـغـ	غـ
fe	ف	f	ـف	ـفـ	فـ
qáf	ق	q	ـق	ـقـ	قـ
káf	ک	k	ـک	ـکـ	کـ
gáf	گ	g (*as in gate*)	ـگ	ـگـ	گـ
lám	ل	l	ـل	ـلـ	لـ
mím	م	m	ـم	ـمـ	مـ
nún	ن	n	ـن	ـنـ	نـ
hamza	ء	, or -*	ء	ـئـ	ئـ
wao	و	o *or* w	ـو	ـو	و
he	ه	h	ـه	ـهـ	هـ
ye	ی	e *or* y	ـی	ـیـ	یـ

* See page 10.

The foregoing Table gives in the third column the English letters by which in transliteration the several letters of the Urdu Alphabet is to be represented.

These forms are with one exception (ch= چ) those agreed upon by the Asiatic Society of Bengal and used in all publications of that Society: There چ is represented by "c" in deference to Continental usage, but as the object of transliteration is to represent sound, "ch" seems the proper form for use in English.

As a necessary consequence of the connection of letters in writing, only the essential part of the letter is written, that is to say, the general form of the letter is indicated, and is distinguished from its fellows by the dots. The letters may be thus divided into classes. Certain of the letters are never joined to the letter following them. These letters are:

ا د ڈ ذ ر ڑ ز ژ و

It is evident that any attempt to join these letters to the left would render them unrecognizable.

Note.—In manuscripts this rule is not always observed, and it should be remembered, that *dál* and *re* are not infrequently found in manuscripts joined to the letter following.

Vowels.

The vowels in Urdu are either short vowels or long vowels. The former are represented by certain marks placed above or below the consonants with which they are pronounced, while the latter are written by means of the letters ا *Alif* و *wao* or ی *ye*, with one or other of the marks used to represent the short vowel sounds, which are as follows:—

The short *u* sound of the English language (as in the word

"butter") is represented in Urdu by a short diagonal stroke from right to left, and from above downwards, written above the consonant with which it is to be pronounced, and called *fatha.*

For example.—The syllable "sun" is written in Urdu letters thus سَن *san*, and has the meaning of *hemp.*

The short *i* sound is represented in Urdu by a short diagonal stroke similar to the above, but written *below* the consonant with which it is to be pronounced, and called *kasra.*

For example.—The syllable "Dikk" is written in Urdu thus, دِقّ *diqq*, and has the meaning of *trouble, annoyance.*

The *u* sound which in English is heard in the words bull, pull, full, is represented in Urdu by a short diagonal stroke with a loop at its upper end, written *above* the letter with which it is pronounced, and called *zamma.*

For example.—The syllable "pull" is written in Urdu, thus پُل *pul*, and has the meaning of "*a bridge.*"

The long vowels are as follows :—

The long *a* sound is represented in Urdu by the letter Alif. At the commencement of a word, this Alif has a second Alif written horizontally over it, while in the middle of a word, the Alif is simply accompanied by the vowel mark *fatha*, written or understood.

For example.—The word "ardour" is represented in Urdu letters, thus آدَر—*ādar*, and has the meaning of *respect* or *honour.*

The word "farm" is represented in Urdu letters, thus فام *fām*, which word means *having-the-colour-of.*

The long *ū* sound is represented in Urdu by the letter *wao* و together with the vowel mark called "*zamma.*"

For example.—The sound "boot" is written in Urdu thus, بُوت *būt*, and is a word meaning *strength, power.*

The long ī sound is represented in Urdu by the letter Ye ی together with the vowel mark "*kasra.*"

For example.—The sound "beer" is written in Urdu thus, بِیر *bīr*, and is a word meaning "*a hero*" "*warrior.*"

These sounds are called معروف *ma'rūf* or "known."

The sound *o*, as in the English word *rope* is represented by the letter و *wao* without any vowel mark.

For example.—The syllable "rope" is written in Urdu thus, روپ *rop* and means *a stalk of grass or corn.*

The *a* sound, represented by the English words *fate, mate,* &c., is represented in Urdu by the letter ی *ye*, without any vowel mark.

For example.—The syllable "pate" is written in Urdu thus, پیٹ *peṭ* and means "*stomach,*" "*belly.*"

These two latter sounds are called مجہول *majhūl*, or "unknown."

DIPHTHONGS.—The above are the simple short and long vowel sounds; there remain certain diphthongs which are as follows:—

The sound *ai*, as in the English word "aisle," is represented in Urdu by the letter ی combined with the vowel "fatha," thus the word "aisle" would be written in Urdu letters اَیل *ail.*

The word for a bullock is بَیل =*bail* pronounced to rhyme with *aisle* as above.

The sound *ow*, as in the English word "cow," is represented in Urdu by the letter و *wáo*, with *Fatha.*

For example.—The word "now" would be in Urdu letters نَو *nau* and is a Persian word meaning "*new.*"

The above give all the sounds of the vowels and diphthongs.

The following words are given as further examples, and as an exercise in reading.

مَطلَب - مِنشار - لُوٹنا - کھیوَٹ - پَیٹھنا - پَنگُو - پَنکھا

Pankhā - *Pangū* - *Paiṭhnā* - *Khewaṭ* - *Lūṭnā* - *Minshār* - *Maṭlab.*
Fan - Cripple - To enter - A rower - To rob - A saw - Object.

روپنا - رونا - رَولا - بَیٹھنا - سینا - سِینا - کُنجی

Kunjī - *Sīnā* - *Senā* - *Baiṭhnā* - *Raulā* - *Ronā* - *Ropnā.*
A key - To sew - Army - To sit - Noise - To weep - To plant.

Pronunciation of Consonants.

It is necessary to say a few words upon the pronunciation of certain letters which are not represented in their transliteration by exactly equivalent English letters. These are

ت ٹ ث چ خ ڈ ذ ڑ ش ص ض ط ع غ ق

To take these in order.

ت This letter is softer in pronunciation than our English "t" and has a sound somewhat more nearly approaching to "th." Practice will alone suffice for its due pronunciation.

ٹ This letter (which may be also written ٹ, *e.g.*, in manuscripts), answers more nearly to our English "t."

ث This letter only occurs in words of Arabic origin, and has a sound exactly answering to the English "s" pronounced with a "lisp." In Hindūstānī however this accurate distinction is very rarely made, and the letter is pronounced as "s" Thus باعث *bā'is̤*.

چ This letter has the sound of "ch" in "chin" or "cheese."

خ This letter has no exact equivalent in English.

The "ch" of the Scottish "*loch*," represents it exactly. Also the "ch" of German, as in the words "*durch*" "*nicht*" very closely approaches the sound.

د The soft *dál* د bears the same relation to "d" and "dh" that the soft ت does to "t" and "th."

ڈ This letter may also be written ڐ, and its sound is that of an English "d" before another consonant, as in "mad man," *i.e.*, more accentuated than when preceding a vowel.

ذ This letter is pronounced in Urdu as the English "z," though its true Arabic value is between "z" and "dh."

ژ This letter is of very infrequent occurrence, and is only found in Persian words. Its sound has no English letter answering to it, though the "z," as pronounced in the word "azure," approaches very near it. The French "j" in the words "jour" - "joli" is exactly equivalent to it, this last word might be written ژولی.

ش This letter is equivalent to our English "sh," for example,

شا باش = *s̲h̲ābās̲h̲* = Bravo.

ص For ordinary purposes it is sufficient, if this letter be pronounced as "s." But in the mouth of a native it has a trace of the "w" sound, as in our word "suavity." Its pronunciation is facilitated by approximating the inner surface of the cheeks to the side teeth, and slightly protruding the lips while pronouncing the "s" sound, the sides of the tongue falling against the inner surface of the teeth.

ض This is even more difficult to pronounce accurately than the foregoing letter, but if the "z" sound be aimed at with cheeks and tongue in the abovementioned position, a very close approximation to the proper pronunciation will result.

ط In pronouncing this "t" sound, the rule given for ص should also be followed.

ع Is strongly guttural, but is usually pronounced like Alif-hamzá at the commencement of a word, and like an abbreviated Alif in the middle of a word. At the end of a word it has a faint "e" sound, but is practically unheard.

In words beginning with ع the tongue must be depressed and the throat well open, the sound emitted will then be fairly representative.

غ The pronunciation of this letter is a matter of considerable difficulty. It is a back-guttural, and there is no sound in English corresponding with it. It bears the same relationship to the "g" sound that خ does to the "k" sound.

Thus—if in the word "loch" we substitute "g" for the "k" sound and pronounce the word thus formed in accordance with the substituted letter, we shall get an approximation to the sound of غ, *e.g.*, تغمه *tag͟hma*, medal.

ق This letter has a sound very like the "q" in "quoit." It is enunciated by uttering a "k" sound with the cheeks applied to the sides of the teeth and the lips slightly protruded, *e.g.*, قابل *qābil*, able. قاعده *qā'ida*, a rule.

Platts' Hindustani Grammar gives a good example by saying it closely resembles the sound uttered by a crow in its "caw."

The letter ر (r) is generally so carelessly pronounced in English that great care must be taken to pronounce this letter fully in Hindustani; even with a slight "roll."

The letters و and ی have a double value, either as consonants or vowels, as the case may be.

If followed by a vowel sound they are consonants, as in the words واجب *wājib* and یونان *yūnān*.

If followed by a consonant they are vowels, as in the words مَوکب *maukib*, میزان *mīzān*.

ALIF HAMZA.—Alif, at the commencement of a word has no sound value, but is merely a graphic sign, a prop for the *hamza* ء which is pronounced. It has therefore only an exponential value, and the sound will differ according as the hamza ء is to be pronounced with one or other of the three vowels before mentioned.

Thus أَ = *a* إِ = *i* أُ = *u*

Hamza is, as will be seen from its form, simply an abbreviated ع.

Hamza when unaccompanied by ا is merely a breathing as in the words طاؤس *ṭá-ús* a peacock, where it is necessary to separate the two vowel sounds *ā* and *ū*. In this position it is to be represented in transliteration by a hyphen, as above shewn. At the beginning of words it is represented in transliteration simply by the vowel which it represents in sound, that is by a, i, or w (*see* pages 20-21).

Alif, with a horizontal Alif written above it at the beginning of a word, forms the long syllable ā. *E. g.*, آسمان *āsmān*, the sky. The Alif written above is called *madda*, or prolongation, and the two together are called *Alif mamdūda*, the prolonged Alif.

Care should be taken in pronouncing this long Alif to avoid a too common European vulgarism by which the sound ā is perverted to *aw*: Thus the word ڈاک meaning "post" is to be pronounced *Dāk* not *Dawk*: thus ڈاک آیا ھی = *ḍāk āyā hai.* When two *wáos* occur together the first is pronounced almost like a "v" thus قوّت power, is pronounced *quv-wat*; اوّل first, is pronounced *av-wal*.

ORTHOGRAPHICAL SIGNS.

TASHDĪD.—When any letter is required to be doubled the sign ّ is written above it. This sign is called تشدید *tashdīd*, or strengthening, and represents the letter ش.

For example, in the words:—

مُشَرَّف *musharraf*, honoured, exalted.

تَكَلُّم *takallum*, conversation.

مُرَبِّی *murabbī*, a teacher, tutor.

TANWĪN.—When a vowel mark *Fatha*, *Kasra* or *Zamma* is required to be doubled it is written double and then acquires an additional sound of "n." Thus, ً *an* ٍ *in* ٌ *un*.

For this reason it is called تنوین *tanwin*, "giving the sound of *n*." In Urdu the *Fatha* is the only vowel mark that undergoes this change: as for example—

فوراً *fauran*, at once. اتّفاقاً *ittifāqan*, by chance.

But in phrases of Arabic which will be met with in reading, both *Tanwín zamma* and *Tanwín kasra* will also be found to occur.

Jazm.—When it is intended that any consonant is to be silent, that is to say, not accompanied by any vowel sound, this fact must be signified in writing by inserting a mark called جَزْم *jazm*, or سُكُون *sukūn* above the consonant.

This sign is either a small circle ٥, or an incomplete circular mark ° placed above the quiescent consonant.

Example.—بولْنا *bolnā*, to speak.

Here, if it were not for the "*jazm*," we might read this word as *bolanā*, as unless there is some indication to the contrary the vowel mark *fatha* is to be understood in all syllables.

A consonant thus made quiescent is called ساكِن *sākin*, *i.e.*, resting; while a consonant pronounced with a vowel is called مُتَحَرِّك *mutaḥarrik*, moving.

There is another mark called وَصله *waslah* which is used only in phrases from the Arabic. It has this form ٮ and is placed over the initial *Alif* of a word in construction with another, to shew that the *Alif* is elided in pronunciation: Thus عبدُ الله, *'Abdu'llah*, not *'Abdu Allah*, which is the full value of the letters.

Numerals.

Every letter in the alphabet has a special numerical value attached to it, but the following figures are those which are ordinarily used to denote the date, year, page of a book, &c., &c. : they are as follows :—

۱	۲	۳	۴	۵	۶	۷	۸	۹	۰
1	2	3	4	5	6	7	8	9	0

they are compounded in exactly the same way as our numerals ; *e.g.*, ۱۰ = 10, ۱۸۷۷ = 1877.

Hindi Numerals.

1	2	3	4	5	6	7	8	9	10
१	२	३	४	५	६	७	८	९	१०

The figures are compounded just as in English.
Thus 1891 = १८९१.

The Abjad.

The values of the letters are shewn in the following line :—

ابجد هوز حطي كلمن سعفص قرشت ثخذ ضظغ

Where the first ten letters represent the numerals from 1 to 10 the eleventh letter represents 20, the twelfth 30 and so on up to 100, the next after 100 is 200 and so on up to 1,000.

Thus ابجد *abjad* = 1 + 2 + 3 + 4 = 10 and so on.

These values are assigned to the letters for the purpose of enabling dates to be expressed in words, forming Chronograms. *For example:* The date of the death of the author of the Urdú-i-Mu'alla in 1285 Hijrí, is thus expressed :

To-day his speech is ended اج اونکا سخن تمام ہوا

The sum of these letters will be found to give the date 1285.

Alphabet in the Hindi Character.

In writing Hindi the Nāgri or Devanāgri character is employed.

It is written from left to right.

The following gives the forms of the letters with their equivalent sounds in the Roman character.

The written character will be found to differ from the printed forms far less than in Urdu. Examples of it will be found at the end of MSS. exercises—

Vowels.

Character.	Sound.	Note.
अ	a (short)	Medial form ा
आ	ā (long)	
इ	i (short)	,, ,, ि
ई	ī (long)	,, ,, ी
उ	u	,, ,, ु
ऊ	ū	,, ,, ू
ए	e	,, ,, े above the letter.
ऐ	ai	,, ,, ै above the letter.
ओ	o	,, ,, ो
औ	an	,, ,, ौ
अं anusvára	u nasal	,, ,, ं above the letter.
अः visarga		,, ,, ः

Consonants.

Character.	Sound.	Character.	Sound.
क	k	द	d *soft*
ख	kh	ध	dh *soft*
ग	g	प	p
घ	gh	फ	ph
ङ	ng	ब	b
च	ch	भ	bh
छ	chh	म	m
ज	j	य	y
झ or ञ	jh	र	r *soft*
ट	t *hard*	ल	l
ठ	th *hard*	व	w
ड	d *hard*	श initial form	Sh
ढ	dh *hard*	ष medial form	Sh
ण or न	n	स	s
त	t *soft*	ह	h
थ	th *soft*		

Double letters in most common use.

Character.	Sound.	Example.	
क्ष	Ksh	परिक्षित	Parikshit
ज्ञ	gy	आज्ञा	Agyá
त्र	tr	पुत्र	Putr
त्त	tt	उत्तर	Uttar
द्ध	ddh	बुद्ध	Buddh
ऋ (initial form)	ri	ऋतु	Ritu
ृ medial form	ri	भृङ्गी	Bhringi
श्र	Shr	श्री	Shri
भृ	bhr	भृङ्गी	Bhringí
ङ्ग	ng	मङ्गल	Mangal
हु	hú	हुआ	húá
द्व	dw	द्वीप	dwip
ध्य	dhy	बध्य	badhya
द्य	dy	विद्या	vidiyá

The Article.

There is no regular article in Hindustani, the noun when standing alone being either definite or indefinite according to the context. The numeral adjective ایک "*ek*" = "one" is frequently used in the place of our indefinite article "a" or "an:" while the demonstrative pronoun وه "*woh*" supplies the place of the definite article "the."

Accidence.

Some of the words composing a sentence are subject to certain changes or modifications according as the writer or speaker wishes to convey different ideas as to circumstances of person, gender, number, time and place.

Thus the crude form of the following words:

میں I - دیکھنا to see - لڑکا boy -

conveys no definite idea, but when thus modified

میں نے تین لڑکوں کو دیکھا

Maiṇ ne tin laṛkoṇ ko dekhā—an idea is complete, *viz.*, I saw three boys.

The Accidental circumstances affecting words are expressed by the various changes included in the term "Accidence."

The vowels used to express these accidental circumstances in nouns, are as follow:—

ا *ā* denotes a masculine singular in the subjective case.

ی *ī* denotes a feminine singular in the subjective case.

ے *e* denotes a masculine plural.

یاں *īyāṇ* or یں *eṇ* denote a feminine plural.

Thus if a Hindī noun ends in ā, we know it is masculine—

Example:—کتّا کاٹتا ھی *Kuttā kāṭtā hai*—The dog bites.

If a Hindī noun ends in ي ī, we know it is feminine.

Example:—لڑکي کہيلتي ھی *Laṛkī kheltī hai*—The girl plays.

The masculine plural ends in ے e short.

Example:—چھوٹے گھوڑے *Chhoṭe ghoṛe*—Small horses.

The feminine plural ends in يان *īyāṇ* when the singular ends in ی ī.

Example:—لڑکيان تہين *Laṛkīyāṇ thīṇ*—The girls were.

But if the singular of a feminine noun ends in a consonant or ا *alif*, or و *wao* the plural subjective will end in ين *eṇ*.

E.g., کِتاب *kitāb*, book, کِتابين *kitābeṇ*, books.

بلا *balā*, calamity, بلائين *balā-eṇ*, calamities.

ناو *nāo*, a boat, ناوين *nāweṇ*, boats.

N.B.—From the above examples we see that the verbs are similarly inflected, with the exception that the termination يان *īyāṇ* has become obsolete in Urdu in the feminine plural of verbs, and is contracted to ين *īṇ*. It is still persistent in Punjābī.

The formative* cases of nouns both masculine and feminine alike, in the plural add the postpositions to the root form with the affix ون *oṇ*, thus مردون کا *mardoṇ ká*, of men, لڑکيون کو *laṛkīyoṇ ko*, to girls, عورتون کي *'auratoṇ kí*, of women, چڑياؤن کے *chiṛiyáoṇ ke*, of birds.

---

* See page 30.

Gender of Urdu Nouns.

The gender of nouns in Urdu is a matter of some difficulty to the student, and it is most important to acquire a thorough mastery of the rules which govern the gender of nouns. Nouns are masculine or feminine *by form*, the termination being in most cases, the indication of the gender.

A. The following are Masculine terminations :—

(*a*) Hindī nouns ending in *long ā*.

as آٹا *āṭā* flour.

The *exceptions* to this are few, being chiefly nouns implying an abstract quality, as كرپا *kirpā*, kindness, कृपा or किरपा.

(*b*) Nouns ending in و *ū* and او *āo*.

The *exceptions* are—

بالُو *bālū*, sand, دارُو *dārū*, liquor, medicine.

ترازُو *tarāzū*, a pair of scales, روهُو *rohū*, a kind of fish.

ابرُو *abrū*, eyebrow, آبرُو *ābrū*, honour, آرزُو *ārzū*, wish.

هَجو *hajw*, satire, بُو *bū*, smell, خُو *khū*, habit.

جُو *jū*, a river, ناو *nāo*, a boat.

(*c*) Nouns ending in ه (*h mute*).

Except: بنفشه *banafsha*, a violet, صرفه *ṣarfa*, expenditure.

توبه *tauba*, repentance, فاخته *fakhta*, a dove.

دفعه *daf'a*, time, لاشه *lasha*, } a corpse.
لوته *loth*, }

N.B.—Arabic feminines in ة (for ۃ) must also be excepted,

e. g., والدہ *wālidah* mother (fem. of والد).

Such noüns are feminine *by signification.*

GENDER OF ARABIC NOUNS USED IN URDU.

The gender of nouns imported into Urdu from the Arabic does not conform to the gender of the noun in its own language.

Without going into the question of the formation of words in Arabic, it must be understood that a number of words will occur which will be seen to be similar in *form,* with a meaning which bears, in all cases, the same relation to the idea to be expressed; this idea differing with the different roots from which the words are derived.

For simplicity's sake the three letters ف, ع and ل are used to represent the 1st, 2nd and 3rd letters of the tri-literal root; these three letters are constant in all derivatives, changes being made in their meaning by the interpolation of other letters, which always occupy the same position for the same shade of meaning.

The following are some of these derived forms; we will first take those that are masculine when used in Urdu.

N.B.—The student is urged to carefully study the remarks on gender, as this is one of the chief difficulties in Urdu.

The following Arabic derivatives are masculine:—

اِفعال *if'āl*—That is, words in which the root form فعل is augmented by an Alif between the second and third letters, and further augmented by having Alifhamza (*vide* page 3,) pronounced with the vowel *kasra*, prefixed to the first letter.

Exceptions: إِجلاس *ijlās*, a session.

إِكراه *ikrāh*, aversion. إِصلاح *iṣlāḥ*, correction.

إِلحاح *ilḥāḥ*, persistence. إِمداد *imdād*, assistance.

إِيراد *īrād*, citing.

تفعُّل *taf'a'ul.*—Formed by prefixing ت and doubling the second letter of the tri-literal root.

Exceptions: توجُّه *tawajjuh*, turning one's attention to.

توضُّو *tawazzū*, performing one's ablutions.

توقّع *tawaqqu'*, hope.

تمنّا *tamannā*, desire—longing.

تسلّي *tasallī*, consoling.

ترقّي *taraqqī*, promotion.

تجلّي *tājallī*, brightness.

تفاعُل *tafā'ul.*—Formed by prefixing ت and inserting Alif between the first and second letters of the root.

Except: تواضُع *tawāzu'*, humility,

and all of this form which end in ي.

انفعال *infi'āl.*—Formed by prefixing the syllable ان *in*, and inserting Alif between the second and third letters, as انقطاع *Inqiṭā'* being cut off. Words of this form all have a passive sense.

افتعال *ifti'āl.*—Formed by prefixing Alif, and inserting ت between the first and second letters, and inserting Alif between the second and third letters of the root.

Exceptions:

إحتياج *iḥtiyāj*, necessity.	إطّلاع *iṭṭilā'*, report.
إحتياط *iḥtiyāṭ*, caution.	إبتدا *ibtidā*, beginning.
إصطلاح *iṣṭilāḥ*, usage.	إلتفات *iltifāt*, attention.
إلتماس *iltimās*, request.	إنتها *intihā*, ending.

إعتراض *i'tirāẓ*, objection (this is also used as masculine.)

إستفعال *istif'āl.*—Formed by prefixing the syllable إست *ist* and inserting Alif between the second and third letters of the root. Words of this form have the signification of *desiring* or *considering*.

Exceptions:

إستمداد *istimdād*, asking for aid.	إسترضا *istirẓā*, conciliating.
إستكراه *istikrāh*, aversion.	إستعداد *ist'idād*, ability.
إستدعا *istid'ā*, request.	

مفعل *maf'al.*—Prefixing the letter م *mīm*—vocalized with either *kasra* or *fatha* as the case may be.

In the former case the word is an instrumental noun, *e. g.*, مسطر *misṭar*, a ruler (for ruling lines) مقراض *miqrāẓ* shears (for cutting) مِفتاح *miftāḥ*, a key (for opening); in the latter it is a noun of place, *e.g.*, مجلس *majlis* place of sitting,

Exceptions:

مَجال *majāl*, power.

مَحفل *maḥfil*, an assembly.

مَجلس *majlis*, place of sitting—assembly.

مسجِد *masjid*, place of worship—temple.

منزِل *manzil*, place of alighting—stage.

منخر *mankhar*, place of breathing—nostril.

The above includes all the masculine forms with the most usual exceptions.

The following are the principal feminine terminations:—

(*a*) ا (Alif) Arabic nouns ending in *Alif.*

Examples: بقا *baqā*, duration.

بلا *balā*, evil, calamity.

N.B.—Exceptions to this rule are Arabic words of the form تفاعُل *tafā'ul*, ending in ا, as تقاضا *taqāẓā*, dunning, which are masculine. (*See* page 21).

(*b*) یا Hindī diminutives such as چڑیا *chiṛiyā* a bird.

Except: پہیا *pahiyā*, a wheel.

(*c*) ت Arabic nouns ending in ت.

Except :

ثُبُوت *sabūt*, firmness. خِلعَت *khil'at*, a robe of honour.

شَربَت *sharbat*, a draught. يَاقُوت *yāqūt*, a ruby.

وَقت *waqt*, time. تَابوت *tābūt*, a bier.

(*d*) Nouns ending in هٹ *hat*, اهٹ *āhat*, اوٹ *āwat*, all of which are of Hindī origin, as گهبراهٹ *ghabrāhat*, consternation.

(*e*) ش Verbal nouns (Persian) as گَردِش *gardish*, revolution: روش *rawish*, manner, custom.

N.B.—بالش *bālish*, a pillow, is not a verbal noun and is masculine.

(*f*) ي Nouns ending in ي as: صراحي *surāhī*, a goblet.

Except : پاني *pānī*, water. گهي *ghī*, ghee.

جي *jī*, soul life. موتي *motī*, pearl.

دهي *dahī*, sour milk. هاتهي *hāthī*, elephant, and words which are obviously masculine such as آدمي *ādmī*, a man. سپاهي *sipāhī*, a soldier.

In addition to the above, it should be borne in mind that nearly all abstract nouns, formed by dropping the infinitive termination, are feminine. The *exceptions* to this rule are:—

نوچ	*noch*, scratching from	نوچنا	to scratch.
ناچ	*nāch*, dancing „	ناچنا	to dance.
رنگ	*rang*, colouring „	رنگنا	to colour.

کهیل *khel*, playing from کهیلنا to play.

نچور *nichoṛ*, squeezing „ نچورنا to squeeze.

دهکیل *ḍhakel*, shoving „ دهکیلنا to shove.

all of which are masculine.

The following Arabic derivatives are feminine :—

تفعیل *taf'īl.*—Formed by prefixing ت and inserting ي between the second and third letters of the root. This form has always an active signification.

Except : تعوین *ta'wīẕ*, an amulet (that which protects).

مفعال *mif'āl.*—Formed by prefixing م *mīm*, and inserting *Alif* between the second and third letters of the root, as :—

منقار *minqār*, a bird's beak.

مقراض *miqrāẓ*, a pair of scissors.

Except : منشار *minshār*, a saw.

مسمار *mismār*, a nail.

معیار *mi'yār*, a touchstone.

تفعال *taf'āl.*—Formed by prefixing ت and inserting *Alif*, as above, as :—

تکرار *takrār*, a quarrel.

تمثال *timsāl*, an effigy, portrait.

N.B.—It will be found well worth while to study these rules thoroughly, as, otherwise, the question of gender will be found a very puzzling one, and will depend solely on the memory for individual words.

THE FORMATION OF THE FEMININE FROM THE MASCULINE.

Feminines are formed in Urdu in various ways.

1. By adding certain affixes :—

(a) ي —When the word ends in a consonant, the letter ي is simply added, thus, براهمن. masculine, *Brāhman*, براهمني feminine, *Brāhmanī.* If the last letter is ا , or *h* mute, it is elided, and the affix ي substituted for it, thus : لڑكا *laṛkā*, boy, لڑكي *laṛkī*, girl, شاهزاده *shāhzāda*, prince, شاهزادي *shāhzādī*, princess.

(b) نَ *an*, or نِ *in*—This affix is used for rational beings, thus :

دهوبي *dhobī*, a washerman, feminine دهوبِن *dhobin*, or دهوبن *dhoban.* جوگي *jogī* a mendicant, *jogin.*

(c) ني *nī*, or اني *ānī*—This is used both for rational and irrational beings, thus : هاتهي *hāthī*, an elephant, feminine هتهني *hathnī ;* ٹٹو *ṭaṭṭū*, a pony, ٹٹواني *ṭaṭṭuānī* a pony-mare ; مهتر *mehtar*, a sweeper, feminine مهتراني *mehtrānī.*

2. By using distinct words :—

e.g., باپ *bāp*, father, feminine ماں *māṉ*, mother.

* سانڈ *sāṇḍ*, bull, feminine گاے *gā-e*, cow.

---

* It must be borne in mind that the feminine of this word, namely سانڈني *sāṇḍnī*, does not mean a *cow*, but a riding camel.

3. By adding the Persian words نر *nar*, or مادہ *māda*, thus:—

شیرنر *sher-i-nar*, a tiger, شیرمادہ *sher-i-māda*, a tigress. The words نر *nar* and مادہ *māda* are used alone to denote *male* and *female*. In Urdu, *female* is usually مادين *mādīn*.*

FORMATION OF THE PLURAL.

Pure Urdu words form their plurals thus:—

1. Form unchanged.—Masculines ending in a consonant, or in ū, o, or ī, as also proper names or degrees of relationship, or titles of profession ending in ā, *remain unchanged in the nominative plural.*

e.g., گهر *ghar*, a house. بچهو *bichhū*, a scorpion.
موتي *motī*, a pearl. چچا *chachā*, an uncle.
راجا *rājā*, a king. كودو *kodū*, a kind of grain.

2. Masculines ending in ā (except the above classes), or in *h mute*, form the plural nominative *by changing this termination into* ے *e*.

e.g., لڑكا *laṛkā*, boy, pl. لڑكے *laṛke*, boys.
پردہ *parda*, curtain, pl. پردے *parde*, curtains.

N.B.—The word دادا dādā, *though a title of relationship, is inflected: this is the sole exception to Rule* 1.

3. Feminines ending in ي ī, form يان *īyāṇ* in the nominative plural.

e.g., لڑكي *laṛkī*, girl, pl. لڑكيان *laṛkīyāṇ*, girls.

---

* *e.g.*, Is that rabbit male or female?
Wuh khargosh nar hai ki mādīn.

N.B.—This form is used for the nominative plural of diminutives in یا *ia*-دبیا *dibiā*, a little box—*plural* دبیان *dibiyāṇ*. *These form also plurals* دبیاین *dibiyāeṇ* (*as at* 4).

4. All other feminines form their nominative plurals by adding ین *eṇ*, thus :—

کتاب *kitāb*, a book, کتابین *kitābeṇ*, books ; ناو *nāo*, a boat, ناوین *nāweṇ*, boats ; لهر *lahr* a wave, *lahreṇ* waves.

The formative plural is formed by adding the syllable ون *oṇ*, in cases where the nominatives, singular and plural, are the same.

e.g., گهر *ghar*, house—Nominative plural گهر—Formative plural گهرون *gharoṇ*, houses.

In all other cases the feminine termination of the nominative plural is changed into ون *oṇ*.

e.g., لڑکي-لڑکیان—Formative plural لڑکیون *laṛkīyoṇ*, girls.

کتاب-کتابین—Formative plural کتابون *kitāboṇ*, books.

ARABIC AND PERSIAN PLURALS.

Certain of these will be met with in reading.

Persian plurals are formed by adding the syllable ان, *ān*, for animate , and ها *há* for inanimate objects, *as a general rule.*

e.g., گل *gul*, rose, گلها *gulhā*, roses ; نامه *nama*, letter, نامها *nāmahā*, letters ; but درخت *dirakht*, tree, forms درختها *dīrakht-hā*, and درختان *dirakhtāṇ*, trees ; and اسپ *asp*, a horse, forms اسپان *aspān*, and اسپها *asphā*.

Some also (nouns of multitude) add ات* *āt*, in the plural.

e.g., دیہ *deh*, a village. دیہات *dehāt*, the villages around.

کاغذ *kāghaz*, paper. کاغذات *kāghazāt*, documents.

نامہ *nāma*, a letter. نامجات *nāmajāt*, despatches.

Notice the euphonic interpolation of ج after the silent *h*—in the last example.

Arabic broken plurals† must be learnt by practice; they *follow the gender of the singular* in Urdu, whereas in Arabic all broken plurals are feminine.

Declension of Nouns.

There are but two declensions :—

I. That in which the formative singular is the same as the nominative.

II. That in which the formative singular is inflected.

In the first are included *all* feminines, and all masculines *except* those ending in ة (*h* mute) and long *ā* (not being professional titles or degrees of relationship) which, with the exception of دادا *dādā*, are uninflected. (*See* page 27.)

---

* This is the regular form of the feminine plural in Arabic—

., والدة *wālida*, mother والدات *wālidāt*, mothers.

† By broken plurals are meant plurals formed by a change in the form of the word, not simply by the addition of a plural termination—

e.g., اهل *ahl* (people) forms اهلُون *ahlūna* (regular plural) and اهالي *ahālī* (broken plural).

In the second are classed all masculines excepted from the first declension, as above, including دادا, as above stated. (For examples of declensions I and II *see* page 32.)

CASE OF NOUNS.

The various cases are formed by certain postpositions, which are added to the formative singular and plural, as the case may be.

N.B.—The "formative" is the condition of the noun in another case than the nominative, or "subjective" case.

1ST DECLENSION.—It has already been stated that in the first declension the *formative* singular is identical in form with the nominative. Accordingly in the *first declension* the singular number of the noun is declined by adding to the uninflected nominative form one or other of the postpositions which indicate the case in which the noun is used. The plural number is declined in the same way, with this change, that to the nominative singular form is added the syllable "*oṇ*" (*n* nasal), pronounced as in the French "bon," "ton," and to the word thus formed the postposition is added.

POSTPOSITIONS.

The following are the postpositions:—

	masc.		*fem.*	
Genitive singular	کا	*kā*	کی	*kī*
" plural	کے	*ke*	کی	*kī*
Dative (sing. and plural) ...	کو	*ko*	کو	*ko*
Accusative (sing. and plural) ...	کو	*ko*	کو	*ko*
Agent (sing. and plural) ...	نے	*ne*	نے	*ne*

		masc.	*fem.*
Ablative (sing. and plural)	...	سے *se*	سے *se**
Locative (sing. and plural)	...	میں *meṉ*	میں *meṉ*

It will thus be seen that the Genitive postposition is the only one which is inflected to agree with the noun which it qualifies, *e.g.*, *the man's horse* would be *ādmī kā ghoṛā ;* here *kā* agrees with the masculine *ghoṛā*, which it qualifies. Again *the man's mare*, is *ādmī kī ghoṛī*. *Ghoṛī* being feminine, requires the feminine postposition *kī*.

THE USE OF اضافت IẒĀFAT. The genitive may also be expressed by the use of the Persian construction termed *iẓāfat*.

This form of genitive is usually an adjectival qualification of a noun of Persian origin, for example:—

تختِ مبارک *Takht-i-mubārak.*

The auspicious throne.

شہرِ بزرگ *Shahr-i-buzurg.*

The large city.

This *Iẓāfat* has three forms. (*a*) After a consonant it is written as a *kasra* as in the above examples. (*b*) After a long alif or wao it is written ی: thus جای نماز *jā-e-nāmaz*, a prayer carpet داروي مُجرّب *dārū-i-mujarrab*, a medicine of proved efficacy.† (*c*) After ه mute it is written in an abbrevia-

* This postposition has also an idiomatic use, meaning "as soon as" *e.g.*, *As soon as he arrives*, may be expressed *uske āne se.*

In this sense it is used with the inflected infinitive.

† *Note.* In many Manuscripts this Iẓāfat will be found written as mentioned at (c), but the above is the general rule in printed works.

ted ی form so as to closely resemble *hamza*, thus قلعۂ عالي *qil'ah-i-'ālī* a lofty fort.

2ND DECLENSION.—Nouns of this class are declined by changing the final letter of the nominative singular into *e short*, and adding the postposition to this in the inflected cases of the singular. *E.g.*, لڑکا *laṛkā*, a boy, لڑکے کو *laṛke ko*, to the boy.

The nominative plural is formed by changing the final letter of the singular nominative into *e short;* the inflected cases of the plural are formed by adding the postpositions to the root form augmented by the syllable "*oṇ*," as in the first declension.

Example—

گھوڑا *ghoṛā*, a horse. گھوڑے *ghoṛe*, horses.

گھوڑوں پر *ghoṛoṇ par*, on horses.

EXAMPLES OF DECLENSIONS.

1st Declension.—گھر *ghar*, a house.

Singular.

Nom.	گھر ...	*ghar* ...	... a house.
Gen.	گھر کا - کي ...	*ghar-kā* (or *kī*)	... of a house.
Dat.	گھر کو ...	*ghar-ko*	... to a house.
Acc.	گھر - گھر کو ...	*ghar-ko* (or *ghar*) ...	a house.
Agent	گھر نے ...	*ghar-ne*	... by a house.
Abl.	گھر سے ...	*ghar-se*	... with, from, out of, a house.

Loc.	گھر مین / گھر پر	... *ghar-meṇ* (or) / *ghar-par* * †	... in a house. / * to a house.
Voc.	ای گھر	... *ai-ghar*	... O house!

Plural.

Nom.	گھر	... *ghar* ...	... houses.
Gen.	گھرون کا	... *gharoṇ-kā* (or *kī*)	of houses.
Dat.	گھرون کو	... *gharoṇ-ko*	... to houses.
Acc.	گھرون کو	... *gharoṇ-ko*	... houses.
Agent	گھرون نے	... *gharoṇ-ne*	... by houses.
Abl.	گھرون سے	... *gharoṇ-se*	... from houses.
Loc.	گھرون مین	... *gharoṇ-meṇ* (or *par*)	in, or to, houses.
Voc.	اي گھرو	... *ai-gharo*	... O houses!

2nd Declension.—لڑکا *Laṛkā*, a boy.

	Singular.		*Plural.*	
Nom.	لڑکا	*Laṛkā* a boy	لڑکے	*Laṛke* boys.
Gen.	لڑکے کا	*Laṛke-ka*	لڑکون کا	*Laṛkoṇ-ka*
Dat.	لڑکے کو	*Laṛke-ko*	لڑکون کو	*Laṛkoṇ-ko*
Acc.	لڑکے کو	*Laṛke-ko*	لڑکون کو	*Laṛkoṇ-ko*
Agent	لڑکے نے	*Laṛke-ne*	لڑکون نے	*Laṛkoṇ-ne*

---

* *Par* often signifies *to*, taking the place of *ko*. Thus "*ghar par jāo*," "go to the house," or more idiomatically "*ghar jāo*."

† Two of these postpositions may be used together: thus گھر مین سے *ghar meṇ se*, from within the house, میز پر سے *mez par se*, from upon the table.

Abl.	لڑکے سے	*Laṛke-se*	لڑکون سے	*Laṛkoṇ-se*
Loc.	لڑکے مين	*Laṛke-meṇ*	لڑکون مين	*Laṛkoṇ-meṇ*
	لڑکے پر	*Laṛke-par*	لڑکون پر	*Laṛkoṇ-par*
Voc.	اي لڑکا	*ai-laṛkā*	اي لڑکو .	*ai-laṛko*

Adjectives.

The adjective may either precede or follow the noun it qualifies, generally the former, unless it is wished to lay stress upon the quality indicated by the adjective.

Adjectives ending in consonants undergo no change of form to suit the gender of the noun. Those ending in long *ā* are changed, as are also some ending in *h* mute, and are inflected thus :—

Masculine Singular.

Nom. اچّھا آدمي *achchā ādmī*, a good man.

Inflected cases *الخ, اچّھے آدمي کا, کو, سے *achche ādmī kā, ko, se, &c., &c.*

Plural.

Nom. اچّھے آدمي *achche ādmī*, good men.

Inflected cases الخ, اچّھے آدميون کا, کو *achche ādmīyoṇ kā, ko, &c.*

Feminine Singular.

Nom. اچّھي عورت *achchī ʻaurat*, a good woman

---

* الخ These three letters are an abbreviation for an Arabic phrase signifying "and so on for the rest"—It is used in Urdu as the equivalent of our "&c."

Inflected cases اچّھی عورت کا, کو, الخ *achchī 'aurat kā, ko, &c., &c.*

Plural.

Nom. اچّھي عورتين *achchī 'auraten*, good women.

Inflected cases اچّھي عورتون کا, الخ *achchī 'auraton kā, &c., &c.*

فلانه *fulāna* and جدا *judā* are also declined, the latter generally in the language of women.

The following adjectives are inflected :—

دیوانه * *dīwāna* نادیده *nādīdā* شرمنده *sharminda.*

رانده *rānda* بیچاره *bechāra* کمینه * *kamīna.*

ناکاره *nākāra* تازه * *tāza* گنده * *ganda.*

حرامزاده *ḥarāmzada* مانده *mānda.*

COMPARISON OF ADJECTIVES.

Adjectives are compared in the following way :—

1. By putting the noun with which the comparison of another noun is made in the ablative case, the adjective agreeing with the noun it qualifies and following it, thus :— the sentence,

"*My horse is bigger than this*" is expressed as follows :—

میرا گھوڑا اس سے بڑا هی

Merā ghoṛā is-se baṛā hai.

My horse (compared) with this is big.

* Declined only by women.

"*This box is heavier than that*"

یہ صندوق اوس سے بھاري هی

Yih ṣandūq us-se bhārī hai.

This box (compared) with that is heavy.

2. By using the word *ba-nisbat* (in comparison with) the genitive, thus:—

"*My horse is bigger than this*" might be expressed—

میرا گھوڑا بنسبت اسکے بڑا هی

Merā ghoṛā banisbat is-ke baṛā hai.

My horse in-comparison-with this is big.

The former, however, is more usual in ordinary colloquial Urdu.

Adjectives are used to express variety or plurality in Urdu by simply repeating the adjective.

E.g., اوس لڑاي مین بڑے بڑے بیر مارے گئے

Us laṛāī men̤ baṛe baṛe bīr māre ga'e.

In that battle very many brave heroes fell.

اس کتابخانے مین اچھي اچھي کتابین هین

Is kitāb khāne men̤ achchī achchī kitāben̤ hain̤.

In this library are all sorts of excellent books.

This repetition of the adjective may also express intensity, thus:

اس تلاو مین چھوٹي چھوٹي مچھلیان هین

Is talāo men chhoṭī chhoṭī machhlīyān̤ hain̤.

There are (only) very small fish in this tank.

Numerals.

FIGURES.		NAMES.	FIGURES.		NAMES.
1	۱	ایک *ek.*	16	۱۶	سوله *solah.*
2	۲	دو *do.*	17	۱۷	ستره *satrah.*
3	۳	تین *tīn.*	18	۱۸	اتّهاره *aṭhārah.*
4	۴	چار *chār.*	19	۱۹	اُنیس *unīs.*
5	۵	پانچ *pānch.*	20	۲۰	بِیس *bīs*
6	۶	چهه *chha.*	21	۲۱	اکّیس *ikkīs.*
7	۷	سات *sāt.*	22	۲۲	بائیس *bā-īs.*
8	۸	آتّهه *āṭh.*	23	۲۳	تیئیس *te-īs.*
9	۹	نو *nau.*	24	۲۴	چَوبیس *chaubīs.*
10	۱۰	دس *das.*	25	۲۵	پچیس *pachīs.*
11	۱۱	اگاره *igārah.* / گیاره *gyārah.*	26	۲۶	چهبّیس *chhabbīs.*
12	۱۲	باره *bārah.*	27	۲۷	ستائیس *satā-īs*
13	۱۳	تیره *terah.*	28	۲۸	اتّهائیس *aṭhā-īs.*
14	۱۴	چوده *chaudah.*			
15	۱۵	پندره *pandrah.*			

FIGURES.		NAMES.	FIGURES.		NAMES.
29	۲۹	اُنتیس *untīs.*	43	۴۳	تیتالیس *tetālīs.*
30	۳۰	تیس *tīs.*	44	۴۴	چوالیس *chau,ālīs.*
31	۳۱	اِکتیس *iktīs.*	45	۴۵	پینتالیس *paiṇtālīs*
32	۳۲	بتّیس *battīs.*	46	۴۶	چھیالیس *chhiālīs.*
33	۳۳	تینتیس *teṇtīs.*	47	۴۷	سینتالیس *saiṇtālīs.*
34	۳۴	چونتیس *chauṇtīs.*	48	۴۸	اٹھتالیس *aṭhtālīs.*
35	۳۵	پینتیس *paiṇtīs.*	49	۴۹	اُنچاس *uṇchās.*
36	۳۶	چھتّیس *chhattīs.*	50	۵۰	پچاس *pachās.*
37	۳۷	سینتیس *saiṇtīs.*	51	۵۱	اِکاون *ikāwan.*
38	۳۸	اٹھتیس *aṭhtīs.*	52	۵۲	باون *bāwan.*
39	۳۹	اُنتالیس *untālīs.*	53	۵۳	ترپن *tirpan.*
40	۴۰	چالیس *chālīs.*	54	۵۴	چون *chauwan.*
41	۴۱	اِکتالیس *iktālīs.*	55	۵۵	پچپن *pachpan.*
42	۴۲	بیالیس *be,ālīs.*	56	۵۶	چھپن *chhappan.*
			57	۵۷	ستاون *sattāwan.*

FIGURES.		NAMES.	FIGURES.		NAMES.
58	۵۸	اٹھاون *āthāwan.*	73	۷۳	تہتّر *tihattar.*
59	۵۹	اُنسٹھ *unsaṭh.*	74	۷۴	چوہتّر *chauhattar.*
60	۶۰	ساٹھ *sāṭh.*	75	۷۵	پچہتّر *pachhattar.*
61	۶۱	اِکسٹھ *iksaṭh.*	76	۷۶	چھِہتّر *chhihattar.*
62	۶۲	باسٹھ *bāsaṭh.*	77	۷۷	ستہتّر *sathattar.*
63	۶۳	تِرسٹھ *tirsaṭh.*	78	۷۸	اٹھہتّر *aṭhhattar.*
64	۶۴	چوسٹھ *chausaṭh.*	79	۷۹	اُناسي *unāsī.*
65	۶۵	پینسٹھ *paiṇsaṭh.*	80	۸۰	اسّي *assī.*
66	۶۶	چھیاسٹھ *chhī,āsaṭh.*	81	۸۱	اِکاسِي *ikāsī.*
67	۶۷	سرسٹھ *sarsaṭh.*	82	۸۲	بیاسِي *be,āsī.*
68	۶۸	اٹھسٹھ *aṭhsaṭh.* / ارسٹھ *arsaṭh.*	83	۸۳	تِراسي *tirāsī.*
69	۶۹	اُنہتّر *unhattar.*	84	۸۴	چوراسِي *chaurāsī.*
70	۷۰	ستّر *sattar.*	85	۸۵	پچاسِي *pachāsī.*
71	۷۱	اِکہتّر *ikhattar.*	86	۸۶	چھیاسِي *chhīāsī.*
72	۷۲	بہتّر *bahattar.*	87	۸۷	ستاسِي *satāsī.*
			88	۸۸	اٹھاسي *aṭhāsī.*

FIGURES.		NAMES.	FIGURES.		FIGURES.
89	٨٩	نواسي *nau,āsī.*	96	٩٦	چھیانوے *chhi,ānawe.*
90	٩٠	نوّے *nawwe.*	97	٩٧	ستانوے *satānawe.*
91	٩١	اِکانوے *ikānawe.*	98	٩٨	اٹھانوے *aṭhānawe.*
92	٩٢	بانوے *bānawe.*	99	٩٩	ننانوے *ninānawe.*
93	٩٣	تِرانوے *tirānawe.*	100	١٠٠	سو *sau.* or سیکڑا *saikṛā.*
94	٩٤	چورانوے *chaurānawe.*			
95	٩٥	پچانوے *pachānawe.*			

ORDINAL NUMBERS.

	Masculine.			*Feminine.*
First	*pahlā*	پہلا	پہلي	*pahlī*
Second	*dūsrā*	دوسرا	دوسري	*dūsrī*
Third	*tīsrā*	تیسرا	تیسري	*tīsrī*
Fourth	*chauthā*	چوتھا	چوتھي	*chauthī*
Fifth	*pānchwān*	پانچوان	پانچوین	*panchwīn*

(inflected *pānchwen*) and so on adding وان (or وین *wīn* for *feminine*) to the cardinals, except in the following,

Sixth	*chheṭhā*	چھٹھا	چھٹھي	*chheṭhī*

DISTRIBUTIVE NUMERALS.

Each may be expressed by the use of the word *pīchhe* پیچھے thus :—

Give the coolies two annas each,

قلي پیچھے دو آنه دینا

Qulī pīchhe do āna denā; or thus *Ek ek* ایک ایک one each, *do do,* دو دو two each, and so on.

MULTIPLICATIVE NUMERALS.

These are formed, (1). By adding.

گُنا (feminine گُني) to the cardinals, as, دوگُنا *dogunā* = دونا *dūnā* two fold. (fem.) دوگُني *dogunī* or دوني *dūnī.*

2. By adding هرا as دوهرا *doharā,* double. تِهرا *tiharā* threefold.

The number of times a thing occurs is expressed as in English ; thus they use the words بار *bār,* دفعه *daf'ā,* or مرتبه *martaba,* each of which means "time," in combination with the numeral adjective; thus, twice دوبار *dobār,* three times تین دفعه or تین مرتبه *tīn daf'a* or *tīn martaba.*

COLLECTIVE NUMERALS.

These are expressed by putting the numeral in the inflected formative plural thus :—

Hundreds of rupees سیکڑون روپئے *Saikroṇ rūpa-e.*

Lakhs of rupees لاکهون روپئے *Lakhoṇ rūpa-e.*

Thousands of men هزارون آدمي *Hazāroṇ ādmī.*

This form also is used to express collective results—

The whole twenty died بیسون مرگئے *Bīsoṇ marga-e.*

The whole five arrived پانچون آگئے *pānchoṇ āga-e.*

Bring all three تینون کو لے آؤ *Tīnoṇ ko le āo.*

Fractions are expressed as follows:—

One-quarter ایک پاو or ایک چوتھاي *ek pau* or *ek chauthāī.*

One-third ایک تهاي *ek tihāī.*

One-half ادها *ādhā*, or نصف *niṣf* (Arabic), or نیم *nīm* (Persian).

A quarter more سوا, *e.g.*, $1\frac{1}{4}$ rupees سوا روپیه *sawā rūpaya.*

A quarter less پون, *e.g.*, 12 annas پون روپیه *paun rūpaya.*

A half more ساڑھے * *sāṛhe*, *e.g.*, 350 ساڑھے تین سو *sāṛhe tīn sau.*

One-and-a-half ڈیڑه *ḍeṛh.* *e.g.*, 150 ڈیڑه سو *ḍeṛh sau.*

Two-and-a-half ڈهاي *ḍhāī* or اڑهاي *aṛhāī.*

Three-and-a-half ساڑھے تین *sāṛhe tīn.*

One-eighth ادہ پاو *ādh pau* $(\frac{1}{4}\times\frac{1}{2})$.

Three-quarters تین پاو *tīn pau* $(\frac{1}{4}\times 3)$.

Five-eighths اڑهاي پاو *aṛhāī pau* $(2\frac{1}{2}\times\frac{1}{4})$.

COLLECTIVE NUMBERS.

The following terms are used to denote:—

A collection of two —A pair جوڑا *Joṛā.*
or جوڑي *Joṛī.*

---

* Only used of numbers above three.

A collection of four	گنڈہ	*Ganḍa.*
„ „ five	گاهي	*Gāhī.*
„ „ twelve	درجن	*Darjan.*
(corruption of "dozen")		
„ „ twenty —a score—	کوڑي	*Koṛī.*
„ „ a hundred	سیکڑا	*Saikṛā.*

MONEY TABLE.

ایک مہر { *Ek muhar* } One Mohur or ashrafī =
ایک اشرفي { *Ek ashrafī* }
سولہ روپیہ *Solah rūpaya* Sixteen rupees.

ایک روپیہ *Ek rūpaya* One rupee = سولہ آنہ *Solah āna* Sixteen annas.

ایك اٹهني *Ek aṭhannī* One eight-anna piece = Half a rupee or eight annas.

ایک چواني *Ek chauannī* One four-anna piece = four annas.

ایك دواني *Ek duannī* One two-anna piece = two annas.

ایك آنہ *Ek āna* One anna = دو ٹکا *do ṭakā* two ṭakās.

ایك ٹکا *Ek ṭaka* One ṭakā = دو پیسا *Do paisā* two paisās (pice).

ایک پیسا *Ek paisā* One paisā (pice) = دو ادهیلا *Do adhelā* Two half paisā.

ایک ادهیلا *Ek adhelā* One half-paisā =

دو چهدام *Do chhadām*, Two pieces of six dāms each.

ایک چهدام *Ek chhadām* One chhadām =

دو دمڑي *Do damṛī*, Two damrīs.

ایك دمڑي *Ek damṛī* One damrī =

دو ادهي *Do addhī* Two addhīs.

ایک ادهي *Ek addhī* One addhī =

چار کوڑي char kauṛī Four cowries.

ایک کوڑي *Ek kauṛī* One cowrie.

The shell of *Cypræa moneta* is used as the lowest unit of money by the very poor.

ایک پسیري *Ek paserī* A weight of five sers (pānch ser).

BAZĀR WEIGHT TABLE (for liquids and solids).

ایک من *Ek man* one maund =

چالیس سیر *Chālīs ser* Forty sers.

ایک سیر *Ek ser* one ser (seer) =

چار پاو *Chār pāo* Four pāos.

ایک پاو *Ek pāo* one pāo =

چار چهٹانک *Char chhiṭāṇk* Four chittacks.

آده پاو *Ādh pāo* half a pāo =

دو چهٹانك *Do chhiṭāṇk* Two chittacks.

دو پیسا بهر *Do paisā bhar* two pice weight=

ادها چهٹانک *adhā chhiṭāṇk* Half a chittack.

پیسا بھر *Paisā bhar* A pice weight =
پاو چھٹانک *Pāo chhiṭāṅk* Quarter of a chittack.

Table of weights for Gold, Silver, Jewels and Drugs.

ایک تولہ *Ek tola* One tola (The weight of a rupee is roughly taken as a tola).

بارہ ماشہ *Bārah māsha* Twelve māshas.

ایک ماشہ *Ek māsha* one māsha =
چار رتي *Chār rattī* Four rattīs.

The weight of the seed of *Abrus precatorius* (scarlet variety), گھونگچي *ghūngchī*, is taken as the standard for the *rattī* weight.

MEASUREMENT OF LAND.

ایک بیگھا *Ek bīghā* one bīghā = 1,600 square yards.
= بیس کٹّھا *Bīs kaṭṭhā* Twenty katthas (cottas).

DIVISIONS OF TIME.

ایک صدي *Ek ṣadī* A century.

ایک جگ *Ek jug* A period of twelve years.

ایك سال *Ek sāl* or ایك برس *Ek baras* } A year of twelve months.

ایک سہ ماهي *Ek sih māhī* Three months, as we say, "a quarter."

ایک مہینہ *Ek mahīna* or ایک ماہ *Ek māh* } A (lunar) month.

ایک پکھ *Ek pakh* A fortnight.

ایک عشرہ *Ek 'ashra* A ten days' period.

يك هفته	*Ek hafta*	A week — "sen'night."
ايك دن ايك روز	*Ek din* or *Ek roz*	A day.
ایک پہر	*Ek pahar*	An eighth of a day, a "watch."
ایک گھنٹہ	*Ek ghanta*	An hour.
يك گهڑي	*Ek ghaṛī*	A space of 22·5 minutes, or the $\frac{1}{64}$th part of a day.
ایک پل	*Ek pal*	$\frac{1}{60}$ of a ghaṛī.

Pronouns.

There are only two personal pronouns, میں *maiṇ*, "I," and تو *tū* "thou," in the singular, and هم *ham* "we" and تُم *tum* "you" in the plural. The *n* in *maiṇ* is nasal, and this must be carefully remembered; a good practical rule is that final *n* is nearly always nasal.*

The place of the third personal pronoun is supplied by the demonstrative pronoun وہ *woh* he, it or they.

The personal pronouns are thus declined:—

1st Person Singular.

Nom.	میں	*maiṇ*	I.
Gen.	میرا	*merā*	of me, mine.
	Feminine میري	*merī*.	
Dat.	مجهکو - مجھے		to me.
Acc.	*mujh-ko* or *mujhe*		me.

* Nasal n, is represented in transliteration by a dotted n,—thus ṇ.

Agent	مین نے	*maiṇ-ne*	by me.
Abl.	مجھسے	*mujh-se*	by, from me.
Loc.	مجھه مین	*mujh-meṇ*	in, on me.
	مجھه پر	*mujh par*	

Plural.

Nom.	هم	*ham*	we.
Gen.	همارا	*hamārā*	of us, our.
Fem.	هماري	*hamārī.*	
Dat.	همکو	*hamko* or	to us.
Acc.	همین	*hameṇ*	us.

Plural.

Agent	هم نے	*ham-ne*	by us.
Abl.	هم سے	*ham-se*	from us.
Loc.	هم مین	*ham-meṇ*	in, on us.
	هم پر	*ham par.*	

2nd Person Singular.

Nom.	تو	*tū*	thou.
Gen.	تيرا تيري	*terā, terī (fem.)*	thy.
Dat.	تجھکو	*tujhko*	to thee.
Acc.	تجھے	*tujhe*	thee.
Agent	تونے	*tū-ne*	by thee.
Abl.	تجھسے	*tujh-se*	from thee.

Loc.	تجھمین تجھپر	*tujh-meṇ* *tujh-par*	in, on thee.

Plural.

Nom.	تم	*tum*	you.
Gen. (fem.)	تمہارا تمہاري	*tumhārā* *tumhārī (fem.)*	your.
Dat.	تمکو	*tumko*	to you.
Acc.	تمہين	*tumheṇ*	you.
Agent	تمنے	*tum-ne*	by you.
Abl.	تمسے	*tum-se*	from you.
Loc.	تم مين تم پر	*tum-meṇ* *tum par*	in, on you.

N.B.—Colloquially the singular is rarely used except by an inferior addressing a superior, when he speaks of himself in the singular.

The second person singular is rarely used and generally as a mark of contempt or displeasure—or, on the other hand, of great submission, as in prayer to the Deity.

The pronoun *āp* is used by inferiors addressing superiors or by people of the same rank on formal terms and by a European conversing with a Native gentleman. It is declined thus:—

Nom.	آپ	*āp*	your honour.
Gen.	آپ کا	*āp-kā*	of your honour.
&c.	&c.	&c.	&c.

The form does not change in the plural.*

* With Āp thus, the verb must be in the 3rd person plural.

This honorific pronoun آپ *āp*, must not be confounded with the *emphatic possessive pronoun* اپنا *apnā* اپني *apnī*, which is used as follows:—

This is my own horse.

يهه ميرا اپنا گهوڑا هى

Yeh merā apnā ghoṛā hai.

He gave me his own book.

اوسنے مجهے اپني كتاب دي

Usne mujhe apnī kitāb dī.

I will sell my house.

مين اپنا گهر بيچونگا

Maiṇ apnā ghar bechūṇga.

Apná if repeated means *each his own:*

Example:—

اپني اپني كتاب ليكے كهڑے هين

Apnī apnī kitáb leke khaṛe haiṇ.

They have each brought their own book and are present.

N.B.—It will be seen from these examples that *apnā* is used as a posśessive pronoun with special relation to the person indicated by the foregoing substantive or pronoun in the sentence, accordingly it must always be used instead of the direct possessive pronoun when an imperative is used, thus:—

Shut your eye اپني انكهه بند كرو

Apnī (not *tumhārī*) *āṇkh band karo.*

Ap is also used for purposes of introduction, thus:—

Ap Dehlī se āyā,—This gentleman has come from Dehli.

Āp is also used to denote the word "self" as *main āp*, I myself or *āp āyā hūn̤*, I have come myself. The word خود *khud**, self, may be used instead of آپ *āp* in this sense.

DEMONSTRATIVE PRONOUNS.

These are two, *yeh* 'this,' *woh* 'that,' and are declined thus :—

Singular.

Nom.	یهه	*yeh*	this, he, she, it.
Gen.	اِسکا	*is-kā* or *kī*	of this.
Dat.	اِس کو	*is ko*	to this.
Acc.	اِسکو *ise* اِسے	*is ko, ise*	this.
Agent	اِس نے	*is ne*	by this.
Abl.	اِس سے	*is se*	from this.
Loc.	اِس مین	*is men̤*	in this.
	اِس پر	*is par*	on this.

Plural.

Nom.	یهه	*yeh*	these, they.
Gen.	اِن کا - کی	*in-kā* or *ki*	of these.
Dat.	اِنکو	*in-ko*	to these.
Acc.	اِنهین - انکو	*in-ko* or *inhēn̤*	these.
Agent	اِنهون نے	*inhon̤-ne*	by these.
Abl.	ان سے	*in-se*	from these.
Loc.	اِن مین - پر	*in-men̤, par*	in or on these.

* *Note.*—In this word and some others the و wāo is not sounded خود *khwud* pronounced *khud* خواب *khwāb* pronounced *khāb*.

Singular.

Nom.	وہ	*woh*	that, he, she, it.
Gen.	اُسکا - اُسکي	*uskā, uskī*	of him—his
Dat.	اُسکو	*usko*	to him.
Acc.	اُسکو اُسے	*usko, use*	him.
Agent	اُسنے	*us-ne*	by him.
Abl.	اُس سے	*us-se*	from him.
Loc.	اُس مین - پر	*us-meṇ, par*	in or on him.

Plural.

Nom.	وہ - وے	*woh*, or *we**	those, they.
Gen.	اون کا - کي	*un kā, un kī*	of those.
Dat.	اُنکو	*un ko*	to those.
Acc.	اُنکو - انھین	*unko, unhēṇ*	those.

Plural.

Agent	اُنھون نے	*unhoṇ ne*	by those.
Abl.	اُن سے	*un se*	from those.
Loc.	اُن مین - پر	*un meṇ, par*	in or on those.

The plural number is used respectfully. The form *inhoṇ*, *unhoṇ* is generally used in speaking of a number more than two.

RELATIVE PRONOUN, *jo* جو (or *jaun*) جون who, which.

Gen. sing. *jiskā* Gen. plural *jinkā*.

---

* The author of the *Urdū-i-Mu'alla* lays down the rule that وہ should be used both for Singular and Plural.

CORRELATIVE PRONOUN, *so* سو (or *taun*) he, &c

Gen. Sing. *tiskā* Gen. plural *tinkā*.

INTERROGATIVE PRONOUN,* *kaun*? who?

Gen. Sing. *kiskā* Gen. plural *kinkā*.

The remainder of the cases are formed as usual with post-positions.

Which? is expressed by کَون سا *kaun sā* (fem. *sī*) as *Yeh kaun sī ghoṛī hai*—Which mare is this?

INTERROGATIVE PRONOUN, of *things only*, *kyā*? what?

Gen. sing. کاهے کا *kāhe kā*. No plural.

Dat. sing. کاهے کو *kāhe ko*

کاهے کا *kāhe kā* is used to signify *of what material*, *e.g.*, یہہ صندوق کاهے کا هے *yeh ṣandūq kāhe kā hai?*

Of what is this box made.

کاهے کو *kāhe-ko*, is used colloquially to signify why? for what reason? *but should be avoided* as a rule; *kyūn?* being used instead. In addition we sometimes hear

کاهے کے لئے *kāhe ke liye?* why?

INDEFINITE PRONOUN, *ko-ī* کوئي 'some one,' some.

کسي کا - کو - سے sing. *kisī kā*, *ko*, *se*. No plural.

kuchh کچهہ 'something' (indeclinable).

---

* This interrogative کَون *kaun* is used both for persons and things.

COMPOUND PRONOUNS—

Indefinite—

كوئي نہين	*ko-ī nahīṇ*	no one.
كچهه نہين	*kuchh nahīṇ*	nothing.
دوسرا كوئي	*dusrā ko-ī*	some one else.
اور كوئي	*aur ko-ī*	some one else.
كوئي نه كوئي	*ko-ī na ko-ī*	some one or other.
كچهه نه كچهه	*kuchh na kuchh*	something or other.
كُچهه كا كُچهه	*kuchh kā kuchh*	something quite different.
جو كوئي	*jo ko-ī*	whoever.
جو كچهه	*jo kuchh*	whatever.
سب كوئي	*sab ko-ī*	every one.
سب كچهه	*sab kuchh*	every thing.

Interrogative—

اور كون	*aur kaun*	who else?
اور كيا	*aur kyā*	what else?

used in answer to a question, means *of course.**

Definite—ايك اور *ek aur* one more.

* A syce, for example, asks صاحب اج سواري كرينگے *ṣāhib āj sawārī karenge.* Will the master ride to-day. The answer اوركيا *aur kyā* = (of course he will.)

اور سب	*aur sab*	all the rest.
اور کچھہ	*aur kuchh*	something else.
اور کوئي	*aur ko-ī*	someone else.

Verbs.

The Urdu Verbs are of two kinds :—

Transitive, those which need an object expressed or understood, as مارنا *mārnā*, to beat. رکھنا *rakhnā* to place.

Intransitive, those which have no need of an object, as بولنا *bolnā* to speak. دوڑنا *dauṛna*, to run.

There is but one Conjugation in Urdu.

Transitive Verbs have two voices, the *Active* and *Passive.*

Parts of the Verb.

All Infinitives end in the syllable نا *nā*, and are formed by the addition of this syllable to the root of the verb.

E.g., چلنا *chal-nā* to go, آنا *ā-nā* to come, بولنا *bol-nā* to speak, مارنا *mār-nā* to strike, کاٹنا *kāṭ-nā* to cut, &c., &c.

There are two *genders*, two *numbers*, three *persons.*

There are three *moods*, as follow :—

Indicative ; Imperative ; Conditional (or Subjunctive.)

The Participles are two :—

Imperfect as	بولتا	*boltā*	speaking.
Past as	بولا	*bolā*	spoken.

There are also Compound Participles :—

Progressive چلتا هوا *chaltā hūā* moving, in a state of motion.

COMPOUND TENSES.

Past Conjunctive. This has three forms, چلکے - چلکر - چل *chal, chalkar, chalke* having moved.

TENSES.

The Tenses are nine in number :—

Aorist ... ... Simple Future	Formed from Root by means of terminations.
Past Absolute ... ... Present Perfect ... ... Past Perfect ... ... Future Perfect	Formed from Past Participle either used alone or with auxiliary verbs.
Past Conditional ... Present Imperfect ... Imperfect	Formed from Imperfect Participle as in the tenses formed from the Past Participle.

Of these tenses the *Aorist, Imperfect, Simple Future, Past Absolute,* and *Past Conditional* are simple tenses, the others are compound tenses formed by the aid of the Auxiliary Verb ہونا *honā* to be.

FORMATION OF TENSES.

1. *Tenses formed from the Root—*

The Aorist is formed from the root by adding certain inflectional terminations. This will be best understood by reference to the following :—

Verb.—بولنا *bolnā* to speak. Root بول *bol.*

Aorist—

مَیں بولُوں	*maiṇ bolūṇ*	I speak,
تُو بولے	*tū bole*	thou speakest.
وہ بولے	*wuh bole*	he speaks.

هم بولین	*ham bolen̤*	we speak.
تم بولو	*tum bolo*	you speak.
وه بولین	*wuh bolen̤*	they speak.

The first persons singular and plural of this tense are often used in the sense of Let me, or Let us, speak. With the conjunction اگر *agar*, this tense becomes a conditional present, *e.g.*, *Agar main̤ bolūn̤* = If I should speak.

The Simple Future is formed from the root as in the case of the aorist, with the addition of the termination گا to the singular, and گے to the plural.

Example :—

Root بول *bol.* Aorist بولون *bolūn̤.*

Simple Future—

مین بولونگا	*main̤ bolūn̤gā*	I shall speak.
هم بولینگے	*ham bolen̤ge*	we shall speak.

The other persons are formed similarly; see Aorist, above.

The IMPERATIVE * is formed simply from the root, the singular being identical with the root, and the plural having the same form as the 2nd person plural of the Aorist.

Example :—

لکهنا *likhnā* to write. Root لکه *likh.*

---

* *Note.* The Infinitive may be used as an Imperative, see Colloquial Sentences page 87, last line.

Imperative—

لکھ *likh* *write thou, لکھو *likho* write ye.

2. *Tenses formed from the Imperfect Participle*—

The past Conditional is formed from the Imperfect Participle, which in all verbs consists of the root with the syllable تا *tā* affixed, or for the feminine تی *tī*.

Example:—دوڑنا *dauṛnā* to run. Root دوڑ *dauṛ*.

Imperfect Participle—دوڑتا *dauṛtā*, (fem.) دوڑتی *dauṛtī*.

Past Conditional or *Habitual* from جیتنا *jītnā* to win.

میں جیتتا	*main jītā*	I used to win.
تو جیتتا	*tū jītā*	thou usedst to win.
وہ جیتتا	*wuh jītā*	he used to win.
ہم جیتتے	*ham jītte*	we used to win.
تم جیتتے	*tum jītte*	you used to win.
وہ جیتتے	*wuh jītte*	they used to win.

Example:—(see page 221.)

جب جیتتا تب مارے خوشی کے غافل ہو جاتا

Jab jītā tab māre khushī ke ghāfil ho jātā.

Whenever he won (when he used to win) from joy he used to get careless.

As a Conditional the conjunction اگر *agar*, if, is used with this tense, thus:—

---

* *Note.* There is also in use a respectful Imperative formed by adding یے, *iye* for the singular and یو *iyo* for the plural, to the root: thus—آپ جائیے *Āp jāiye*, Be pleased to go, Sir. See page 84, line 5. The plural form is little used.

اگر مین دوڑتا *agar main dauṛtā.*

If I had run.*

As an Optative, it is used thus :—

کاشکہ مین اوسکو دیکھتا

Kāsh ki main usko dekhtā.

Would that I had seen him!

3. *Tenses formed from the Past Participle.*

The Past Absolute is formed from the Past Participle, which is simply the root with the addition of the syllable *ā*.

Example:—

بولنا *bolnā* to speak. Root بول *bol.*

Past Participle—

بولا *bolā* spake, (*fem.*) بولي *bolī.*

Past Absolute—

مین بولا (بولي)	*main bolā* (f.) *bolī*	I spake.
تو بولا	*tū bolā*	thou spakest.
وہ بولا	*wuh bolā*	he spake.
هم بولے	*ham bole*	we spake.
تم بولے	*tum bole*	you spake.
وہ بولے (بولین)	*wuh bole* (f.) *bolīn*	they spake.

اگر مین دوڑتا تو اوسکو پکڑ لیتا

* If I had run I should have caught him.

COMPOUND TENSES.

The compound tenses are as follows:—

Present Imperfect, formed from the Imperfect Participle of the verb, with the present of the Auxiliary Verb هونا *honā* to be, which is thus conjugated:

مین هون	*maiṇ hūṇ*	I am.
تو هے	*tū hai*	thou art.
وه هے	*wuh hai*	he is.
هم هین	*ham haiṇ*	we are.
تم هو	*tum ho*	you are.
وه هین	*wuh haiṇ*	they are.

Present Imperfect of بولنا *bolnā* to speak—

مین بولتا هون	*maiṇ (boltā) hūṇ*	I (speaking) am.
تو بولتا هے	*tū (boltā) hai*	thou (speaking) art.
وه بولتا هے	*wuh (boltā) hai*	he (speaking) is.
هم بولتے هین	*ham (bolte) haiṇ*	we (speaking) are.
تم بولتے هو	*tum (bolte) ho*	you (speaking) are.
وه بولتے هین	*wuh (bolte) haiṇ*	they (speaking) are.

The *Imperfect* is formed from the Imperfect Participle with the past tense of the Auxiliary Verb هونا *hona* to be, which is conjugated thus:

مین تها	*maiṇ thā*	I was.
تو تها	*tū thā*	thou wast.
وه تها	*wuh thā*	he was.

ہم تھے	*ham the*	we were.
تم تھے	*tum the*	you were.
وہ تھے	*wuh the*	they were.

Hence the Imperfect comes to have a habitual or continuous sense, though تھا *thā* is more idiomatically omitted.

Imperfect of the verb دوڑنا *dauṛnā*—

میں دوڑتا تھا	*maiṇ dauṛtā thā*	I was running, or used to run.	
تو دوڑتا تھا	*tū dauṛtā thā*	thou wast	&c.
وہ دوڑتا تھا	*woh dauṛtā thā*	he was	&c.
ہم دوڑتے تھے	*ham dauṛte the*	we were	&c.
تم دوڑتے تھے	*tum dauṛte the*	you were	&c.
وہ دوڑتے تھے	*wuh dauṛte the*	they were	&c.

The Past Tense of the Auxiliary Verb ہونا *honā*, has also a feminine form, thus :—

میں تھی	*maiṇ thī*	I (a woman) was.	
تو تھی	*tū thī*	thou ,,	wast.
وہ تھی	*wuh thī*	she was.	
ہم تھین	*ham thīṇ*	we (women) were.	
تم تھین	*tum thīṇ*	you ,,	were.
وہ تھین	*wuh thīṇ*	they ,,	were.

Thus the Imperfect feminine will be—

مین دوڑتی تھی	*maiṇ dauṛtī thī*	I was running.
وہ روتی تھین	*wuh rotī thīṇ*	they were weeping.

The *Present Perfect* is formed from the Past Participle by the addition of the present tense of the Auxiliary Verb ھونا *honā* to be: Thus—

مین بولا ھون	*maiṇ bolā hūṇ*	I have spoken.
تو بولا ھے	*tū bolā hai*	thou hast spoken.
وہ بولا ھے	*wuh bolā hai*	he has spoken.
ھم بولے ھین	*ham bole haiṇ*	we have spoken.
تم بولے ھو	*tum bole ho*	you have spoken.
وہ بولے ھین	*wuh bole haiṇ*	they have spoken.

In the feminine the terminations of the participle must be changed to *ī*, *e.g.*, مین بولی ھون *maiṇ bolī hūṇ*.

The construction of the past participle in Active Transitive Verbs is different to the above, as the particle نے *ne* of the Agent Case must always be used with it: Thus—

I struck مین نے مارا *maiṇ ne mārā*.

I have struck مین نے مارا ھی *maiṇ ne mārā hai*.

This will be explained in its proper place, *see* page 63.

The *Past Perfect* (*Pluperfect*) is formed from the Past Participle together with the past tense of the Auxiliary Verb ھونا *honā* to be.

Example:—

مین بولا تھا	*maiṇ bolā thā*	I had spoken.
تو گیا تھا	*tu gayā thā*	thou hadst gone.
وہ آیا تھا	*wuh āyā thā*	he had come.
ہم لیگئے تھے	*ham legaye the*	we had gone away with.
تم ھنسے تھے	*tum haṇse the*	you had laughed.
وہ روئے تھے	*wuh ro-ye the*	they had cried.

Feminine.

مین بولي تھي	*maiṇ bolī thī*	I had spoken.
وہ آئي تھي	*wuh ā-ī thi*	she had come.
وہ روئین تھین	*wuh rō-īn thīṇ*	they had cried.

The *Future Perfect* is formed from the Past Participle together with the future of the Auxiliary Verb ھونا *honā*.

Example:—

مین گیا ھوگا	*maiṇ gayā hogā*	I shall have gone.
تو گیا ھوگا	*tu gayā hogā*	thou shalt have gone.
وہ گیا ھوگا	*wuh gayā hogā*	he shall have gone.*
ھم گئے ھونگے	*ham ga-ye hoṇge*	we shall have gone.
تم گئے ھونگے	*tum ga-ye hoṇge*	you shall have gone.
وہ گئے ھونگے	*wuh ga-ye hoṇge*	they shall have gone.

* This tense has an idiomatic use signifying probability, *e.g.*, وہ گیا ھوگا = I expect he has gone, he has probably gone.

In addition to these there are certain other forms which are rather to be called phrases than true tenses. These are called by grammarians—

Future Imperfect, expressing future continuous action.
Present Potential, expressing contingent action.
Past Continuous Potential, } expressing past contingent
Past Perfect Potential. } action.

They need only be indicated briefly, thus—

Future Imperfect—

میں چلتا ہونگا *maiṇ chaltā hūṇgā* I shall be going.

Present Potential—

میں لکھتا ہوں *maiṇ likhtā hoṇ* I may be writing.

Past Continuous Potential—

میں چلتا ہوتا *maiṇ chaltā hotā* I might have been going, with اگر *agar* if, this becomes a conditional = If I had been going.

Past Perfect Potential—

میں چلا ہوتا *maiṇ chalā hotā* I might have gone.

Example :—

If you had been going I might have gone with you.

Agar tum chalte hote to maiṇ bhī tumhāre sāth chalā hotā.

Conjugation of Active Transitive Verbs.

An Active Transitive Verb is conjugated exactly in the same way, except that in the perfect and pluperfect tenses, the object of the action is put in the accusative case with the postposition *ko*, and the verb in the past absolute, the person acting being indicated by the pronoun in the agent case with نے *ne* thus—

I killed the tiger.*

میں نے شیر کو مارا

Maiṇ ne s̲h̲er ko mārā.

There is another form in which it may be expressed—thus, by putting the object in the nominative, and the verb in the past absolute form, agreeing in gender with the noun to which it refers, thus—

I killed a tigress.

میں نے شیرنی ماری

Maiṇ ne s̲h̲ernī mārī.†

I saw a horse.

میں نے گھوڑا دیکھا

Maiṇ ne ghoṛā dekhā.

The grammatical difference is merely that in the 1st case the verb is impersonal; in the 2nd, it is personal; the two constructions are closely represented by the Latin forms, *viz.*—

1. Delendum est Carthaginem.
2. Delenda est Carthago.

Analysis of the Agent Case.

Whenever it is desired to express that an action has been completed, and this action is one which requires an object either expressed or understood, and this object is governed by an *active transitive verb*, there is but one way in which this idea can

* This construction puts the object of the action in a more definite form, and implies a previous mention or knowledge of the object in most cases.

† This construction is used where the connection between the verb and its object is very close and is to be emphasised, *viz.*, It was a tigress I killed; or where the object is indefinite, or has not been previously mentioned.

be expressed in Urdu, and that is by using the past tense in the third person. The subject is put first with the postposition نے *ne*, and the object is either put (*a*) in the formative with the postposition کو *ko*, or (*b*) in the subjective, thus—

(*a*). The king dismissed the wazír.

راجا نے وزیر کو معزول کیا

Rājā ne wazīr ko ma'zúl kīyā.

(*b*). The Maulaví wrote a letter.

مولوي صاحب نے چٹھي لکھي

Maulavī Ṣāḥib ne chiṭṭhī likhī.

(*c*). The thief drove the horses.

چور نے گھوڑوں کو ھانکا

Chor ne ghoroṇ ko hāṇkā.

It will thus be seen that where the object is put in the formative with *ko*, whether it be masculine or feminine, singular or plural, the verb is used in the 3rd person masculine singular; but where the object is put in the nominative (subjective) case, the verb must agree with it in gender and number.

Example:—

Masc. S.—He sang a song.

اوسنے ایک گیت گایا *usne ek gīt gāyā.*

Masc. Pl.—He shot five tigers.

اوسنے پانچ شیر مارے *usne pānch sher māre.*

Fem. S.—He caught a fish.

اوسنے ایک مچھلي پکڑي *usne ek machhlī pakṛī.*

Fem. Pl.—He killed all the flies.

اوسنے سب مکھیان مارین *usne sab makkhiyāṇ mārīṇ.*

The reason of this seems to be as follows:—

In the first case the predominant idea is the action expressed by the verb used, thus in example (*a*) the idea is

Rājā ne ma'zūl kīyā.
The king dismissed.

This is obviously incomplete, and the mind asks "Whom?" The answer is given, *Wazīr ko* = the wazīr. The wazīr is a well-known officer, and consequently is defined, and is therefore put in the objective case with *ko.*

In the second case the object of the action is the predominant idea: thus in (*b*) *chiṭṭhī likhī*—A letter was written.*

This is not complete in itself, as from the construction it is seen that it is not a passive, so that the writer must be mentioned, and this is supplied by the words *Maulavī Ṣāḥib ne.*

This construction with the particle نے *ne* is one of the greatest sources of stumbling to beginners in Urdu—owing to there being certain verbs which are at first sight transitive (such for instance as ليجانا *lejáná* to take away,) but are really intransitive grammatically speaking, and mistakes will never be possible if it is remembered that *certain verbs are transitive in English but intransitive in Urdu.* For instance—

The verbs to *bring* and to *take away* are in English active transitive verbs, but in Urdu are intransitive. Why is this?

---

* Another instance of this construction is:—

يهه عرض وزير كي پادشاه نے سني *Yeh 'arz wazīr kī pādshāh ne sunī*

The king listened to this representation of his wazīr.

Here the representation is the predominant idea.

Simply because they are translated by words whose meaning is respectively *having taken to come* and *having taken to go.*

Here the first part of the verb, لے *le* is merely a participle, and it is the latter part جانا *jáná* of the really compound verb which determines the construction.

Hence we translate—

The servant took away the book.

نوکر کتاب لیگیا

Naukar kitāb le gayā.

i.e., the servant (having taken the book) went. نوکر گیا *Naukar gayā* is the actual statement, کتاب لے *kitāb le* is simply a parenthesis.

The same applies to *lānā* which is really *le-ānā* = having taken to come.

The verbs سوچنا *sochnā* to think, سمجھنا *samajhnā* to understand, are in Urdu active transitive verbs with the object understood; thus for example—

مین نے نہین سمجھا *main ne nahīn samjhā.* I did not understand (his meaning).

اوس نے یون سوچا *Us ne yūn sochā.* He thought thus.

The Passive Verb.*

The passive in Urdu is formed by combining the *past participle* of transitive or intransitive verb with the verb

---

* *N. B.*—The passive construction is not allowable in Urdu in cases where the agent is known.

Thus, He was killed, will be وہ مار ڈالا گیا *wuh mār ḍālā gayā*, but, He was killed by a tiger, will be translated شیر نے اوسکو مار ڈالا *Sher ne us ko mār ḍālā.*

جانا *jānā* to go; as from لینا *lenā* to take, لیا جانا *līyā jānā* to be taken; بولنا *bolnā* to speak, بولاجانا *bolā jānā* to be spoken.

The verb is then conjugated like the ordinary verb, with such changes in the termination of the past participle as may be necessitated by the person and number. A few examples will illustrate the use of the passive verb. دیکھنا *dekhnā* to see, دیکھا جانا *dekhā jānā* to be seen:

مین دیکھا جاونگا	*maiṇ dekhā jāūṇgā*	I shall be seen.
وہ دیکھي جایگي	*wuh dekhī jāegī*	She will be seen.
مین دیکھا گیا	*maiṇ dekhā gāyā*	I was seen.

ایسي بات نہین بولي جاتي

Aisī bāt nahīṇ bolī jātī.

Such a word is not spoken.

This will serve as a guide to the formation of the rest of the tenses of the passive verb, the verb جانا *jānā* being conjugated regularly throughout.*

Derived Verbs.

Causal Verbs.—(*a*) A neuter verb is converted into a transitive verb by adding *alif* to the root, shortening a preceding long vowel.

Thus بولنا *bolná* to speak, بلانا *bulānā* to call, the *wao* و being shortened to *zamma.*

Also by lengthening the short vowel in the root supplying its place by the corresponding weak consonant thus

کَٹنا *kaṭnā* to be cut, becomes کاٹنا *kāṭna* to cut.

* *Note.*—The student is advised to practise the formation of these tenses with various verbs.

چھلنا *chhilnā* to be peeled, becomes چھیلنا *chhīlnā* to peel.

مڑنا *muṛnā* to be turned, becomes موڑنا *moṛnā* to turn.

(*b*) A transitive verb treated in the same way as at (*a*) becomes *Causal* thus پڑھنا *paṛhnā* to read, پڑھانا *paṛhānā* to teach.

Double causals are formed by inserting the syllable وا between the root and infinitive ending thus: پڑھوانا *paṛhwānā* to cause to teach, to get taught.

کاٹنا	*kaṭnā*	to cut (anything).
کٹانا	*kāṭānā*	to get (a thing) cut.
کٹوانا	*kaṭwānā*	to some one else to get (a thing) cut.

Example of Causals and Double Causals:—

اج بال کٹاونگا	*āj bāl kaṭāūṇgā*	I will have my hair cut to-day.
یه کتاب چھپواو	*yeh kitāb chhapwāo*	Get this book printed.
اپنی سبق سناو	*apnī sabaq sunāo*	Make me hear (*i.e* repeat) your lesson.
یه روپئے گنواو	*yeh rupa-e ginwāo*	Get these rupees counted.

COMPOUND VERBS.

The most important of these are the following :—

Intensives.—Formed by adding an infinitive form to the root form of another verb.

Example:—	پی جانا	*pī jānā*	to drink off.
	بول اٹھنا	*bol uṭhnā*	to speak (unexpectedly).

گر پڑنا *gir paṛnā* to fall down.

کاٹ ڈالنا *kāṭ ḍālnā* to cut to pieces.

Potentials.—Formed by adding the verb سکنا *saknā* (to be able) to either the root form or inflected infinite of another verb. بولنے سکنا *bolne saknā* or بول سکنا *bol saknā* to be able to speak, e.g., *wuh bolne nahīn saktā.* He cannot speak.

Completives.—By adding the verb چُکنا *chuknā* (to finish) to the root form of another verb.

e.g., لکھہ چکنا *likh chuknā* to finish writing.

N.B.—It must be remembered that the verb چُکنا *chuknā* is intransitive میں لِکھہ چکا ھوں *maiṇ likh chukā hūṇ* I have finished writing.

Continuatives.—By adding one of the verbs جانا *jānā*, or رهنا *rahnā* to an inflected present participle.

as, بکتے جانا *bakte jānā* to go on talking.

پڑھتے رهنا *paṛhte rahnā* to keep on reading.*

Frequentatives or Habituals.—By adding the verb کرنا *karnā* to a past participle uninflected, *e.g.*, رویا کرنا *royā karnā* to repeatedly weep, سویا کرنا *soyā karnā* to be in the habit of sleeping.

---

* See also page 221 Urdu line 4. Closely connected with this is the statical form of the past participle of the verb *rahnā* combined with the root of the verb: thus

وہ سورهاهی *wuh so rahā hai*, he is asleep.

Examples of all these verbs will be found in the passages for translation, pp. 213 to 252.

Inceptives.—By adding the verb لگنا *lagnā* to an inflected infinitive, *e.g.*, بولنے لگنا *bolne lagnā* to begin to speak.

Imminents.—By adding the verb چاهنا *chāhnā* (to wish) to an inflected infinitive, *e.g.*, وه آنے چاهتا هی *wuh āne chāhtā hai* he is just coming.

N.B.—This verb چاهنا constructed with the past participle forms a *desiderative*, *e.g.*, آیا چاهنا *āyā chāhnā* to wish to come.*

The construction of a sentence in Urdu differs considerably from the English as the order to be observed is either.

Subject——Object——Verb. For example—

راجا نے شیر کو مارا *Rājā ne sher ko mārā.*

or ——Agent——Subject——Verb.

راجا نے شیرني ماری † *Rājā ne shernī mārī.*

The use of the Infinitive.

The Infinitive is used in Urdu as a verbal noun, to express abstract ideas.

For example:

پادشاه کو وزیر کا کهنا یاد آیا *Pādshāh ke vazīr kā kahnā yād āyā* The king remembered *the saying* of the wazīr.

کسي عزيز کا مرنا سخت نا گوار هی *Kisī 'azīz kā marnā sakht nā guwār hai.*

The death of any beloved one is very hard to bear.

جي کا متلانا *Jī kā matlānā.* Feeling sick.

---

* This rule is however not invariably observed, *vide* p. 230 Urdu line 7.

† *Vide* pages 63 to 66 for the explanation of these several constructions.

When thus used it is naturally subject to inflection for the various cases: thus

سوائے رونے کے *Siwāe rone ke.* Except weeping.

It also takes the feminine termination when compounded with substantives of feminine gender: *e.g.*

دعا مانگنی *du'ā māngnī* Asking a blessing.

سرنگ اڑانی *Surang uṛānī* Springing mines.

Constructed with the verb هونا *honā* to be, the uninflected infinitive gives the idea of *necessity*, *e.g.*

ایک روز مرنا هی *Ek roz marnā hai.* Death is necessary some day or other.

ایسا کہنا هوگا *Aisā kahnā hogā.* We must say.

همارا جانا هوا *Hamārā jānā hūā.* I had to go.

Concord of the Verb.

It must be remembered, (*a*) that the verb must always agree in gender and number with its subject if that subject be not more than one. *See* Examples (*a*)(*b*)(*c*), pp. 73 and 74.

(*b.*) If the subjects be more than one and are rational beings, the verb is plural, the natural order of persons being preserved, and if they are of different genders the masculine is preferred.

(*c.*) If the subjects are numerous, impersonal, and of varying genders, the verb should always agree with the nearest subject, though a singular verb is permissible after a number of impersonal subjects each of which is in the singular.

If these few rules be borne in mind and those relating to the concord of the adjective and the qualified noun, there will be found no difficulty in constructing a thoroughly grammatical sentence in Hindustani.

Examples:—

(*a.*) Subject, Masculine Singular.

یهه پاني بهت جلد بهتا هی

Yeh pānī (m.) *bahut jald bahtā hai.*

This water flows very fast.

(*a.*) Subject, Feminine Singular.

میري گهوڑي تیزي کرتي هی

Merī ghoṛī tezī kartī hai.

My mare is impetuous.

(*b.*) Subjects, Rational of the same genders.

میرا چچا اور اوسکا بیٹا آ گئے هین

Merā chachā aur uskā beṭā ā ga-e haiṇ.

My uncle and his son have arrived.

(*b.*) Subjects, Rational of different genders.

میرا بهای اور بهن دهلي کے رهنیوالے هین

Merā bhāī (m.) *aur bahiṇ* (f.) *Dihlī ke rahne wāle haiṇ.*

My brother and sister are inhabitants of Dihlī.

(c.) Subjects numerous, impersonal, of varying gender.

اس باغ کے پھول پھل روشین کیاریان اور
فوارے بہت اچھے لگتے ہین

Is bāgh ke phūl (m.) *phal* (m.) *rawishen* (f.) *kīyārīyān* (f.) *aur fawwāre* (m.) *bahut achche lagte hain.*

The flowers, fruit, paths, beds and fountains of this garden are very pleasant.

(c) Subjects numerous, each in the singular and impersonal.

اوسکي بندوق بلم تلوار اور خنجر چوري گیا هی

Uskī bandūq, ballam, talwār aur khanjar chorī gayā hai,
His gun, spear, sword and dagger have been stolen.

Adverbs.

Adverbs are particles used to qualify any word or sentence in connection with which they occur, and have reference either to time, place, or manner.

The following is a list of those of most ordinary occurrence.

آج	*āj*	to-day.
کل	*kal*	yesterday, (or in future) to-morrow.
آجکل	*ājkal*	nowadays.
پرسون	*parson*	day before yesterday (or in future) the day after to-morrow.*
ترسون	*tarson*	three days hence.
همیشه	*hamesha*	always.
نت	*nit*	always.

* "The day before," is to be translated گئے دن *ga'e din*, that is the by-gone day. Similarly "the night before" is گئي رات *ga'ī rāt*.

جونهین	*joṇ hīṇ*	as soon as.
جهت	*jhaṭ*	instantly.
تُرت	*turt*	quickly, soon.
آگے	*āge*	before (of time.)
آگے	*āge*	in front, before (of place.
سامهنے	*sāmhne*	in front, before (of place.
پاس	*pās*	near, at the side of.
اوپر	*ūpar*	over, above, upon.
نیچے	*nīche*	below, under.
پار	*pār*	beyond.
وار پار	*wār pār*	through and through.
شاید	*shāyad*	possibly, perhaps.
البته	*albatta*	certainly.
بے شکّ	*be shakk*	undoubtedly.
دهیرے	*dhīre*	gently.
زور سے	*zor se*	violently.
بس	*bas*	enough.
زیاده	*ziyāda* vulgo *jāstī*	} more.
جون تون	*joṇ toṇ*	the best way he could.

TABLE OF A QUINTUPLE SERIES OF ADVERBS OF TIME, PLACE, MANNER, QUANTITY, AND NUMBER, FORMED FROM THE FIVE PRONOUNS, یہہ YIH, وہ WUH, کون KAUN, جون JAUN, تون TAUN, AS UNDER:

	NEAR.	REMOTE.	INTERROGATIVE.	RELATIVE.	CORRELATIVE.
	یہہ *yih*, this.	وہ *wuh*, that.	کون *kaun*, who.	جون *jaun*, who, which	تون *taun*, that same.
1	اب *ab*, now.	اُسوقت *us-waqt*, then.	کب *kab*, کد *kad*, when?	جب *jab*, جد *jad*, when.	تب *tab*, تد *tad*, then.
2	یہان *yahāṇ*, here.	وہان *wahāṇ*, there.	کہان *kahāṇ*, where?	جہان *jahāṇ*, wherever.	تہان *tahāṇ*, there.
3	ادہر *idhar*, hither.	اُدہر *udhar*, thither.	کدہر *kidhar*, where?	جدہر *jidhar*, whither.	تدہر *tidhar*, thither.
4	یون *yūṇ*, this.	وون *wūṇ*, in that way.	کیون *kyūṇ*, how?	جیون *jyūṇ*, as.	تیون *tyūṇ*, so, same.
5	ایسا *aisā*, like this.	ویسا *waisā*, like that.	کیسا *kaisā*, like what?	جیسا *jaisā*, like, which.	تیسا *taisā*, like that.
6	اتّا *ittā*, ایتا *etā*, this much.	اُتّا *uttā*, اوتا *otā*, that much.	کتّا *kittā*, کیتا *ketā*, how much?	جتّا *jittā*, جیتا *jetā*, as much.	تتّا *tittā*, تیتا *tetā*, so much.
7	اِتنا *itnā*, اِیتنا *etnā*, this many.	اُتنا *utnā*, اُوتنا *ūtnā*, that many.	کتنا *kitnā*, کیتنا *ketnā*, how many?	جتنا *jitnā*, جیتنا *jetnā*, as many.	تتنا *titnā*, تیتنا *tetnā*, so many.

N.B.—*This table is known as Dr. Gilchrist's Philological Harp.*

Postpositions.

These parts of speech follow the noun, which is put in the genitive inflected form. Most of them take the masculine form کے *ke*, but a few take کي *kī*. These latter are—

بابت	*bābat*	on account of.	طرف	*ṭaraf*	in direction of.
خاطر	*khāṭir*	for the sake of.	طرح	*ṭarah*	after manner of.

معرفت	*ma'rfat*	by means of.
نسبت	*nisbat*	in comparison with.
مانند	*mānind*	like.

These four: مانند *mānind*, نسبت *nisbat*, معرفت *ma'rfat*, بابت *bābat*, sometimes *precede* the noun, in which case they take کے *ke* like the others; a few of the most common of which are here given—

آگے	*āge*	before (both of time and place.)
بدلے	*badle*	instead of.
برابر	*barābar*	equal to, level with.
باهر	*bāhar*	outside.
بعد	*ba'd*	after (of time.)
پیچھے	*pīchhe*	after (of time or place.)
لائق	*lā'iq*	worthy.
لئے	*li'ye*	for the sake.
موافق	*muwāfiq*	like.
مطابق	*muṭābiq*	in accordance with.

بر خلاف	*bar khilāf*	in opposition to.
نزدیك	*nazdīk* vulgo *nagīch*	near,
نیچے	*nīche*	beneath.
پاس	*pās*	near, in the possession of.
سامهنے	*sāmhne*	before (of place only).
ساته	*sāth*	with.
سنگ	*sang*	with.
اوپر	*ūpar*	above.
واسطے	*wāsṭe*	for the sake of.
یہاں هاں	*yahāṇ, hāṇ*	with, at the home of.
ذریعے	* *zari'e*	by means of.
وسیلے	* *wasīle*	by means of.
سبب	* *sabab*	by reason of.

Conjunctions.

اگر *agar* followed by تو *to* if—then, in that case.†

---

* These are compounded with *ba*, and *precede* the noun, or with the ablative preposition *se* and *follow* it, *e.g.*:—

Mohan ke zari'e se or *Bazari'e Mohan ke.*	by Mohan's aid.
Ba sabab muflisī ke or *Muflisī ke sabab se.*	by reason of poverty.

† Example:—

Agar wuh ātā to main khush hotā. If he had come I should have been pleased.

اگرچه	*agarchi*	followed by	لیکن *lekin*, or by توبهي *to bhī* or تاهم *tā ham*		although—still
اور	*aur*	followed by	اور	*aur*	both—and.
بهي	*bhī*	,,	بهي	*bhī*	both—and.
چونكه	*chuṇki*	,,	لهذا *lihāza* or اس لئے *Is līye*		since—therefore
جب تک	* *jab tak*	,,	تب تک	*tab tak*	while.
جو	*jo*	,,	تو	*to*	if—then.
خواه	*khwāh*	,,	خواه	*khwāh*	either—or.
هرچند	*harchand*	,,	لیکن *lekin* or تو بهی *to bhī.*		although—yet
چاهے	*chāhe*	,,	چاهے	*chāhe*	whether—or.†

Interjections.

خبردار	*khabardār.*	take care!
شاباش	*shābāsh.*	bravo—well done.
واه واه	*wāh wāh.*	dear me! bravo.
افسوس	*afsos*, or حيف *ḥāif.*	alas!

---

* *Jab tak sāṇs tab tak ās.* While there is life there is hope.

† *Chāhe jīūn chāhe marūn.* Whether I live or die.
Harchand (see page 248, Urdu line 13).

Names of Months Hindū and Muḥammedan.*

English.	Hindū.	Muḥammedan.	Remarks.
January.	پوس *Pūs.*	محرّم *Muḥarram.*	*The correspondence of these months with the English months is only approximate owing to the different systems of reckoning
February.	ماگهه *Māgh.*	صفر *Ṣafār.*	
March.	پھاگن *Phāgun.*	ربیع الاوّل *Rabī'ul-awwal.*	
April.	چیت *Chait.*	ربیع الثاني *Rabī'uṣ-ṣānī.*	
May.	بیساکه *Baisākh.*	جمادي الاوّل *Jamādīu-l-awwal.*	
June.	جیٹه *Jeṭh.*	جمادی الثاني *Jamādīu-ṣ-ṣānī.*	
July.	اساڑه *Asaṛh.*	رجب *Rajab.*	
August.	ساون *Sāwan.*	شعبان *Sha'bān.*	
September.	بهادون *Bhādoṉ.*	رمضان *Ramaẓān.*	
October.	کوار *Kuār.*	شوّال *Shawwāl.*	
November.	کاتک *Kātik.*	ذي القعده *Zil Qa'dah.*	
December.	اگهن *Agahan.*	ذی الحجه *Zil Hijjah.*	*N.B.*—The Hindū year commences with the month بیساکه *Baisākh*; The Muḥammedan year commences with the month محرّم *Muḥarram.*

Days of the week.

English.	Urdū.	Hindī.	Pronunciation.
Sunday.	اتوار	इतवार	*Itwār.*
Monday.	سوموار - پیر	सोमवार	*Pīr* or *Somwār.*
Tuesday.	منگل	मङ्गल	*Maṇgāl.*
Wednesday.	بدھ	वुध	*Budh.*
Thursday.	جمعرات	बिफै	*Juma'rāt* or *Biphai.*
Friday.	جمعہ	सूक्र	*Jum'ah* or *Sūk.*
Saturday.	سنیچر - ھفتہ	सनीचर	*Sanīchar* or *Hafta.*

The following formula is given for converting the Christian into the corresponding Muḥammedan year, and *vice versâ*:—

$$H \times \cdot 97 + 621\cdot 54 = C$$

$$\frac{C - 621\cdot 54}{\cdot 97} = H$$

where H is the Muḥammedan year—*year of the Hegira* (A.H.) Hijrí هجري (ھ)

C. is the Christian year. (A.D.) عيسوي *'Isawī* (ع).

For example, 1894 A.D. by this formula will be found to correspond to 1312 A.H.

If from the Muḥammedan year thus found we deduct eleven we get the Hindu year (Sambat), 1312 – 11 = 1301 (Sambat).

PART II.

COLLOQUIAL SENTENCES.

N.B.—The student is advised to study this portion of the book very carefully—paying especial attention to those sentences to which an asterisk is prefixed, as they contain examples of specially important idioms or constructions.*

General Phrases.

Guft-o-gū. Bāt chīt. — گفت وگو- بات چیت

Who are you?
Tū kaun hai? — تو کون هی

Who is that man?
Wuh kaun shakhṣ hai? — وه کون شخص هی

What is your name?
Tumhārā kyā nām hāi? — تمهارا کیا نام هی

Where do you come from?
Tum kahāṇ se āte ho? — تم کهان سے آتے هو

What do you want?
Kyā māṇgte ho? — کیا مانگتے هو

Where do you live?
Tum kis jagah rahte ho? — تم کس جگهه رهتے هو

What is your trade?
Tumhārā kyā pesha hai?
تمہارا کیا پیشہ ہے

Where are you going?
Kidhar jāte ho?
کدھر جاتے ہو

Where is my servant?
Hamārā naukar kahāṇ
ہمارا نوکر کہاں ہے

Call my syce (groom).
Hamāre sā-is ko bulāo.
ہمارے سائس کو بلاو

When will you return?
Tum kab tak phir āoge?
تم کب تک پھر آوگے

In a week's time.
Ek hafte ke 'arṣe men.
ایک ہفتے کے عرصے میں

In a few days.
Thoṛe roz ba'd.
تھوڑے روز بعد

Do you know my house?
Tum mere baṇgle ko paḥchānte ho?
تم میرے بنگلے کو پہچانتے ہو

It is near the Fort.
Qil'e ke pās hai.
قلعے کے پاس ہے

On the bank of the river.
Daryā ke kināre par.
دریا کے کنارے پر

Not far from the Church.
Girjā ghar se thoṛī dūr.
گرجا گھر سے تھوڑی دور

You go on in front.
Tum āge jāo.
تم آگے جاو

I will follow after. *Ham pīchhe se āwenge.*	هم پیچھے سے آوینگے
How far is the Post Office? *Dāk-khāna kitnī dūr hai?*	ڈاک خانہ کتني دور هی
* About a mile from here. *Yahāṇ se ko-ī ek mīl hai.*	یہان سے کوئي ایك میل هی
Send for a carriage. *Ek gāṛī māṇgāo.*	ایک گاڑي منگاو
I want a closed carriage. *Band gāṛī chāhiye.*	بند گاڑي چاهئے
Now I am ready. *Ab maiṇ ṭaiyār hūṇ.*	اب مین طیار هون
Your horse is lame. *Tumhārā ghoṛā laṇgṛātā hai.*	تمہارا گھوڑا لنگڑاتا هی
He goes very slowly. *Wuh bahut mīṭhā jātā hai.*	وہ بہت میٹھا جاتا هی
* I shall be late. *Ham ko der lagtī hai.*	هم کو دیر لگتي هی
Look sharp—whip up. *Jaldī karo—chābuk māro.*	جلدي کرو - چابک مارو
Open the windows. *Khiṛkiyoṇ ko khol do.*	کھڑکیون کو کھول دو
* Shut the door. *Darwāze ko band karnā.*	دروازے کو بند کرنا

* Observe the construction.

Drive to the Telegraph Office. *Tār-ghar par hāṇk kar le jāo.*	تار گهر پر هانک کر لیجاو
Afterwards to the railway station. *Ba'd us ke, rel ke isṭeshan par jāo.*	بعد اوسکے - ریل کے استیشن پر جاو
Ask if there is a letter for me. *Pūchho, mere līye ko-ī chiṭṭhī hai yā nahīṇ?*	پوچهو میرے لیئے کوئي چٹهي هی یا نهین
Where is the Pay Office? *Bakhshī Ṣāḥib kā daftar kidhar hai?*	† بخشي صاحب کا دفتر کدهر هی
On the other side of this street. *Is raste kī dūsrī ṭaraf.*	اس رستے کي دوسري طرف
Opposite the Staff Office. *Birgid Mejar ke daftar ke sāmne.*	برگد میجر کے دفتر کے سامنے
Beyond the Cavalry Mess. *Risāle ke Messkoṭ kī parlī ṭaraf.*	رسالے کے میس کوٹ کي پرلي طرف
This side of the European Infantry Mess. *Lāl Kurtī ke Messkoṭ kī warlī ṭaraf.*	لال کرتي کے میس کوٹ کي ورلي طرف
On the right of the road. *Saṛak kī dāhnī ṭaraf par.*	سڑک کي داهني طرف پر
To the left of the shops. *Dukānoṇ kī bāīṇ ṭaraf.*	دکانون کي بائین طرف

† بخشي خانه *Bakhshīkhāna.* Pay Office.

This is the Native Infantry Mess. *Yeh Kālī Palṭan kā Messkoṭ hai.*	یہہ کالي پلٹن کا میس کوٹ ھی
The Lieutenant-Governor's house. *Lāṭ Ṣāḥib kī koṭhī.*	لاٹ صاحب کي کوٹھي
Is Mr. ——— at home? ——*Ṣāḥib ghar meṇ haiṇ?*	صاحب گھر مین ھین
Not at home, Sir. *Ḥuzūr, darwāza band hai.*	حضور دروازہ بند ھے
Very well, take my cards. *Achchhā, ṭikaṭ le lo.*	اچھا ٹکٹ لے لو
Put this box into the gāṛī. *Yeh ṣandūq gāṛī meṇ rakho.*	یہہ صندوق گاڑي مین رکھو
*Be careful not to break it. *Khabardār, usko mat toṛo.*	خبردار اوسکو مت توڑو
Sir, a gentleman has called. *Ḥūzūr, ek bāhar kā Ṣāḥib āyā hai.*	حضور ایک باھر کا صاحب آیا ھی
Very well, admit him. *Bahut achchhā, salām do.*	بہت اچھا سلام دو
What o'clock is it? *Kitne baje haiṇ?*	کتنے بجے ھین
Twenty minutes past eight. *Aṭh baj ke bīs minaṭ haiṇ.*	آٹھہ بج کے بیس منٹ ھین
A quarter to six. *Paune chhe baje.*	پونے چھہ بجے

* Observe the construction. We may also say مت توڑنا *mat toṛnā*. This use of the infinitive in the negative gives increased emphasis to the command.

Call me at seven to-morrow. مجھے کل صبح کے سات بجے جگاو
Mujhe kal ṣubḥ ke sāt baje jagāo.

Order my horse. گھوڑے کے واسطے حکم دو
Ghoṛe ke wāsṭe ḥukm do.

Which saddle—the parade saddle? کون سا زین صاحب - پریتي زین
Kaun sā zīn Ṣāḥib, pareṭī zīn?

No—a plain saddle and the new girths. نہ ,سفات - اور نئے تنگ
Na, safāt, aur na-e taṇg.

This bridle is dirty. یہہ لگام میلي هی
Yeh lagām mailī hai.

My stirrup is too long. رکاب لمبي هی
Rikāb lambī hai.

Shorten it two holes. اوسے دو گھر چھوٹا کرو
Use do ghar chhoṭā karo.

Bring the chestnut pony. سرنگ ٹٹو لے آو
Suraṇg ṭaṭṭū le āo.

Take the gray to the Polo ground. سبزے ٹٹو کو پولو کي جگہ لے جاو
Sabze ṭaṭṭū ko Polo kī jagah le jāo.

*Wait there for me. وهان هما را رستہ دیکھو
Wahāṇ hamārā rasta dekho.

*Take the new sticks with you. نئي لکڑیان ساتھہ لے جانا
Na-ī lakṛiyāṇ sāth le jānā.

---

* Observe the construction.

Change the pony mare's bridle. تٹواني کي لگام بدل دو
Ṭaṭnānī kī lagām badal do.

*You must get the dun pony shod. سمند ٹٹو کا نعل بندھوانا چاھئے
Samand ṭaṭṭu kā na'l baṇdhwānā chāhiye.

How did his back get rubbed. پیٹھ کس طرح لگ گئي
Pīṭh kis ṭaraḥ lag ga-ī?

Mind and rub him down well. خبردار خوب مالش کرو
Khabardar, khūb mālish karo.

Put bandages on his legs. چارون پانون پر پٹي باندھو
Chāron paṇoṇ par paṭṭī bāṇdho.

*Have one or two mouthfuls of water given him. ایك دو گھونٹ پاني دِلوادو
Ek do ghoṇṭ pānī dilwā do.

Be at the Club at four precisely. چار بجے ٹھیك کلب گھر حاضر هو
Chār baje ṭhīk Kalab ghar ḥāẓir ho.

What clothes will you wear, Sir. حضور کون سے کپڑے پہنینگے
Ḥuẓūr kaunse kapṛe pahneṇge?

Uniform. Khākī uniform. وردي کپڑا خاکي وردی
Wardī kapṛā. Khākī wardī.

Give me the warm suit I wore yesterday. وہ گرم جوڑا دینا جو کل پہنا تھا
Woh garm joṛa denā jo kal pahnā thā.

---

* Observe the doubly causal verb.

Where are my gloves?
Kahāṇ haiṇ dastāne?
کہاں ہیں دستانے

Give me my helmet and sword and sash.
Wardī ṭopī aur jāl kirich do.
وردي توپي اور جال کرچ دو

Is my horse at the door?
Ghoṛā darwāze par hai?
گھوڑا دروازے پر ھی

Parade is at half-past seven.
Pareṭ sāṛhe sāt baje hogī.
پریٹ ساڑھے سات بجے ھوگي

There's plenty of time yet.
Abhī bahūt waqt hai.
ابھي بہت وقت ھی

I want breakfast at ten.
Das baje ḥāẓirī chāhiye.
دس بجے حاضري چاھئے

*What is there for lunch?
Tifin ke wāsṭe kyā kyā hai?
تفن کے واسطے کیا کیا ھی

Show me the bill of fare.
Bil fel dekhlāo.
بل فیل دکھلاو

Give me whatever is ready.
Jo kuchh ṭaiyār hai le āo.
جو کچھه طیار ھی لے آو

Has the dhobi brought my clothes from the wash?
Kyā dhobī jugān lāyā hai yā nahīṇ?
کیا دھوبي جگان لایا ھی یا نہین

What is this delay?
Yeh kyā derī hai?
یهه کیا دیري ھی

---

* Observe the construction: the repetition of *kyā* implies an expectation that there will be several things to choose from.

This shirt is badly washed.
Yeh qamīṣ achchhī ṭaraḥ se nahīṇ dhoyā gayā.

یه قمیص اچھي طرحسے نہین دھویا گیا

Tell him he must do better.
Kah do ki is se achchhā kām karnā hogā.

کہه دو که اس سے اچھا کام کرنا هوگا

Discharge him—he is of no use.
Use jawāb do, kuchh kām kā nahīṇ hai.

اوسے جواب دو - کچھه کام کا نہین هی

Engage another from to-day.
Āj se kisī dūsre ko bhartī karo.

آج سے کسي دوسرے کو بھرتي کرو

*Pay him his due.
Jo kuchh ṭalab denī hai so de denā.

جو کچھه طلب دیني هی سو دے دینا

*Are there any arrears due?
Us kī kuchh chaṛhī hūī ṭalab hai?

اوسکي کچھه چڑهي هوئي طلب هی

*He has a few days' pay due.
Kuchh chhīṭ kī kauṛī bāqī hai.

کچھه چھیت کي کوڑي باقي هی

Is there a good Munshi here?
Yahāṇ ko-ī achchhā Munshī hai?

یہان کوئي اچھا منشي هی

*Look out for one and send for him.
Kisī Munshī ko tālāsh kar ke bulā bhejo.

کسي منشي کو تلاش کر کے بلا بھیجو

---

* Observe the construction.

*I want to learn Hindustani.
Maiṇ Urdū zabān sīkhā chāhtā hūṇ.
مین اُردو زبان سیکها چاهتا هون

Sir, I will teach you.
Janāb, maiṇ āp ko sikhā dūṇgā.
جناب مین آپکو سکها دونگا

You must first listen to me.
Pahle merī bātoṇ ko sunnā chāhiye.
پهلے میري باتون کو سننا چاهیئے

*Then try to speak yourself.
Ba'd us ke āp bolne kā qaṣd kījiyegā.†
بعد اوسکے آپ بولنے کا قصد کیجئیگا

I cannot understand you.
Maiṇ āp kī bāt ko nahīṇ samajh saktā hūṇ.
مین آپکي باتکو نهین سمجهه سکتا هون

Please to speak more slowly.
Āp, mihrbānī kar ke, zara āhista boliye.
آپ مهرباني کرکے ذرا اهسته بولئے

Will you kindly repeat that?
Mihrbānī se us bāt ko phir kahiye.
مهرباني سے اوس بات کو پهر کهئے

I said it is a fine day.
Maiṇ ne kahā thā ki āj mausim ṣāf hai.
مین نے کها تها که آج موسم صاف هی

*I will say every thing twice.
Maiṇ har ek bāt ko do bār bolā karūṇgā.
مین هر ایک باتکو دوبار بولا کرونگا

---

* Observe the construction.

† The (future) precative imperative used respectfully.

*If you paid attention you would soon learn to speak.
Agar āp tawajjuh karte to jaldī se guft-gū karnā sīkhte.

اگر آپ توجه کرتے تو جلدي سے گفتگو کرنا سیکھتے -

*I would write if I had leisure.
Agar furṣat hotī to maiṇ likhtā.

اگر فہرست هوتي تو مین لکھتا

*I used to write a little every day.
Maiṇ thoṛā bahut har roz likhtā.

مین تہوڑا بہت هر روز لکھتا

I was waiting for you.
Maiṇ āp ke intiẓār meṇ thā.

مین آپکے انتظار مین تھا

I will ask for a pen and ink.
Maiṇ qalam dawāt maṇgātā hūṇ.

مین قلم دوات منگاتا هون

He had brought me a pen already.
Woh peshtar se ek qalam mere wāsṭe lāyā thā.

وہ پیشتر سے ایک قلم میرے واسطے لایا تھا

How much did you give for this?
Ap ne is ke liye kitnā dām diyā.

آپ نے اسکے لیئے کتنا دام دیا

I bought it from my Munshi.
Maiṇ ne apne Munshī se kharīdā.

مین نے اپنے منشي سے خریدا

I saw your books on the table.
Maiṇ ne āp kī kitābeṇ mez par dekhīṇ.

مین نے آپکي کتابین میز پر دیکھین

---

* Observe the construction, noting the *conditional* and *habitual* use of the imperfect.

He heard a sound.
Us ne ek āwāz sunī.

اوسنے ایک آواز سنی

*He thought it must be the report of a gun.
Us ne yūṇ khiyāl kiyā ki albatta top kī āwāz hai.

اوسنے یون خیال کیا که البته توپ کي آواز هی

*He wrote and said he was ill.
Us ne likhā aur kahā ki maiṇ bīmār hūṇ.

اوسنے لکھا اور کہا که مین بیمار هون

*He said he could not perform that duty.
Us ne 'arẓ kiyā ki woh kām mujh se nahīṇ ho saktā.

اوسنے عرض کیا که وه کام مجھسے نہین هوسکتا

I do not understand this word.
Maiṇ is lafẓ ko nahīṇ samajhtā hūṇ.

مین اس لفظ کو نہین سمجھتا هون

Kindly explain the meaning of this sentence.
Is jumle kā ma'na āp mihrbānī kar ke bayān kījiye.

اس جمله کا معني آپ مهرباني کرکے بیان کیجئے

I am much obliged to you.
Maiṇ āp kā bahut mamnūn hūṇ.

مین آپ کا بہت ممنون هون

This is not right.
Yeh durust nahīṇ.

یهه درست نہین

I am very thankful to you.
Maiṇ āp kā bahut shukr-guz̲ār hūṇ.

مین آپکا بہت شکرگذار هون

---

* Observe the construction. *Oratio recta* used in Urdu.

It seems as if it would rain. *Aisā ma'lūm hotā hai ki shāyad pānī barsegā.*	ایسا معلوم هوتا هی که شاید پانی برسیگا
You are right. It is raining now. *Āp bajā haiṇ. Abhī meṇh barastā hai.*	آپ بجا هین ابهی مینه برستا هی
It will soon clear. *Jald ṣāf hogā.*	جلد صاف هوگا
*The clouds are breaking. *Bādal khule jāte haiṇ.*	بادل کهلے جاتے هین
The sun is shining again. *Dhūp phir nikal āī hai.*	دهوپ پهر نکل آئی هی
It is thundering and lightning. *Bādal garajtā hai aur bijlī chamak rahī hai.*	بادل گرجتا هی اور بجلی چمك رهی هی
*I fear it will hail. *Maiṇ ḍartā hūṇ, mabādā ole na pareṇ.*	مین ڈرتا هون مبادا اولے نه پڑین
It will do much harm to the crops. *Faṣl ko bahut nuqṣān karegā.*	فصل کو بهت نقصان کریگا
Grain will become very dear. *Anāj bahut mahange ho jāenge.*	اناج بهت مهنگے هو جاینگے

---

* Observe the construction.

What is the bazar rate for rice?
Bāzār meṇ chāṇwal kā kya nirkh hai?
بازار مین چانول کا کیا نرخ هی

*Flour is cheaper than it was.
Aṭe ka nirkh baṛh gayā hai.
آٹے کا نرخ بڑه گیا هی

*It will soon become dearer.
Nirkh jaldī se ghaṭ jāegā.
نرخ جلدي سے گهٹ جایگا

I must go now.
Ab muj'h ko jānā hai.
اب مجهکو جانا هی

I will return to-morrow as usual, Deo volente.
Kal dastūr ke muwāfiq, inshā 'Allāh maiṇ phir āūṇgā.
کل دستور کے موافق انشاء الله مین پهر آونگا

I hope you will not get wet.
Umīd hai ki ḥuzūr bhīg na jāeṇ.
امید هی که حضور بهیگ نه جائین

Can you lend me an umbrella?
Ap chhātā 'āriyatan de sakte ho?
آپ چهاتا عاریةً دے سکتے هو

There is only this old one.
Faqaṭ ye ek purānā chhātā hai.
فقط یهه ایک پرانا چهاتا هی

That will do very well.
Achchhā, is se kām ba-khūbī chalegā.
اچها اس سے کام بخوبي چلیگا

---

* This is a very important idiom نرخ *Nirkh*, means the amount of any given commodity sold for a given sum.

Hence نرخ بڑهنا *Nirkh baṛhnā*, means that you get more for your money, hence to be cheaper.

*I will return it immediately.
Maiṇ us ko fauran wāpas bhejtā hūn.
مین اوسکو فوراً واپس بہیجتا هون

If I had known I would have sent for a tikka gari.
Agar maiṇ jāntā to ẓarūr ṭhikā gāṛī mangwātā.
اگر مین جانتا تو ضرور ٹہیکه گاڑي منگواتا

It does not matter.
Kuchh muẓāyaqa nahīṇ.
کچهه مضايقه نهين

Do not distress yourself, Sir.
Ap na ghabrāiye.
آپ نه گهبرائیے

Military Phrases.

He drew his bayonet from the scabbard.
Us ne apnī sangīn miyān se nikālī (khenchī).
اوسنے اپني سنگين ميان سے نکالي (کهينچي)

He made a blow at me with his sword.
Us ne apnī talwār se mere ūpar wār kiyā.
اوسنے اپني تلوار سے ميرے اوپر وار کيا

I warded it off and killed him.
Maiṇ ne us kā wār khālī diyā aur use mār ḍālā.
مين نے اوسکا وار خالي ديا اور اوسے مار ڈالا

The edge of his sword was notched.
Us kī talwār kī dhār kirī huī thī.
اوسکي تلوار کي دهار کري هوي تهي

---

* Observe the use of the present tense in Urdu, to express an action in the immediate future.

Fortunately the blade broke. حسن اتفاق سے پهل توت گيا
Ḥusn-i-ittifāq se phal ṭūṭ gayā.

*Otherwise he would have certainly killed me. ور نہ مجهکو ضرور مار ڈالتا
Warna mujh ko zarūr mār ḍāltā.

Many of our men fell in action. هماري فوج کے بہت سے جوان کام آے
Hamārī fauj ke bahut se jawān kām āe.

*They had taken three days' ration. تين روز کي رسد ساتهه ليئے هوے تهے
Tīn roz kī rasad sāth līye hue the.

We had no water for 24 hours. ايک شبانہ روز تک پاني نہ ملا
Ek shabāna-roz tak pānī na milā.

*Many horses, mules and camels died. بہت سے گهوڑے خچر اور اونٹ سقط هو گئے
Bahut se ghore, khachchar, aur ūnṭ saqaṭ ho ga-e.

*The wounded man died of his wounds. وہ زخمي زخموں کے مارے فوت هوا
Wuh zakhmī zakhmoṇ ke māre faut huā.

The Pioneers carry spade and pickaxe. بيلداروں کے پاس بيلچہ اور گينتي رهتي هے
Bel-dāroṇ ke pās belcha aur gaiṇtī rahtī hai.

---

* Observe the construction.

*The lance is a very useful weapon. *Hathyāron meṇ se neza bahut kām kā hai.*	هتهيارون مين سے نيزه بهت کام کا هی
The English sword is straight and pointed. *Aṇgrezī kirich sīdhī hai aur pīplā-dār hai.*	انگريزي كرچ سيدهي هی اور پيپلا دار هی
The cavalry sword is curved. *Sawāroṇ kī talwār khamdār hai.*	سوارون كي تلوار خمدار هی
I galloped after him. *Maiṇ ne us ke pichhe ghoṛā sarpaṭ pheṇkā (dauṛāyā).*	مين نے اوسکے پیچھے گھوڑا صرپٹ پھینکا (دوڑایا)
His horse stumbled and fell. *Us kā ghoṛā ṭhokar khā kar gir gayā.*	اوسکا گھوڑا ٹھوکر کھاکر گر گیا
My horse crushed his head with his hoof. *Mere ghoṛe ne sum se us kā sar kuchal ḍālā.*	میرے گھوڑے نے سم سے اوسکا سر کچل ڈالا
As he fell he fired a shot at me. *Girte hī us ne mere ūpar apnī bandūq chalāī.*	گرتے هي اوسنے میرے اوپر اپني بندوق چلائي
The bullet passed through my helmet. *Golī merī ṭopī se wār pār huī.*	گولي ميري توپي سے وار پار هوئي

* Observe the construction.

The enemy fled in all directions. — دشمن تتر بتر هوکر بهاگ گئے
Dushman tittar bittar ho kar bhāg ga-e.

We learned their strength from spies. — همنے جاسوسون سے اونکي قوت معلوم کي
Ham ne jāsusoṇ se un kī quwwat mā'lūm kī.

*Their infantry were armed with breech-loaders. — اونکي پيادہ فوج کوتهي دار بندوقون کو رکهتے تهے
Un kī piyāda fauj koṭhī-dār bandūqoṇ ko rakhtē thē.

Their guns were of cast-iron. — اونکي توپين ڈهلے هوے لوهے کي تهين
Un kī topeṇ ḍhale hue lohe kī thīṇ.

They were encamped to the eastward. — وہ پورب کي طرف خيمہ زن تهے
Wuh pūrab kī ṭaraf khīma-zan the.

How did you attack the stockade? — تمنے سنگر پر کس طرحسے حملہ کيا
Tum ne saṇgar par kis ṭaraḥ se ḥamla kiyā?

They fought very bravely. — وہ بهت جوان مردي سے لڑتے رهے
Wo bohut jawāṇ-mardī se laṛte rahe.

Many were killed and wounded. — بهت سے مقتول اور مجروح هوے
Bahut se maqtūl aur majrūḥ hūe.

---

* Observe the construction.

They gave way very reluctantly.
Wuh nihāyat mus͟hkil se pīchhe ko haṭ ga-e.

وہ نہایت مشکل سے پیچھے کو ہٹ گئے

On what sort of ground was the battle fought?
Jahāṇ laṛāī huī wahāṇ zamīn kaisī thī?

جہان لڑائی ہوئی وہان زمین کیسی تہی

Was there much cover for the men?
Jawānoṇ ke līye bahut āṛ thī yā nahīṇ?

جوانون کے لیئے بہت آڑ تہی یا نہین

There were some sugarcane fields.
Kītne ek ganne (īkh) ke khet the.

کتنے ایک گنے (ایکھہ) کے کھیت تہے

*In which we hid as we advanced.
Jin meṇ ham chhipte chhipte āge baṛhte ga-e.

جن مین ہم چھپتے چھپتے آگے بڑھتے گئے

*They did not see us till we were close.
Jab tak ki ham nazdīk na ā-e the unhoṇ ne nahīṇ dekhā.

جبتک کہ ہم نزدیک نہ آئے تہے اونہون نے نہین دیکھا

*Then we fired volleys and charged.
Pher ham ne bāṛeṇ uṛāīṇ aur hallā kiyā.

پہر ہمنے باڑین اڑاین اور ہلا کیا

The hills were very steep and rough.
Pahāṛ bahut ṭhāṛh aur behaṛ the.

پہاڑ بہت ٹہاڑہ اور بیہڑ تہے

---

* Observe the construction.

*The battle lasted till nightfall.
Shām tak laṛāī barābar hotī rahī.

شام تک لڑائي برابر هوتي رهي

Many deserters came over to us.
Bahut se bhagoṛe hamārī fauj meṇ ā mile.

بهت سے بهگوڑے هماري فوج مين آملے

Immediately at daybreak we crossed the river.
Ṣubḥ hote hī ham ne daryā ko 'ubūr kiyā.

صبح هوتے هي همنے دريا كو عبور كيا

We found a ford a little way off.
Thoṛī dūr par ek pāyāb ham ne pāyā.

تهوڑي دور پر ايک پاياب همنے پايا

Over which our cavalry crossed.
Ki jis se hamāre sawār utar ga-e.

كه جس سے همارے سوار اُتر گئے

Some of our heavy guns stuck in the mud.
Bhārī topoṇ meṇ se kāī ek kīchaṛ meṇ phaṇs ga-īṇ.

بهاري توپون مين سے كئي ايک كيچڑ مين پهنس گئين

*The whole force had crossed by midday.
Dopahar tak tamām fauj utar ga-ī thī.

دوپهر تک تمام فوج اوتر گئي تهي

*By forced marches we reached the capital.
Yalghār kar ke ham pāe-takht ko pahuṇche.

يلغار كرکے هم پاے تخت كو پهنچے

---

* Observe the construction.

We left all camp-followers behind.
Ham ne sab bahīr o bungāh ko pīchhe chhoṛ diyā.

همنے سب بہیرو بنگاہ کو پیچھے چھوڑ دیا

*The garrison capitulated without opposition.
Ahl-i-qil'ah ne baghair muqābala kīye taslīm kī.

اهل قلعه نے بغیر مقابله کیئے تسلیم کي

At what time did the prisoner go on guard?
Quidī kis waqt pahre par gayā?

قیدي کس وقت پہرے پر گیا

When did you notice he was drunk?
Tum ne kab mā'lūm kiyā ki woh matwālā hai?

تمنے کب معلوم کیا که وه متوالا هی

To whom did you report the fact?
Tum ne is bāt kī ittilā' kis ko dī?

تمنے اس بات کي اطلاع کسکو دي

Had he all his proper accoutrements?
Us kā sab kīl kāṇṭā durust thā.

اوسکا سب کیل کانٹا درست تها

You say he was asleep near his sentry box.
Tum yeh kahte ho ki wuh apnī gumtī ke pās so rahā thā.

تم یهه کهتے هو که وه اپني گمتي کے پاس سو رها تها

Yes sir, and his rifle was lying on the ground.
Hāṇ Janāb, aur us kī bandūq zamīn par paṛī thī.

هان جناب اور اوسکي بندوق زمین پر پڑي تهي

* Observe the construction.

When you awoke him was he drunk?
Jub tum ne us ko jagāyā to nas͟he meṇ thā?

جب تمنے اوسکو جگایا تو
نشے مین تھا

*Can you repeat his exact words?
Kyā tum us kī ṭhīk ṭhīk bātoṇ ko i'āda kar sakte ho?

کیا تم اوسکي ٹھیک ٹھیک
باتون کو اعادہ کر سکتے ہو

*Where was his pouch belt found?
Us kā tosh-dān kahāṇ se barā-mad hūā?

اوسکا توشدان کہان سے
برامد ہوا

This is a crime punishable with death, transportation, corporal punishment, imprisonment or dismissal.
Yeh ek aisā gunāh hai jis kī sazā yā qatl, yā jalā-waṭanī, yā mār khānā, yā qaid, yā barṯaraf honā hai.

یہہ ایک ایسا گناہ ہے جسکي
سزا یا قتل یا جلا وطني یا
مار کہانا یا قید یا بر طرف
ہونا ہی

The articles of war—
Āīn-i-las͟hkarī.—

آین لشکري

It is thus written in the articles of war—
Āīn-i-las͟hkarī meṇ yoṇ likhā hai ki—

آین لشکري مین یون لکھا
ہی کہ

---

* Observe the construction.

A sentry who in time of war or alarm shall sleep upon his post.

Jo sipāhī pahre-dār laṛāī ke waqt yā kisī aur khatre ke waqt apni chaukī pahre kī jagah par so jāwe.

جو سپاهي پهريدار لڑائي کے
وقت يا کسي اور خطرے
کے وقت اپني چوکي
پهرے کي جگه پر سو جاوے

Shall on conviction suffer death or transportation for life.

Agar us kā gunāh ṣābit ho, to qatl yā 'umr bhar tak jalā-waṭanī us kī sazā hogī.

اگر اسکا گناه ثابت هو تو قتل
يا عمر بهر تک جلاوطني
اوسکي سزا هوگي

Or other punishment as by a General Court-Martial shall be awarded.

Yā koī dusrī sazā, jaisī Janral Korṭ Mārshiāl kī tajwīz meṇ ṭhahre.

يا کوئي دوسري سزا جيسي
جنرل کورٹ مارشيال کي
تجويز مين ٹهرے

Whenever any Officer or Soldier shall commit a crime deserving punishment by Court-Martial, he shall, by his Commanding Officer, be put under arrest, if an officer: or, if a soldier, be confined.

Jab kabhī koī 'uhda-dār yā sipāhī aisā gunāh kare ki jis kī sazā Korṭ Mārshiāl ke hukm ke qābil hai, jo wuh 'uhda-dār ho, to us kā Kamān Afsar Ṣāḥib us ko naẓr-band karegā, aur jo wuh sipāhī ho, to qaid kiyā jāegā.

جب کبهي کوئي عهده دار
يا سپاهي ايسا گناه کرے
که جسکي سزا کورٹ
مارشيال کے حکم کے قابل
هی جو وه عهده دار هو تو
اوسکا کمان افسر صاحب
اوسکو نظر بند کريگا اور جو
وه سپاهي هو تو قيد کيا جايگا

Courts Martial—
Faujī 'Adālat
(or) *Jangī 'Adālat*—

فوجي عدالت
جنگي عدالت

Proceedings of a General Court-Martial, by order of the General Officer Commanding the District, dated ——— held ——— at ——— on ——— Wednesday, the ——— of ——— 1889.
Ek Janral Korṭ Mārshiāl kī rū-ba-kārī Disṭrikṭ ke Janral Afsar Kamānīr ke ḥukm se jo fulānī tārīkh ko ṣādir huā, fulānī chhāonī men, ba-tārikh fulān, māh fulān, San 1889 *'Īsawī, Budh ke roz jam'a huā.*

ايک جنرل کورٹ مارشيال کي روبکاري ڈسٹرکٹ کے جنرل افسر کمانير کے حکم سے جو فلاني تاريخ کو صادر هوا - فلانے چهاوني مين بتاريخ فلان ماه فلان سنه ١٨٨٩ ع بده کے روز جمع هوا

President.
Mīr-i-Majlis.

مير مجلس

Members.
Ṣāḥibān-i-Majlis.

صاحبان مجلس

At eleven o'clock the Court opens.
Gyārah baje Korṭ jam'a huā.

گياره بجے کورٹ جمع هوا

The prisoner ———, is, brought before the court. ——— appears as prosecutor and takes his place.
Sipāhī fulān qaidī ho kar Korṭ ke sāmhne pesh kiyā jātā hai; fulān Ṣaḥib mudda'ī ḥāẓir huā aur apnī jagah par baiṭhtā hai.

سپاهي فلان قيدي هوکر کورٹ کے سامهنے پيش کيا جاتا هی فلان صاحب مدعي حاضر هوا اور اپني جگهه پر بيٹهتا هی

The order for convening the Court and Appointment of President is read. *Korṭ ke jam'a hone kā ḥukm aur Mīr-i-Majlis ke muqarrar hone kī sanad sunāī jātī hai.*	کورٹ کے جمع هونیکا حکم اور میر مجلس کے مقرر هونے کي سنن سنائي جاتي هی
Have you any objection to be tried by me as President, or by any of the Members whose names you have heard read? *Maiṇ jo Mīr-i-Majlis hūṇ, aur dīgar Ṣāḥibān-i-Majlis jin hon ke nām tumhāre rū-ba-rū sunāe gae haiṇ, un meṇ se kisī par i'tirāẓ karte ho yā nahīṇ?*	مین جو میر مجلس هون اور دیگر صاحبان مجلس جنهون کے نام تمهارے روبرو سنائے گئے هین اون مین سے کسي پر اعتراض کرتے هو یا نهین

The Charge Sheet.

Fard-i-Ilzām. فرد الزام

The prisoner is arraigned on the following charge, *viz.*:— *Qaidī is jurm par pesh kīyā gayā hai, ya'ne ki:—*	قیدي† اس جرم پر پیش کیا گیا هے یعني که
Are you guilty or not guilty of the charge made against you? *Jis jurm kī tuhmat tum par lagāī jātī hai, tum us jurm ke gunah-gār ho yā nahīṇ?*	جس جرم کي تهمت تم پر لگائي جاتي هے تم اوس جرم کے گنهگار هو یا نهین

† or مجرم, *mujrim.*

The Court find the prisoner to be guilty of the charge? *Korṭ ne yūṇ ṭhahrāyā ke qaidī gunah-gār hai.*	کورٹ نے یون ٹھہرایا کہ قیدي گنہگار هے
The Court consider the charge is not proved. *Korṭ ki yeh tājwīz hai ki jurm ṣābit nahīṇ hūā.*	کورٹ کي یهہ تجویز هے کہ جرم ثابت نہین هوا
The sentence of the Court is that the prisoner be imprisoned with hard labour for two years. *Korṭ kā yeh fatwā hai ki qaidī do baras kī mī'ād tak qaid bā-mashaqqat kī sazā pāwegā.*	کورٹ کا یهہ فتوی هے کہ قیدي دوبرس کي میعاد تک قید با مشقت کي سزا پاویگا
The finding of the Court-Martial is confirmed by the Commander-in-Chief. *Korṭ kī tajwīz jo us qaidī ke ḥaqq meṇ ṭhahrāī gāī Kamānīr-in-Chīf Ṣāḥib bahādur ne manẓūr kī.*	کورٹ کي تجویز جو اوس قیدي کے حق مین ٹھہرائي گئي کمانیر این چیف صاحب بہادر نے منظور کي
On the assembly of a Court-Martial, the Judge Advocate shall administer to the Interpreter the following solemn affirmation— *Jab Korṭ Mārshiāl ke ijlās kā shurū' ho, tab Jaj Aiḍvokeṭ ko Korṭ ke Mutarjim se īman kī rū se yeh iqrār lenā chāhiye.*	جب کورٹ مارشیال کے اجلاس کا شروع هو تب جج ایڈوکیٹ کو کورٹ کے مترجم سے ایمان کي رو سے یهہ اقرار لینا چاهیئے

All persons, who give evidence at a Court-Martial, are to be examined on oath according to the forms of their respective religions, or affirmation.

Jo gawāh gawāhī ke liye Korṭ Mārshiāl ke ḥuẓūr āwe, us kī zabāṇ-bandī us ke dīn dharram kī rīt rasm ke muṭābiq qasam kī rū se, yā iqrār kī rū se lī jāegī.

جو گواه گواهي کے ليئي
کورٹ مارشيال کے حضور
آوے اوسکي زبان بندي
اوسکے دين دھرم کي
ريت رسم کے مطابق قسم
کي رو سے يا اقرار کي رو
سے لي جايگي

Hindoos and Musalmans shall make affirmation as follows—

Hindū Musalmānoṇ se iqrār is ḍhab par liyā jāegā.

هندو مسلمانون سے اقرار اس
ڈھب پر ليا جايگا

I solemnly affirm in the presence of Almighty God, that what I shall state shall be the truth, the whole truth, and nothing but the truth.

Maiṇ īmān (dharam) *kī rū se Ḥaqq Ta'ālā Khudā ko ḥāẓir aur nāẓir jān kar* (Parmeshwar Bhagwān ko jān mān ke), *iqrār kartā hūṇ ki wuh bāt jo maiṇ kahūṇ so sachchī kahūṇgā, aur binā lagāo thoṛe bahut ke sab sach kahūṇgā, aur siwā sach ke kuchh aur na kahūṇgā.*

مين ايمان (دھرم) کي رو سے
حق تعالى خدا کو حاضر
اور ناظر جانکر * [پرميشور
بھگوان کو جان مانکے]
اقرار کرتا هون که وه بات
جو مين کهون سو سچي
کهونگا اور بنا لگاو تھوڑے
بهت کے سب سچ کهونگا
اور سوا سچ کے کچھه اور
نه کهونگا

* *Note.*—The words within brackets are for Hindūs.

The effects of deserters are to be publicly sold, and the proceeds, after payment of regimental debts, remitted to the Treasury.

Bhagoroṉ kā māl nīlām meṉ bechnā chāhiye, aur bikrī se jo kuchh ḥāṣil ho us se Rijminṭ ke dain adā kar ke jo bāqī bache, Sarkārī khazāne meṉ dākhil kiyā jāe.

بھگوڑون کا مال نیلام مین بیچنا چاھیئے اور بکري سے جو کچھه حاصل ھو اوس سے رجمنٹ کے دین ادا کر کے جو باقي بچے سرکاري خزانے مین داخل کیا جاے

List of Crimes.

Jarāim kī Fihrist.

جرائم کي فہرست

Disobeying lawful command.

Wājibi ḥukm kā na mānnā.

واجبي حکم کا نه ماننا

Sleeping upon his post.

Apnī chaukī pahre kī jagah par so jānā.

اپني چوکي پہرے کي جگهه پر سو جانا

Leaving his post before regularly relieved.

Apne pahre se ba-ghair ba-qā'ida badlī ke uṭh jānā.

اپنے پہرے سے بغیر بقاعدہ بدلي کے اٹهه جانا

To shamefully abandon.

Be-ghairatī se chhoṛ denā.

بي غیرتي سے چھوڑ دینا

Treacherously making known watchword.

Daghā-bāzī se chaukī pahre kī bāt batā denā.

دغابازي سے چوکي پہرے کي بات بتا دینا

Being drunk when on or for duty.
Naukarī par ho ke, yā naukarī kī taiyārī par ho ke matwālā honā.

نوکري پر هوکے يا نوکري کي طياري پر هوکے متوالا هونا

To be insubordinate or insolent in the ranks.
Ṣaff meṇ ho ke gustākhī se ḥukm na mānnā yā be-adabī karnā.

صف مين هوکے گستاخي سے حکم نه ماننا يا بي ادبي کرنا

To behave in a manner unbecoming the character of an Officer.
Aisī chāl nikālnī jo 'uhda-dār kī 'izzat ābrū par na phabe.

ايسي چال نکالني جو عهده دار کي عزت آبرو پر نه پهبي

To malinger, feign or intentionally produce disease or infirmity.
Makr ya bahāne se apne ko bīmār banānā, jān būjh ke apne par koī bīmārī yā 'illat paidā karnā.

مکر يا بهانے سے اپنے کو بيمار بنانا جان بوجهکے اپنے پر کوئي بيماري يا علت پيدا کرنا

Illegally and against the will of.
Ghair-wājibī ṭaur se aur be-marẓī logoṇ kī.

غيرواجبي طور سے اور بي مرضي لوگون کي

To exact carriage, porterage or provisions.
Bār-bardārī yā moṭyā qulī yā khānā sīdhā zabardastī se lenā.

باربرداري يا موتيا قلي يا کهانا سيدها زبردستي سے لينا

Wantonly and intentionally to insult religious prejudices.
Jān būjh ke sharārat se kisī ko dīn dharam ki baton ke sabab chheṛnā.

جان بوجھکے شرارت سے کسي کو دین دہرم کي باتون کے سبب چھیڑنا

Designedly or through neglect.
Jān būjh ke yā ghaflat se.

جان بوجھکے یا غفلت سے

To sell, pawn, lose or injure his horse, arms, cloths, accoutrements or regimental necessaries.
Apne ghoṛe, yā hathyār, yā poshāk, yā saz-sāman ko, ya Rijminṭ ke kisī zarūrī āsbāb ko bechnā yā giro rakhnā, ya nuqṣān pahunchānā.

اپنے گھوڑے یا ہتھیار یا پوشاک یا ساز سامان کو یا رجمنٹ کے کسي ضروري اسباب کو بیچنا یا گرو رکھنا یا نقصان پہنچانا

To embezzle or fraudulently misapply public money.
Sarkārī rūpaya khājanā yā khiyānat se be-jā kharch karnā.

سرکاري روپیہ کہا جانا یا خیانت سے بیجا خرچ کرنا

To connive at or be concerned in.
Jurm mensharīk honā yā ana-kānī denā.

جرم مین شریک ہونا یا انا کاني دینا

Disgraceful conduct.
Fazīḥatī chāl-chalan.

فضیحتي چال چلن

Wilfully maiming or injuring himself.
Jān būjh ke apne ko langṛā lūlā karnā.

جان بوجھکے اپنے کو لنگڑا لولا کرنا

Purloining or selling Government Stores. *Sarkār ke āsbab ko chorī karnā (mūsnā) yā bechnā.*	سرکار کے اسباب کو چوري کرنا (موسنا) یا بیچنا
Stealing money or goods. *Naqd rūpaya yā āsbāb yā dūsre māl kī chorī karnā.*	نقد روپیه یا اسباب یا دوسرے مال کي چوري کرنا
Directly or indirectly. *Āp yā aur kisī ke wasīle se.*	آپ یا اور کسي کے وسیلے سے
Accepting bribe, present or gratification. *Rishwat yā nazr bhenṭ yā mā-bihil-iḥtiẓāẓ lenā.*	رشوت یا نذر بهینٹ یا ما به الاحتظاظ لینا
Beating or illtreating any person. *Kisī ko mār pīṭ karnā yā izā denā.*	کسي کو مار پیٹ کرنا یا ایذا دینا
Without being regularly relieved in time of peace. *Baghair ba-qā'ida badlī ke ṣulḥ ke dinoṇ meṇ.*	بغیر بقاعده بدلي کے صلح کے دنون مین
In camp, Garrison or Cantonments. *Lashkar yā qil'ah yā chhāonī meṇ.*	لشکر یا قلعه یا چهاوني مین
Intentionally raising false alarms. *Jān būjh ke dhokā dilānā.*	جان بوجهکے دهوکا دلانا

To absent himself without leave.
Baghair parwānagī ke ghair-ḥāẓir honā.

بغیر پروانگي کے غیرحاضر هونا

To allow ammunition to be wasted.
Golī bārūt ko barbād hone denā.

گولي باروت کو برباد هونے دینا

Using, menacing or disrespectful words, signs or gestures.
Bāton se, yā ishāron se, yā aur be-jā ḥarakaton se dhamkānā yā be-imtiyāzī karnā.

باتون سے یا اشارون سے یا اور بیجا حرکتون سے دهمکانا یا بی امتیازي کرنا

Causing disorder or riot.
Balwā-ārāī (or) *hangāma-pardāzī.*

بلوا آراي or هنگامه پردازي

Disturbing the proceedings.
Rū-bakārī men khalal pahunchānā.

روبکاري مین خلل پهنچانا

Purposely giving false evidence.
'Amadan jhūṭhī gawāhī denī.

عمداً جهوتهي گواهي دیني

Conduct to the prejudice of good order and military discipline.
Chāl chalan jo nek qā'ida aur fauj ke achchhe intiẓām ke bar-khilāf hai.

چال چلن جو نیک قاعده اور فوج کے اچهے انتظام کے برخلاف هے

A grave crime—trivial crime.
Jurm-i-sangīn—jurm-i-khafīf.

جرم سنگین جرم خفیف

Civil Offences.

Arson. — اتش زني
Ātash-zanī.

Perjury. — حلف دروغي (دروغ حلفي)
Ḥalaf daroghi (or) *Darogh-i-ḥalafī.*

Assault and battery. — مارپيٹ - حمله آوري
Mār pīṭ—ḥamla-āwarī.

Burglary. — نقب زني
Naqb-zanī.

Inciting. — اشتعالک
Ishti'ālak.

Wilful murder. — قتل عمد
Qatl-i-'amad.

Homicide. — قتل نفس مستلزم السزا †
Qatl-i-nafs-i-mustalzimu-s-sazā.

Manslaughter. — قتل شبهه عمد
Qatl shibh-i-'amad.

Hurt. — ضرر رساني
Zarar-rasānī.

Grievous hurt. — ضرب شديد
Ẓarb-i-shadīd.

Forcible attainment. — استحصال بالجبر
Istiḥṣāl bil-jabr.

---

† Literally—killing so as to be deserving of punishment.

Unlawful appropriation. استحصال بیجا
Istiḥṣāl-i-bejā.

Unlawful imprisonment. حبس بیجا
Ḥabs-i-bejā.

Criminal breach of trust. خیانت مجرمانه
Khiyānat-i-mujrimāna.

Sedition. بلوا
Balwā.

Rioting. هنگامه پردازي
Hangāma-pardāzī.

Rape. زنا بالجبر
Zinā bil-jabr.

Defamation of character. ازالۀ حیثیت عرفي
Izāla-i-ḥaisīyat-i-'urfī.

Coining. جعلسازي - قلبسازي
Ja'l-sāzī, qalb-sāzī.

Punishment. سزا
Sazā.

Death—To be hanged. قتل - پهانسي پانا
Qatl—phāṇsī pānā.

Transportation for life. عمر بهر تك جلاوطني (دیسنکالا)
'Umr bhar tak jalā-waṭanī (des-nikālā.)

Transportation. عبور دریاي شور - کالاپاني
'Ubūr-i-daryā-shor—Kālā pānī.

Dismissal from service. *Naukarī se bar-ṭaraf honā.*	نوکري سے بر طرف هونا
Imprisonment with hard labour. *Qaid sakht mihnat ke sāth (bā-mashaqqat).*	قيد سخت محنت کے ساتهه (با مشقت)
Imprisonment without hard labour. *Qaid bidūn sakht mihnat ke (be-mashaqqat).*	قيد بدون سخت محنت کے (بی مشقت)
For a term of five years. *Pāṇch baras kī mī'ād tak.*	پانچ برس کي ميعاد تک
Solitary confinement. *Qaid tanhāī ke sāth.*	قيد تنهائي کے ساتهه
Corporal punishment. *Sazā-i-badanī—Sazā-i-bed.**	سزاي بدني - سزي بيد
Suspension from rank, pay and allowances. *'Uhde se aur sab ṭalab tankhwāh ke pāne se mu'aṭṭal honā.*	عهدے سے اور سب طلب تنخواه کے پانے سے معطل هونا
He shall be fined to the extent of his arrears of pay. *Apnī sab ṭalab tankhwāh jitnī nikaltī ho ḍanḍ ke ṭaur se bhar degā.*	اپني سب طلب تنخواه جتني نکلتي هو ڈنڈ کے طور سے بهر ديگا
He shall make good such loss or damage. *Us kā harja us se liyā jāegā jis qadar nuqṣān aur ṭoṭā pahuṇchā ho.*	اوسکا هرجه اوس سے ليا جايگا جس قدر نقصان اور توٹا پهنچا هو

* بيد *bed*—a cane.

Reduction to the ranks.
Sipāhī ke darje meṇ utārā jānā.

سپاهي کے درجے مین اوتارا جانا

Amenable to the Articles of War.
Āīn-i-lashkarī kā tābi'-dār.

آئین لشکري کا تابعدار

To be placed lower on the list of his rank.
Apne darje kī fard meṇ us kā nām kuchh utārā jānā.

اپنے درجے کي فرد مین اوسکا نام کچهه اوتارا جانا

*To put under stoppages of pay.
Ṭalab tankhwāh ko dabā rakhnā.

طلب تنخواه کو دبا رکهنا

The sentence will take effect.
Yeh ḥukm 'amal meṇ āwegā.

يهه حکم عمل مين آويگا

*The prisoner will be put under stoppages not exceeding half of his pay and allowances until the amount of such loss or damage be made good.
Qaidī kī ṭalab tankhwāh (ādhī se ziyāda na ho) dabā rakkī jāwegī jab tak ki nuqṣān yā ṭoṭe kā miqdār chukāyā na jāwegā.

قيدي کي طلب تنخواه (آدهي سے زياده نه هو) دبا رکهي جاويگي جب تلک که نقصان يا توٹے کا مقدار چکايا نه جايگا

The prisoner is to be released and to return to his duty.
Qaidī qaid se chhoṛā jāegā aur apnī naukarī par baḥāl kiyā jāegā.

قيدي قيد سے چهوڑا جايگا اور اپني نوکري پر بحال کيا جايگا

---

* Observe the idiom.

To commute a sentence. *Kisī ḥukm ko badal denā.*	كسي حكم كو بدل دينا
To mitigate a sentence. *Kisī ḥukm ko ghaṭānā.*	كسي حكم كو گهٹانا
To remit a sentence. *Kisī ḥukm ko mu'āf karnā.*	كسي حكم كو معاف كرنا
To confirm a sentence. *Kisī ḥukm ko manẓūr karnā.*	كسي حكم كو منظور كرنا
To revise a sentence. *Kisī ḥukm ko naẓar-i-s̤ānī karnā.*	كسي حكم كو نظر ثاني كرنا
To quash a sentence. *Kisī ḥukm ko bāṭil karnā.*	كسي حكم كو باطل كرنا

Specimen Court-Martial.

At a general Court-Martial assembled at Sealkote, on Tuesday, the 29th April 1869, Havildar Ram Singh was arraigned on the following charge:— *Ek Jarnal Korṭ-Mārshiyāl ke rū-ba-rū, jo Aprail kī untīswīṉ tārīkh, san aṭhārah sau unhattar, Mangal ke roz Shālkoṭ kī chhāonī jam'a hūā, Rām Singh Ḥavāl-dār is jurm par pesh kiyā gayā, ya'ne.*	ايك جرنل كورٹ مارشيال كے رو برو - جو اپريل كي انتيسوين تاريخ سنه اٹهاره سو انهتر منگل كے روز شيالكوٹ كي چهاوني جمع هوا - رام سنگه حوال دار اس جرم پر پيش كيا گيا يعني -

---

Charge.
Ilzām kī tafṣīl.

Conduct to the prejudice of good order and military discipline, in having, on or about the 15th February when on duty with a detachment of the Regiment, wilfully neglected to obey the written orders of his superior officer Captain Smith of the same Regiment, to see that the Government transport mules returning from Sealkote to Jhelum were not overloaded, whereby, and in consequence of his wilful neglect as aforesaid, twenty of the said mules or thereabouts were overloaded with the baggage of the men of the detachment, and eight of the said mules were injured on the march to Jhelum, by reason of their being so overloaded.

Chāl chalan jo nek qā'ida aur fauj ke achchhe intiẕām ke bar-khilāf hai, ki us ne māh Ferwarī kī pandrahwīṇ tārīkh ko yā us ke qarīb, jab wuh apnī palṭan kī ek ta'ināti ke hamrāh naukarī par thā, apne baṛe 'uhda-dār, usī Palṭan ke Kaptān Ismit Ṣāḥib Bahādur

الزام کي تفصيل

چال چلن جو نیک قاعدہ اور
فوج کے اچھے انتظام کے
برخلاف هی که اوسنے
ماہ فروري کي پندرهوین
تاریخ کو یا اوسکے قریب
جب وہ اپني پلٹن کي
ایک تعیناتي کے همراہ
نوکري پر تها - اپنے بڑے
عهدہ‌دار اوسي پلٹن کے کپتان
اسمت صاحب بهادر کے
لکھے هوے حکم کو جان
بوجهکے نهین مانا - وہ کیا
حکم تها که خبرداري کرنا
که سرکاري باربرداري کے
جو خچر شیالکوٹ کي
چهاوني سے جهلم کي
چهاوني کو واپس آتے هین
اونپر زیادہ بوجهه نه لدنے
پاوے - اس عدول حکمي

ke likhe hū-e ḥukm ko jān būjh ke nahīṇ manā—woh kyā ḥukm thā ki khabar-dārī karnā ki Sarkārī bār-bardārī ke jo khachchar Shālkoṭ kī chhāonī se Jhelam kī chhāonī ko wāpas āte haiṇ un par ziyāda bojh na ladne pāwe—is 'udūl-ḥukmī ke sabab se, aur us ne jo 'amadan (jān būjh ke) ghaflat kī jaise ke pahle mazkūr hūā hai, un khachcharoṇ meṇ se bīs to, yā us ke qarīb, ta'īnātī ke sipahiyoṇ ke māl o asbāb se ḥadd se ziyāda lāde ga-e, chunānchi un khachcharoṇ meṇ se āṭh 'adad basabab isī ziyāda bojh paṛne ke zakhmī ho ga-e.

کے سبب سے اور او سنے جو عمداً (جان بوجھکے) غفلت کي جیسے کہ پہلے مذکور ہوا ھی اون خچرون مین سے بیس تو یا اوسکے قریب تعیناتي کے سپاھیون کے مال واسباب سے حد سے زیادہ لادے گئے - چنانچہ اون خچرون مین سے اٹھہ عدد بسبب اسي زیادہ بوجھہ پڑنے کے زخمي ہوگئے

The Court find the prisoner is guilty of the charge against him, omitting from it the word "wilful."

Korṭ ne yūṇ tajwīz kī hai ki mujrim is jurm kā gunahgār hai, siwāe is ke da'wā kī fard se "jān būjh ke" ke lafz bar-taraf karnā chāhiye.

کورٹ نے یون تجویز کي ھی کہ مجرم اس جرم کا گنہگار ھی سواے اسکے دعوی کي فرد سے جان بوجھکے کے لفظ برطرف کرنا چاھیئے

And sentence the prisoner to be suspended from rank, pay, and

کورٹ کا یہہ حکم ھی کہ

allowances for a period of three months.
Kort kā yeh ḥukm hai ki qaidī sab ṭalab tankhwāh ke pāne se tīn mahīnoṇ kī mī'ād tak mu'aṭṭal rakhā jāwegā.

قيدي سب طلب تنخواه کے پانے سے تين مہينون کي معياد تک معطّل رکہا جاويگا -

The prisoner is to be released from arrest. The sentence will take effect from the 29th July.
Qaidī qaid se chhoṛā jāegā. Yeh ḥukm Jūlāī kī untīs tārīkh se 'amal meṇ āwega.

قيدي قيد سے چہوڑا جايگا - يهہ حکم جولائي کي ۲۹ تاريخ سے عمل مين آويگا -

Indian Army Regulations, Vol. II, Part II, Discipline, para. 2214.

Every recruit, prior to his being enrolled in his regiment and sworn in according to the Indian Articles of War, is to have the accompanying declaration made to him by the Commanding Officer in front of the regiment or corps, and in presence of the officers and soldiers :—

"In time of peace, after having served for 3 years, on making application for your discharge through the Commanding Officer of your Company (troop or battery), it will be granted to you in two months from the date of application, provided it does not cause the vacancies in the Company (troop or battery) to exceed ten, in which case you must remain until that objection be removed, or waived by competent authority ; but in time of war you have no claim to a discharge, and you must remain and do your duty until the necessity of retaining you in the service shall cease. In the event of your re-enlisting you have no claim to reckon your previous service to discharge."

بوقت صلح بعد اسکے که تمنے تین برس تک نوکري کي
هی اپني کمپني کے کمانير صاحب کي معرفت جو نام کٹنے
کي درخواست کروگے تو اوسي درخواست کي تاريخ سے ليکر
دو مهينے کے بعد منظور هوگي نظر برينکه اوس کمپني مين
خالي اسامي دس سے زيادہ نه هو اور جو زيادہ هو تو چاهيئے
که تم رهوگے جب تک که وہ اعتراض بر طرف نهين هو يا که
کسي سرکار کے قاعدہ يا حکم سے معاف هو جاوگے - لکن
جنگ کے ايام مين تمکو مطلقا نام کٹانے کا حق نهين اور
ضرور هی که تم رهوگے اور اپني نوکري کو پورا کروگے جس
وقت تک که تمکو فوج مين رکهنے کي ضرورت هوچکيگي اور
اگر تم دوسري دفعه بهرتي هوجاوگی تو نوکرئ سابق کو اپني
تئين حساب کرنے کا نام کٹانے کے واسطے بالکل حق
نهين هے -

Translation.

Ba-waqt-i-ṣulḥ, ba'd is ke ki tum ne tīn baras tak naukarī kī hai, apnī Kampanī ke Kamānīr Ṣāḥib kī ma'rifat jo nām kaṭne kī darkhwāst karoge, to usī darkhwāst kī tārīkh se le kar do mahīne ke ba'd manẓūr hogī, naẓar bar-īṇ-ki us Kampanī meṇ khālī asāmī das se ziyāda na ho, aur jo ziyāda ho to chāhiye ki tum rahoge jab tak ki woh i'tirāẓ bar-ṭaraf nahīṇ ho, yā ki Sarkār ke qā'ida yā ḥukm se mu'āf ho jāoge: lekin jang ke aiyām meṇ tum ko muṭlaqan nām kaṭāne ka ḥaqq nahīṇ, aur ẓarūr hai ki tum rahoge aur apnī naukarī ko pūrā karoge, jis waqt tak ki tum ko fauj meṇ rakhne kī ẓarūrat ho chukegī; aur agar tum dūsrī daf'a bhartī ho jāoge, to naukarī-i-sābiq ko apne ta-īṇ ḥisāb karne kā, nām kaṭāne ke wāsṭe bil kull ḥaqq nahīṇ hai.

Medical Phrases.

Are there any new cases to-day?
Āj koī nayā bīmār hai?
آج کوئي نيا بيمار هى

After seeing the new cases I will examine the recruits.
Na-e bīmāron ko dekhne ke ba'd ham rangkrūton ko mulāḥiẓa karenge.
نئے بيمارن کو ديکهنے کے بعد هم رنگکروٹون کو ملاحظه کرينگے

How is the man who fell from his horse yesterday evening?
Wuh jawān kaisā hai jo kal shām ko apne ghoṛe par se gir paṛā?
وه جوان کيسا هى جو کل شام کو اپنے گهوڑے پر سے گر پڑا

He is still unconscious, Sir.
Ḥuẓūr, abhī tak behosh hai.
حضور ابهي تک بيهوش هے

How many men are there in Hospital?
Haspatāl meṇ kitne ādmī bīmār haiṇ?
هسپتال مين کتنے آدمي بيمار هين

Take care that the hospital is clean.
Khabar-dār, Haspatāl ṣāf rahe.
خبردار هسپتال صاف رهے

Open all the windows.
Sab khiṛkiyoṇ ko kholo.
سب کهڑکيون کو کهولو

Keep the beds one foot from the wall.
Chār-pāiyoṇ ko dīwār se ek fuṭ ke fāṣile par rakho.
چار پايون کو ديوار سے ايک فٹ کے فاصلے پر رکهو

That man's bedding is insufficient.
Us ādmī kā bistar kam hai.
اوس آدمي کا بستر کم هى

In future give him clean sheets.
**Āyinda ko ṣāf chādareṇ diyā karo.*

آینده کو صاف چادرین دیا کرو

This matter must be reported to the Adjutant.
Ajīṭan Ṣāḥib ke pās is bāt kī khabar bhejnā chāhīye.

اجیٹن صاحب کے پاس اس بات کي خبر بهیجنا چاهیئے

Are all poisons kept under lock and key?
Kyā sab zahr qufl meṇ band rahte haiṇ?

کیا سب زهر قفل مین بند رهتے هین

This is a strict Government order.
Yeh Sarkār kā sakht ḥukm hai.

یهه سرکار کا سخت حکم هی

*You alone are responsible for the instruments.
Hathyār sab tumhāre hī zimme par haiṇ.

هتیار سب تمهارے هي ذمے پر هین

These instruments are not in good order.
Yeh hathyār durustī par nahīṇ haiṇ.

یهه هتهیار درستي پر نهین هین

The scalpels are blunt and dirty.
Chhuṛīāṇ sab kund aur mailī haiṇ.

چهریان سب کند اور میلی هین

---

* Observe the construction, noting the force of هی *hī*, in the second sentence.

That saw is useless from rust.
Woh āṛā morche ke sabab se kuchh kām kā nahīṇ hāi.
وہ آرا مورچے کے سبب سے کچھ کام کا نہین هی

The latrine is dirty, it must be kept much cleaner.
Ṭaṭṭī mailī hai, isse bahut ṣāf rakhnā hogā.
ٹٹی میلي هی اسّے بہت صاف رکھنا ہوگا

*I will never pass over this matter.
Maiṇ is bāt se hargiz darguzar nahīṇ karne kā.
مین اس بات سے هرگز درگذر نہین کرنے کا

Why did you not obey my order?
Tum ne hamārā ḥukm kyūṇ na mānā?
تمنے همارا حکم کیون نہ مانا

There is a very bad smell here.
Is jagah meṇ baṛī bad-bū hai.
اس جگہ مین بڑي بدبو هی

See that dry earth is more freely used.
Khabar-dār, sūkhī miṭṭī ziyāda-tar ḍālī jāegī.
خبردار سوکھي مٹي زیادہ‌تر ڈالي جایگي

Where is the mortuary?
Lāsh-khāna kis ṭaraf hai?
لاش خانہ کس طرف هی

Open the door and let me see it.
Kholo darwāza ke ham mulāḥiza kareṇ.
کھولو دروازہ کہ هم ملاحظہ کرین

Now show me the bath-rooms.
Ab ghusl-khana dikhlāo.
اب غسل خانہ دکھلاو

---

* Observe the construction. *Maiṇ nahīṇ karne kā.* I am not one to.

* Have fresh water always kept here. *Yahāṇ har waqt tāza pānī bharā rakho.*	یہان ہر وقت تازہ پانی بھرا رکھو
* Fill this water-pot with water. *Is ghaṛe meṇ pānī bhar do.*	اس گھڑے مین پانی بھر دو
* Have the walls freshly plastered. *Dīwāroṇ ko nae sar se lipwā denā.*	دیوارون کو نئے سر سے لپوا دینا
Have sulphur burnt in this room. *Is kamare men kuchh gandhak jalwā-do.*	اس کمرے مین کچھہ گندھک جلوادو
Has this recruit been vaccinated ? *Is umīdwār ko kabhī ṭīkā lagāyā gayā ?*	اس امیدوار کو کبھی تیکا لگایا گیا
I was vaccinated in childhood. *Maiṇ laṛakpan meṇ godā gayā.*	مین لڑکپن مین گودا گیا
* Well, show me your arm and the marks. *Achchhā apnā bāzū aur nishān dekhlāo.*	اچھا اپنا بازو اور نشان دکھلاو
He must be re-vaccinated. *Pher ṭīkā lagānā paṛegā.*	پھر تیکا لگانا پڑیگا
Give me the vaccinating lancet. *Ṭīkā lagāne kā nashtar de denā.*	تیکا لگانے کا نشتر دے دینا

* Observe the construction.

Call in both those recruits.
Un donoṇ rangkrūtoṇ ko bulāo.

اون دونون رنگکروتون کو بلاو

*Not both at once—one at a time.
Donoṇ ko ek sāth mat bulāo—ek ek kar ke.

دونون کو ایکساتهه مت بلاو ایک ایک کرکے

Take off your clothes.
Kapṟoṇ ko utāro.

کپڑون کو اوتارو

*He seems rather short.
Us kā qadd zara chhoṭā ma'lūm hotā hai.

اوسکا قد ذرہ چهوٹا معلوم هوتا

Bring the standard and measure him.
Nāp lāo aur us kā qadd nāpo.

ناپ لاو اور اوسکا قد ناپو

*Examine his eyesight with the dots.
Bindīyoṇ se us kī bīnāī jāṇchnā.

بندیون سے اوسکي بینائي جانچنا

*His chest must be measured.
Us kī chhātī nāpā chāhiye.

اوسکي چهاتي ناپا چاهئے

The tape is on the small table.
Nāpne kā fītā chhoṭī mez ke ūpar hai.

ناپنے کا فیتا چهوٹي میز کے اوپر هی

Walk up and down the room.
Kamare meṇ chalo phiro.

کمرے مین چلو پهرو

Turn round and come back.
Ghum ke lauṭ āo.

گهوم کے لوٹ آو

---

* Observe the construction.

*Hop first on the right foot.
Ek pāṇw par laṇgṛī chalo—pahle dahne pāṇw par.

ایک پانو پر لنگڑي چلو - پہلے دھنے پانو پر

Then back on the left foot.
Pher bāeṇ pāṇw par lauṭ āo.

پھر بائیں پانو پر لوٹ آو

Stretch your arms over your head.
Donoṇ hāthoṇ ko sar ke ūpar pasāro.

دونو هاتهون کو سر کے اوپر پسارو

Let me see your fingers.
Uṇgliyoṇ ko dekhne do.

اونگلیون کو دیکھنے دو

Stand with your heels together.
Eṛiyoṇ ko jor kar khaṛe ho.

ایڑیون کو جوڑ کر کھڑے هو

Stand on one foot, put the other forward.
Ek pāṇw par khaṛe ho, dūsre ko āge rakho.

ایک پانو پر کھڑے هو دوسرے کو آگے رکھو

Bend your ankle joint and toes.
Panja moṛo, aur ṭakhnoṇ ko moṛo.

پنجه موڑو اور ٹخنون کو موڑو

*Kneel on one knee.
Ek ghuṭne ke bal baiṭho.

ایک گھٹنے کے بل بیٹھو-

Up again.
Phir ūṭho.

پھر اوٹھو

Now on the other knee.
Ab dūsre ghuṭne par.

اب دوسرے گھٹنے پر

---

* Observe the construction.

* Down on both knees and spring up with both legs together.
Donoṇ ghuṭnoṇ par baiṭho aur ek dam chhāl mār ke jaldī se uṭho.
دونون گہٹنون پر بیٹھو اور ایک دم چہال مار کے جلدي سے اوٹھو

Turn round — separate your legs.
Ghūm jāo — pāṇoṇ kholo.
گہوم جاو پانون کہولو

Bend down and touch the ground with the hands.
Jhuk ke hāthoṇ ko zamīn par rakho.
جہک کے هاتهون کو زمین پر رکہو

* Stretch out your arms, like this.
Bāzuoṇ ko pasāro, aisā karke.
بازوون کو پسارو - ایسا کر کے

Bend the fingers.
Uṇgliyoṇ ko moṛo.
اونگلیون کو موڑو

Bend your thumbs thus.
Is ṯarah apne aṇgūṭhoṇ ko moṛo.
اس طرح اپنے انگوٹهون کو موڑو

*Bend your wrists.
Pahuṇchoṇ ko moṛ denā.
پہنچون کو موڑ دینا

Now bend your elbows.
Ab kuhniyoṇ ko moṛo.
اب کہنیون کو موڑو

Have you ever had a blow on the head?
Kabhī sar par choṭ lagī hai?
کبهي سر پر چوٹ لگي هی

Are you ever giddy?
Kabhī sar ghūmtā hai? — Chakkar ātā hai?
کبهي سر گہومتا هی - چکر آتا هی

* Observe the construction.

Say how many dots are there?
Batāo, kitnī bindiyāṇ haiṇ?

بتاو - کتنی بندیان هین

Now come to the office.
Ab daftar meṇ chalo.

اب دفتر مین چلو

*Copy this letter and post it to-day.
Is chiṭṭhi kī naql kar ke āj ḍāk meṇ dā<u>kh</u>il karo.

اس چتهي کا نقل کرکے آج ڈاک مین داخل کرو

Fill in all these columns.
In sab <u>kh</u>ānoṇ ko pūrā karnā.

ان سب خانون کو پورا کرنا

Show me all the books.
Sab kitāboṇ ko dekhlāo.

سب کتابون کو دکهلاو

*I hear the regiment marches to-morrow.
Aisā sunne meṇ āyā hai ki Palṭan kal kūch karegī.

ایسا سننے مین آیا هی که پلٹن کل کوچ کریگي

Is all the carriage, &c., ready?
Bār-bardārī wa<u>gh</u>aira sab ṭaiyār hai?

بار برداري وغیره سب طیار هی

*Any man who is too ill to march must be left behind in hospital.
Jo koī jawān bīmārī ke sabab se kūch nahīṇ kar sakta ho, haspatāl meṇ chhor diyā jāegā.

جو کوئي جوان بیماري کے سبب سے کوچ نهین کرسکتا هو هسپتال مین چهوڑ دیا جایگا

---

* Observe the construction.

Are all preparations for the march complete? *Kūch ke sab intiẓām pūre haiṇ?*	کوچ کے سب انتظام پورے هین
Two doolies and two country carts will be required. *Do ḍoliyāṇ aur do bail-gāṛiyāṇ darkār hoṇgīn.*	دو ڈولیان اور دو بیل گاڑیان درکار هونگین
Pitch the hospital tent under a tree. *Haspatāl ka ḍerā kisī dirakht ke nīche khaṛā karo.*	هسپتال کا ڈیرا کسي درخت کے نیچے کھڑا کرو
*The ground is very damp here. *Zamīn is jagah kī bahut gīlī hai.*	زمین اس جگهه کي بهت گیلي هی
Let the men have some straw spread. *Sipāhiyon ke līye kuchh poāl bichhwā denā.*	سپاهیون کے لیئے کچهه پوال بچهوا دینا
Extra carriage is required, Sir. *Ḥuẓūr, ka-ī ek fāltū gāṛī darkar haiṇ.*	حضور کئي ایک فالتو گاڑي درکار هین
How are *gārīs* to be had? *Gāṛīyān kis ṭaraḥ se mileṇgīn?*	گاڑیان کس طرحسے ملینگین
By application to the Quarter-Master. *Quātar Māsṭar Ṣāḥib ke pās likhne se.*	کواٹر ماسٹر صاحب کے پاس لکهنے سے

---

* Observe the construction.

*For every six men one cart of two bullocks can be had. *Chhe chhe bīmāroṇ ke liye ek ek do bail kī gāṛi mil saktī hai.*	چهه چهه بيمارون کے لیئے ایک ایک دو بیل کي گاڑي مل سکتي هی
Where is the original of this letter? *Is chiṭṭhī kī aṣl kahāṇ hai?*	اس چٹھي کي اصل کہان هی
*This is only a duplicate copy. *Yeh to faqaṭ muṣannā hai.*	یهه تو فقط مثنا هی
*Call up the new cases one by one. *Na-e ādmiyoṇ ko ek ek kar ke bulāo.*	نئے آدمیون کو ایک ایک کرکے بلاو
*What is the matter with you? *Kyā hūā tum ko?*	کیا هوا تمکو
†Show your tongue. *Jībh dekhlāo.*	جیبه دکهلاو
Have you pain anywhere? *Kahīṇ kuchh dard hai?*	کهین کچهه درد هی
How is your appetite? *Bhūkh kaisī hai?*	بهوکهه کیسي هی
Do you digest your food? *Kyā khānā hazm hotā (pachtā) hai?*	کیا کهانا حضم هوتا (پچتا) هی

---

* Observe the construction.

† *N.B.*—The word زبان *zabān* is often used instead of جیبه *jībh* by uneducated natives.

Do you ever have fever?
Tum ko kabhī bukhār ātā hai?
تمکو کبھي بخار آتا هی

Draw a long breath.
Lambī sāṇs kheṇcho.
لمبي سانس کھینچو

*Tell me your name.
Apnā nām batāo.
اپنا نام بتاو

Cough, cough once more.
Khāṇso, pher khāṇso.
کھانسو - پہر کہانسو

*Lie down on your bed.
Apnī chār-pāi par leṭ jāo.
اپني چار پاي پر لیٹ جاو

Draw up your knees.
Ghuṭnoṇ ko uṭhāo.
گھٹنوں کو اٹھاو

Turn over on your right side.
Dāhnī ṭaraf ko karwaṭ lo.
داهني طرف کو کروٹ لو

Now turn on your left side.
Ab bāīṇ ṭaraf ko karwaṭ lo.
اب بائین طرف کو کروٹ لو

Lie on your back—on your face.
Chit leṭo—paṭ leṭo.
چت لیٹو - پٹ لیٹو

Show me your gums.
Masūṛā dekhlāo.
مسوڑا دیکھلاو

At what time does the fever attack you?
Kis waqt bukhār chaṛhtā hai?
کس وقت بخار چڑھتا هی

About seven in the evening.
Shām ke waqt, qarīb sāt baje.
شام کے وقت قریب سات بجے

---

* Observe the construction.

And when does it leave you? *Aur kab utar jātā hai?*	اور کب اُتر جاتا هی
† Generally about 4 A.M. *Akṣar koī chār baje fajr ko.*	اکثر کوئي چار بجے فجر کو
* How long have you been suffering? *Kab se tum ko bukhar hūā kartā hai?*	کبسے تمکو بخار هوا کرتا هی
I am very thirsty and perspire profusely. *Mujhe pīyās bahut lagtī aur pasīna bahut nikalta hai.*	مجهے پیاس بہت لگتي اور پسینا بہت نکلتا هي
I am very constipated. *Mujh ko qabẓīat shiddat se hai.*	مجهکو قبضیت شدت سے هی
* Give him five grains every three hours. *Tīn tīn ghanṭe ke ba'd pāṇch pāṇch grain diyā karo.*	تین تین گهنٹے کے بعد پانچ پانچ گرین دیا کرو
He is better now than he was. *Ab pahle se achchhā hai.*	اب پہلے سے اچها هی
How did you catch cold? *Kis ṭaraḥ se sardī lag gaī?*	کس طرح سردي لگ گئے
Four days ago, Sir, I got wet on guard. *Ḥuẓūr, chār roz hue maiṇ pahre par bhīg gayā thā.*	حضور چار روز هوے مین پهرے پر بهیگ گیا تها

---

† N. B.—Observe this use of کوئي signifying "about."

* Observe this idiom.

Have you had any shivering?
Kyā kuchh jāṛā āyā thā?

کیا کچھہ جاڑا آیا تھا

Put his bed in a corner, out of the draught.
Us kī chār-pāī ko goshe meṉ rakh do, ki us par hawā na lagne pāwe.

اوسکي چار پائي کو گوشے مین رکھہ دو که اوس پر هوا نه لگنے پاوے

He will require a sick attendant.
Us ke wāsṭe ek chhuṭṭī wālā chāhiye.

اوسکے واسطے ایک چھٹي والا چاهئے

*Please write a requisition for me.
Ek chhuṭṭī wāle ke liye darkhwāst likhiyegā.

ایک چھٹي والے کے لیئے درخواست لکھیئے گا

Take care there is no communication between this case of small-pox and the regiment.
Khabar-dar ho ki is chechak wāle se koi Palṭan kā shakhṣ milne na pāe.

خبردار هو که اس چیچک والي سے کوئي پلٹن کا شخص ملنے نه پاوے

A report must be sent at once.
Ek ripoṭ fauran bhejā chāhiye.

ایک رپوٹ فوراً بھیجا چاهئے

He is complaining of griping.
Wuh maroroṉ kī bahut shikāyat kartā hai.

وه مرورون کي بهت شکایت کرتا هي

Is this man delirious at night?
Yeh ādmī rāt ko hazyān kī ḥālat meṉ rahtā hai?

یهه آدمي رات کو هذیان کي حالت مین رهتاهي

---

* Observe the construction.

At present he is quite insensible.
Is waqt woh bilkull be-hosh hai.

اس وقت وہ بالکل بے ہوش هی

* Give him iced milk to drink occasionally.
Kabhī kabhī usko baraf dūdh pilāte raho.

کبھي کبھي اوسکو برف دودہ پلاتے رهو

His pulse is very small and irregular.
Nabẓ us kī bahut bārīk aur be-qā'ida hai.

نبض اسکی بہت باریک اور بے قاعدہ هی

Stop this medicine from to-day.
Āj se yeh davā mauqūf karo.

آج سے یہہ دوا موقوف کرو

Isolate the case of Scabies.
Khujlī wāle ko 'alāḥida rakho.

کهجلي والے کو علیحدہ رکھو

That looks like a case of sunstroke.
Yeh bīmārī tamkā sī ma'lūm hotī hai.

یہہ بیماري تمکا سا معلوم هوتي هی

Call the *bhisti* and tell him to bring his *mussuck* full of cold water.
Bhistī ko bulāo aur kah do ki mashk ṭhanḍe pānī se bhar ke jaldī se lāwe.

بهشتي کو بلاو اور کهہ دو کہ مشک ٹھنڈے پاني سے بھر کے جلدي سے لاوے

* Wrap him at once in iced sheets and give him a hypodermic injection of Quinine.
Fauran usko ṭhanḍī chadaron meṇ lipetnā aur chamre ke nīche Quinine pechkārī se dena

فوراً اوسکو ٹھنڈي چادرون مین لپیٹنا اور چمرے کے نیچے کوینین پیچکاري مے دینا

---

* Observe the construction.

PART III.

EXERCISES IN READING MSS.

۱

غریب پرور سلامت

جب سے فدوی یہاں آیا
ہے ہمیشہ بیمار رہتا ہے اور کوئی حکیم اس جگہ نہیں
اور دوا بھی کچھ دستیاب نہیں ہوتی لہذا امیدوار
ہوں کہ تبدیلی غلام کی کسی دوسرے جگہ ہو جاے
ورنہ غلام اس جگہ ضرور مر جائیگا واجب تھا عرض
کیا فقط

عرضی امیر خان
فدوی جمعدار

١

غریب پرور سلامت

حسب الحکم حضور کے فدوی نے
ضلع کانپور جاکر ایک سو دس آدمی قوم رجعت سے
بھرتی کئے ہیں اور ایک ایک روپیہ فی کس خوراک
کے واسطے جو حسب دستور اور حکم حضور کے دیدیا
چنانچہ اونتیس تاریخ اسی مہینے کے فدوی معہ سب
آدمیونکے چھاونی میں حاضر ہوگا لیکن آگرے کے
رستے نہیں آویگا بریلی کی راہ سے آویگا
سنا ہے کہ وہاں بیماری بہت ہے اور آدمی
مرتے ہیں اطلاعاً عرض کیا فقط

عرضی فدوی امیر خان [illegible] حوالدار
[illegible] کمپنی

ر

غریب پرور سلامت

آج فدوی کی طبیعت

بہت بیمار ہے اور طاقت آمد و رفت نہیں لہذا

امیدوار ہوں کہ رخصت دو روز کی مل جاوے

اور جو حضور رخصت نہ دیں تو عوضی اپنا دیدوں

واجب تھا عرض کیا فقط

عرضی فدوی نیاز مند درباری

ملازم حضور

د

غریب پرور سلامت

کل فدوی واسطے لینے شکر
کے بازار کو جاتا تھا جب کوتوالی کے پاس پہنچا تو نرائن
کانسٹبل نے مجھکو گالی دی اور لات گھونسے سے بہت
مارا تمام بازار کے لوگ گواہ ہیں لہذا امیدوار ہوں کہ
حضور نابردی کو عدالت میں طلب فرما کر سزا دیں
نہیں تو سب رعیت سرکار کی تباہ ہو جائیگی واجب
تھا عرض کیا فقط

[illegible]

ل

غریب پرور سلامت

بہت عرصہ ہوا کہ حضور نے زبان

مبارک سے فرمایا تھا کہ پرورش تمہارے بیٹے کی کسی جگہ

وقت خالی ہونے اسامی کے ہوگی سو اب ایک چپراسی

عدالت فوجداری میں خالی ہوئی ہے لهذا امیدوار

ہوں کہ پرورش بندہ زادہ اوس اسامی پر ہو جاوے

مناسب تھا عرض کیا فقط

عرضی

فدوی جواہر لعل محرر عدالت

معظم سرری

لہ

غریب پرور سلامت

عرصہ ایک ہفتے کا گذرا ہوگا کہ مسمی
رامدیال چپراسی ملازم حضور سات من دانہ فدوی کی
سے حضور کے واسطے لیگیا ہے اور قیمت نہیں دے گیا
اج فدوی نے دام نامبردے سے طلب کئے تو گالیان
دینے لگا اور مارنے کو مستعد ہوا غلام نے اپ کے
خوف سے کچھ نکہا لہذا امیدوار ہون کہ حضور
قیمت دانہ فدوی کو چپراسی مذکور سے دلوادیں واجب تہا عرض
کیا فقط

عرضی

[illegible]

۱

غریب پرور سلامت

کل سے فدوی کو تپ و لرزہ آگیا ہے

اور تمام بدن میں درد ہے اور دم بدم قے ہوتی ہے ہر چند کہ

بابو شفاخانہ نے دوائی دی پر کچھ فایدہ نہوا لہذا امیدوار ہوں

رخصت ایک ہفتے کی عنایت ہو جاوے اگر رخصت

نہ ملیگی تو فدوی ضرور مر جائیگا اور یہ بھی واضح ہو کہ فدوی

نے جس روز سے نوکر ہوا ہے کبھی رخصت نہیں لی

اور کوئی بہانہ یا حیلہ نوکری کے وقت نہیں کیا ہمیشہ حکم

سرکار بجالایا واجب تھا عرض کیا فقط

عرضی [illegible]

غریب پرور سلامت

جناب عالی برسوں سے فدوی

بموجب حکم حضور کے عدالت میں حاضر ہے اور گواہ

بھی سب موجود ہیں لیکن مقدمہ فیصل نہیں ہوتا

اور فدوی کا خرچ بہت ہوتا ہے گواہوں کو خوراک

دیتا ہے لہذا امیدوار ہوں کہ مقدمہ آج پیش ہو

بجا ہے واجب تھا عرض کیا فقط

فدوی [illegible] مدعی

ل

غریب پرور سلامت

عرصہ دو سال کا گذرا کہ فدوی کی
بیٹی کی شادی کندن سنار کے گھر ہوئی تھی بعد سب رسوم
شادی کے بھی تمام ہو گئے تھے سو اب نامبردی نے
از راہ دغابازی کے شادی دوسرے جگہ کر دی اور کہا
ہے کہ تم اپنے بیٹی کی شادی اور جگہ کر لو خداوندا جائے
انصاف ہے کہ فدوی نے دو سو روپیہ خرچ کر کے تو شادی کی
ہے اب کہاں سے پھر اتنا روپیہ لاویں جو شادی دوسری
کریں لہذا امیدوار ہوں کہ حضور مدعا علیہ کو عدالت
میں طلب کر کے تحقیقات فرمائیں اور گواہ غلام کے
بہت ہیں واجب تھا عرض کیا فقط

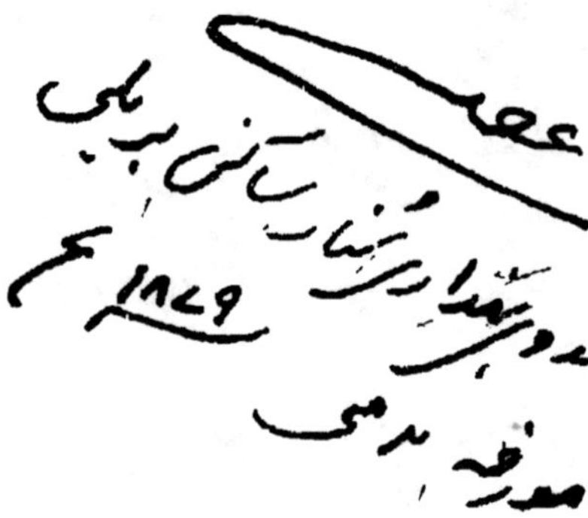

غریب پرور سلامت

کل فدوی کے گہر سے خط آیا ہے
اوس سے دریافت ہوا کہ فدوی کے والد نے اس جہان
سے انتقال کیا اور اب گہر پر کوئی سرپرست
جو سب بندوبست گانو وغیرہ کا کرے کوئی باقی نہیں رہا اس
حالت میں فدوی کسطرح نوکری نہیں کر سکتا لہذا امید
وار ہون کے نام فدوی کا نوکری سرکار سے کاٹا جاوے
ورنہ سب کاروبار میرا ابتر ہوجایگا واجب تہا عرض
کیا فقط

عرضی
فدوی [illegible] علی [illegible] حوالدار
نمبر [illegible] کمپنی

غریب پرور سلامت

عرصہ ایک سال کا ہوا کہ مسمی
سردار نجار درزی نے مبلغ ایک سو دس روپئے فدوی
سے قرض لئے تھے اور تمسک اقرار سات مہینے کا لکھ دیا
تھا چنانچہ اب دس مہینے گزر گئے لیکن نامردہ روپیہ ادا نہیں
کرتا جو آج فدوی نے روپیہ طلب کیا تو کہا ہمارے نام نالش کرو
اگر ہم سے تقاضا کروگے تو ہم تمکو خوب مارینگے لہذا امیدوار
ہوں کہ نامردے کو حضور طلب کر کے روپیہ دلوادیں واجب
تھا عرض کیا

[illegible]

لہ

غریب پرور سلامت

عرض یہ ہے کہ چار مہینے کا ہوا کہ فدوی نے

مبلغ بیس روپئے نندرام لعل حوالدار کمپنی دو کو اسکے گھر جانے کے

وقت دئے تھے اور یہہ کہدیا تھا کہ تم یہہ روپئے ہمارے بھائی بدری

داس کو دیدینا اور رسید لیکے ہمارے پاس روانہ کرنا سو کل فدوی

کے مکان سے خط آیا ہے اوس سے دریافت ہوا کہ حوالدار نے وہ روپئے

نہیں دئے لہذا امیدوار ہوں کہ روپیہ علم کا حوالدار کی طلب

سے دلایا جاوے فقط

فدوی دیال سپاہی

۱

غریب پرور سلامت

کل فضائل الہی سے مشہور ہیں

فدویہ کا فوت ہو گیا اور کوئی شخص دوسرا رشتہ دار
یا وارث فدویہ کا نہیں جو خبرگیری کھانے پینے کی کرے
اور کوئی جائداد بھی پاس فدویہ کے نہیں کہ جس سے گذران
اپنی کروں لہذا امیدوار ہوں کہ حضور دو روپیہ ماہوار
میرے خاوند کی طلب سے مقرر کر دیں کہ اوس سے گذارا
فدویہ کا بخوبی ہو جایگا اور حضور کو دعا کرونگی

عرضی
فدویہ مسماۃ بلاسو دواہ
جدا حسینی بیوی

لہ

غریب پرور سلامت

جب سے فدوی پلٹن میں
بھرتی ہوا ابھی کبھی کوئی قصور نہیں کیا اور نوکری سے کسی
وقت غیر حاضر نہیں ہوا اور اپنے بڑے عہدہ دار کا ہمیشہ
حکم مانا لیکن کل صوبہ دار صاحب نے فدوی کو برا بھلا کہا
جب فدوی نے کہا کہ مجھے کیوں گالی دیتے ہو تو بولے کہ
ہم تمکو فوج سے نکال دینگے خداوندا فدوی کو اب نوکری
منظور نہیں لہذا امیدوار ہوں کہ استعفا فدوی کا
منظور ہو فقط

عرضی عبداللہ سپاہی
فدوی جماعت نمبر اول

15.

غریب پرور سلامت

جب سے مدو گھر پر آیا ہمیشہ
بیمار ہے اگرچہ بہت علاج شفاخانہ وغیرہ کا کیا
لیکن آرام نہیں ہوتا تمام بدن میں بائی کا درد بھی
اور کبھی پسلی میں درد ہو جاتا ہے اور آدھا سینے
کا درد بھی ہوتا ہے تمام بدن درد ہے اور ہاتھ پاؤں
پر ورم آگیا ہمیشہ قبض پیٹ میں رہتا ہے ڈرتا
ہوں کہ کہیں سرسام ہو جائے لہذا امیدوار ہوں کہ رخصت
دو مہینے کی مل جاوے واجب تھا عرض کیا فقط

عرضی
مدو بن [illegible] بخش
جمعدار

لہ

غریب پرور سلامت

زر چوکیداری قدیم سے

فدوی کے نام پر چار آنہ ماہواری مقرر ہیں اور

فدوی ماہ بماہ ادا کرتا ہے لیکن کل بخشی نے فدوی

سے کہا کہ تم سے ہم اس مہینے میں آٹھ آنہ لینگے لہذا

امیدوار ہوں کہ حضور بخشی مذکور سے دریافت فرما

کر حکم مناسب دیں کہ میں اس ظلم سے بچ جاؤں

واجب تھا عرض کیا فقط

عرضی فدوی [illegible]

غریب پرور سلامت

پرسوں دس بجے رات کو فدوی
کے مکان میں چوری ہو گئی اور اسباب مالیت سو روپیہ کا
چوری گیا جب کوتوال صاحب سے اطلاع کی تو انہوں
نے جواب دیا کہ تم فریب کرتے ہو خداوندا جائے
غور ہے کہ فدوی کا اسباب چوری گیا اور فدوی
فریب کرتا حضور موقع پر تشریف لاویں اور گواہوں
سے دریافت کریں تب فدوی کا حال حضور کو کھل
جاوے فقط

عرضی [illegible]

ل

غریب پرور سلامت

آج بھائی فدوی کا گھر سے

آیا ہے اور ارادہ اسکا بھی ہے نوکری سرکار کرے اور عمر

اسکی قریب بیس برس کے ہے اور لکھا پڑھا بھی ہے لہذا

امیدوار ہوں کہ بعد ملاحظہ ڈاکٹر صاحب کے وہ اس

پلٹن میں بھرتی کیا جاوے اسواسطے کہ فدوی کے باپ دادا

قدیم سے فوج میں نوکر رہے ہیں اور فوج ہی کو پسند

کرتے ہیں واجب جانکر عرض کیا فقط

عرضی فدوی [illegible]

[illegible] سپاہی

ر

غریب پرور سلامت

جناب عالی حسب الحکم حضور کے

مدوی نے دو ہاتھی نواب صاحب بہادر سے لیکر کاشی پور میں

پہنچادئے اور چہار گھوڑے سرکاری بھی حضور کے مقام شفاخانہ پر

رکھی ہیں جو وقت آپ کو درکار ہو تیار ہیں اور راجا کاشی

پور بھی کہتی ہیں کہ چار فیل اور شکاری کو تمکو ایک ہاتھی کے

لئے دے سکتے ہیں اگر حضور فرمادیں تو راجہ صاحب سے ہاتھی لیکر

جنگل میں تیار رکھوں اطلاعاً عرض کیا فقط

مدوی عنایت خان

جمعہ ۱ ۱

ر

غریب پرور سلامت

فدوی نے اقبال حضور سے

آج حرما قیدی کو جو سات برس کا میعادی تھا گرفتار
کر لیا اور دوسرے لوگوں کی گرفتاری شب و روز کوشش
کرتا ہوں اطلاعاً عرض کیا مخبروں نے خبر دی ہے کہ تین
اشتہاری ضلع بجنور میں ہیں سو فدوی نے ایک آدمی
معتبر اپنا روانہ کیا ہے وقت ملنے سراغ کے فوراً روانہ
بجنور ہونگا اور فدوی کو پرسوں سے تپ و لرزہ آنے
لگا بہت کمزوری ہے آفتاب دولت تاباں رہے فقط

[illegible]

ا

غریب پرور سلامت

فدوی عرصہ بیس سال سے پنشن
پاتا ہے اور رسالہ سواران ہندوستانی میں نوکر تھا اور اب فدوی
کو عارضہ فالج کا ہو گیا ہے چل نہیں سکتا لہذا امیدوار ہوں کہ
پنشن فدوی کی فدوی کے بیٹے کے نام پر مقرر ہو جاوے وہ گذر
سے لیا کریگا مناسب جانکر عرض کیا آفتاب دولت کا تابان رہے فقط

عرضی
فدوی سید منور خان سوار
پنشنی [illegible]
جوان

غریب پرور سلامت

حضور نے فرمایا تھا کہ

روپیہ تمہارا دس تاریخ کو دینگے سو آج دس تاریخ

کو فدوی حاضر ہوا ہے لہذا امیدوار ہون کہ

روپیہ فدوی کا آج مل جاوے کس واسطے کہ فدوی

اب گھر جاتا ہے مناسب تھا عرض کیا فقط

عرضی مہدی حسن سوداگر

ر

غریب پرور سلامت

پرسوں واقع ۱۲ ماہ ہذا کو مسمی
کندن سنگھ برادر فدوی کا بعلت مارپیٹ کے قید
ہوگیا ہے اور پاس نامردہ کے لوٹہ نہیں اس باعث
سے بہت تکلیف ہے لہذا امیدوار ہوں کہ حکم حضور
واسطے دلانے لوٹہ مذکور کے بنام داروغہ جیل کے
صادر ہو جاوے کہ وہ لوٹہ قیدی کو دلوا دیں
واجب تھا عرض کیا فقط

[illegible]

ادر

غریب پرور سلامت

جناب عالی حضور کی دولت میں یہ معروض ہے کہ آجکل مرض
چیچک کا بس زور ہے — اور میرے چند طفلان ایسے ہیں
کہ جنکو ٹیکا نہیں دیا گیا اور میرے تمنا یہ ہے کہ یہ کام حضور کے
دست مبارک سے انجام پاوے تو عین خاوندی و بندہ
نوازی ہوگی۔ جسکا شکریہ تمام عمر ادا نہ کر سکونگا۔

[illegible]

۵ جنوری ۱۸۸۹ء

غریب پرور عالم جاں حاتم وقت نوشیروان جناب لگن صاحب بہادر دام اقبالہ

جناب عالی حال یہ ہے کہ دو قطعہ پروانہ از راہ غریب پروری و بندہ نوازی

کے سرکار فیض آثار سے بذریعہ ڈاک پر مکان والد فدوی کے مرحمت فرما

تھا۔ اور حال پرورش فدوی کے معلوم ہوا خدا حضور کو اور بابا صاحب

کو سلامت رکھے حال یہ ہے کہ جب سے حضور روانہ ولایت کو ہوئے

فدوی نے نوکری گورنر صاحب بہادر جو کہ فیض آباد میں اسسٹنٹ کمشنر

تھے وہاں پر ملازم رہا عرصہ چند روز کا ہوا کہ وہ مر گئے لہذا فدوی

کچھ تدبیر ریل کے کرایہ کما کے بہت جلد خدمت میں حاضر ہوگا

واجب تھا عرض کیا الہی آفتاب

دولت و اقبال کا چمکتا ہو جیو

معروضہ خانہ زاد امیر حسن خان
خانساماں مورخہ ۲۰
۲۵ اکتوبر ۱۸۸۱ء

ہ

غریب پرور سلامت

فدوی حسن علی صوبہ دار

کی عرض یہ ہے کہ فدوی اور فدوی کے باپ دادے سیکڑوں برس سے مہاراجہ گوالیار کا رعیت ہے اور دس ہزار بلکہ زمین لاخراج فدوی کا موروثی مدت سے ہے جسکی گزاری خزانہ مقرر نہیں تھا اور کسی وقت میں کسی مہاراجہ صاحب نے کوئی خراج طلب نہیں کیا تھا اور نہ اس وقت کے مہاراجہ صاحب نے کبھی کچھ خزانہ لیا مگر انھوں مہاراجہ صاحب کے بھائی نے ناحق مہاراجہ صاحب کے بنا حکم ساری زمین کو ضبط کر لیا ہے اور فدوی کو کوئی عرضی مہاراجہ صاحب تک پہنچنے نہیں دیتے اس لئے فدوی مہاراجہ صاحب کے نام پر ایک عرضی اس عرضی کے ساتھ حضور میں بھیجتا ہوں اور امیدوار ہوں کہ حضور اس عرضی کو گوالیار کے ایجنٹ صاحب بہادر کے حضور میں بھیج دیجئے تاکہ وہ مہاراجہ صاحب کے حضور میں پیش کر دیویں

المرقوم ۳ جنوری ۱۸۸۴ع

غریب پرور خداوند نعمت فیاض زمان دام اقبالہ

جناب عالی حضور سے یہہ ہے کہ جب حضور چھاونی
سیتاپور سے طرف ولایت کے تشریف لے چلے یہہ خانہ زاد بھی حضور کے ہمراہ
چلا شہر کلکتہ تک گیا جب کہ حضور جہاز پر سوار ہوکر روانہ سمت ولایت کو ہوئی
بعد دو روز کے یہہ فدوی مکان روانہ ہوا لیکن شب و روز یہہ دعا مانگتا تھا کہ خدا جلد
حضور کو ہندستان میں لاوی جو حضور اپنی رسالہ میں رونق افروز ہوویں بندہ کو بہت خوشی
حاصل ہووے کہ حق تعالی اپکو بدرجہ علی کے پہونچاوی روز بروز ترقی اپکی عمر درازی بابا کی کرکا

اب فدوی امیدوار ہی کہ کب واسطے اس خانہ زاد کے حکم ہو کہ فدوی خدمت گذاری
اور طابعداری میں حاضر ہو واجب تھا عرض کیا الہی آفتاب اقبال دولت کا چمکتا
ہو جیو کے اور خانہ زاد شہر لکھنو محلہ قطب پور متصل پل ہاہنی لب گومتی بمکان منشی
یوسف خان کے رہتا ہوں

عرضی
خانہ زاد گنہگار سی خان زمان خان
مورخہ تاریخ ۹ ماہ جمادی الاول ۱۸۱۸ع

دو نیاز
خدمت

جناب مکرم معظم فیاض زمان

بعد تسلیم ملتمس ہوں - کہ چندہ شفا خانہ مین دینا ایک کار خیر ہے یہہ چندہ بیکسان
مریضان و محتاجان کے کام اویگا اور ہر ایک ذی شان و معزز جیسے آپ و دیگر
صاحبان ہین اونپر ایک فرض ہے کہ بیماران و ماندگان کو دوا بخشین بعد حسب الحکم
گورنمنٹ عالیہ جو صاحب دس روپیہ سال سے زیادہ دیوینگے

انکا نام تختہ بورڈ پر جو شفا خانہ میں ذریں حروف سے منقش ہو کر
لٹکایا جاویگا — ماسوائے اسکے حسب منشار گورنمنٹ جو مقرب اور اہل
دول چندہ میں شریک ہونگے اونسے قیمت دوائی نہیں لیجاویگی ورنہ قیمت ادویہ
جو لیوینگے دینی پڑیگی چونکہ جناب ہی اہل دول اور ذی شان ہیں اسلئے امید
قوی ہے کہ چندہ شفا خانہ میں دینا منظور کرینگے — اور تختہ بورڈ اب
تیار ہو رہا ہے اور بہت سے نام لکھے گئے ہیں

بحضور جناب برگیڈ میجر صاحب چہاونی سیتاپور دام اقبالہ

عرض بعد سلامت

جناب عالی فدوی چاند خاں امیدوار روزگار ایک برس کی
سے سید محمد صادق صاحب وکیل عدالت کے یہاں روپیہ وکالت کا اج تابہ وصول کیا
کرتا تھا اب کرایہ فی وکالت کے بہت کم ہے اسوجہ سے میری گذر نہیں ہوتی اور تکلیف
میں ہوں چونکہ حضور کے قدردانی اور فیض رسانی کا عام شہرہ ہے اسلئے میں بھی امیدوار ہوا اگر

حضور کے سررشتہ میں کوئی جگہ خالی ہو یا عوضی ہو یا آیندہ ہونیکی امید ہو تو حضور مجھکو
مقرر فرمائیں میں ابھی کار متعلقہ کو مستعدی اور ہوشیاری و دیانت سے انجام دونگا
میری دیانت اور مستعدی کے بارہ میں سید محمد صادق صاحب کہہ سکتے ہیں واجب جانکر عرض کیا

زیادہ حد ادب فقط

فدوی چاندخاں امیدوار روزگار معروضہ

۲۵ - اگست ۱۸۶۸ع

۲۶

بحضور فیض بخش و فیض رساں جناب ڈاکٹر جی - ریں گلگ صاحب بہادر دام اقبالہم

غریب پرور سلامت

چونکہ فدوی عرصہ چند ماہ سے خانہ نشین ہے اور کار تحریر بخوبی سر انجام دے
سکتا ہے حسن اتفاق سے حضور کے دفتر میں ایک اسامی خالی
ہی اگر حضور براہ خاوندی اسامی مذکور پر بندہ کو مامور فرماویں

تو عین غربا پروری ہی تاکہ فدوی اپنی مراد دلی کو پہونچکر
حضور کی جان و مال کو دعا دیتا رہے — الہی آفتاب دولت
کا ہمیشہ درخشان ہو جیو

عرض

فدوی امیر خان امیدوار
مورخہ ۳۰ جنوری ۱۸۸۹ء

بحضور فیض گنجور جناب ڈاکٹر صاحب بہادر دام اقبالہ

غریب پرور سلامت

جناب عالی عرض ضروری کی یہ ہی کہ بندہ بہفتہ عشرہ سے بعارضہ تپ نوبتی
علیل مبتلا ہی باعث شدت گرمی بخار کے از بس مجبور ہوں اکثر شب کو بوجہ
حرارت کے اس درجہ دھشت ہوتی ہی کہ جیسے خواب و خورش مطلق نہیں
ہوتا اور دوران سر ہردم رہتا ہی و خیال امراض دماغ ہی ہوتا ہی —

- علاوہ ازیں فدوی کو تکلیف زیادہ یہ بھی ہے کہ اس جگہ اپنا کوئی
ہم جنس نہیں ہے جو کسی طرح مدد پہونچاوے - لہذا عرضی ہذا گذرانکر امیدوار
ہوں کہ اگر رخصت ایکماہ کی حضور سے عطا فرمائی جاوے تو عین خاوندی
ہے تاکہ اپنے وطن جاکر علاوہ علاج معالجہ کے تبدیل آب و ہوا بھی کروں زیادہ
حد ادب

عرضی فدوی فتح خان تحصیلدار
۲۹ جنوری سنہ ۸۹ ع

غریب پرور سلامت

فدوی حسن رضا خان کوتوال کی

عرض یہہ ہی کہ اج جو پلٹن میرٹھہ سے اس چھاونی
مین پہنچی ہی اسکے چند سپاہی نے ملکر اس ایک غریب
لکڑہارے کو مارا ہی اور اسکی لکڑیان چھین لی ہین وہ بیچارہ
کوتوالی مین نالشی ہونے پر ایا فدوی اس لکڑہارے کو ہمراہ لیکر صوبہ
دار صاحب کے پاس گیا کہ جن سپاہیون نے اس بیچارہ کی لکڑیان
چھین لی ہین اونکی شناخت کرے مگر صوبہ دار صاحب
نے شناخت کرنی کے لئے کسی سپاہی کے خیمہ مین جانے
نہین دیا اسلئے امیدوار ہون کہ صوبہ دار صاحب کے نام
حکم ہو کہ فدوی کے ہمراہ ملکر تحقیقات مین تاکید
کرین فقط

عرضی

حسن رضا خان کوتوال

अर्जी

श्रीयुत महाराजा धिराज श्रीधनधारी सिंह बाहादुर के समीप मे सेनाधिकारी भुपाल सिंह कोराम राम पहुंचे विनती यह है कि आपकी आज्ञानुसार मैने युद्ग भुमि मे अपनी सेना के इतनी सरवय परिमाण भेजी है कि ३००० तीन हजार पैदल सिपाही सस्त्रधारी और २००० दो हजार सवार और बड़े बड़े योधाओं के सहित तोपों और गोला बारुद आदि सब फउज का सामान भी भेज चुका हुं लेकिन एक पत्र और समर भुमि से आयाहे लिखा हुआ रण रंगसिंह का के उहां शत्रु दलका बड़ाजोर है इसमे तुमलोग अन्दाज ५००० पांच हजार सवार और दो तोप रवाना और भेजो तो शत्रु को फौज को हटाय सकते हैं नहीं तो शत्रुओं की सेना हमारी सेना में आय जायगी इससे यह विनती कर कहता हुं कि जो सरकार की आज्ञा होय तो लिखे मा फक सेना और भेजदुं उचित जान के अर्ज किया तारीख १८ मास फागुन सुदी

श्रीयुत म ाहादुर के समीप मे
देवी सिंह ी यह है कि सरकारि
रिसाले के २० बीघा खेत घोड़ों से
चरवाय लि पड़ने से नाकाम होगिया
अब उस खे साल मे सरकारी माल
गुजारी कैसे ी इसलिये अर्ज कर्ता हुं के
येसा हुकुम भी ऐसा अनीतिका काम
सिपाही लो हायता होय के जिस्से
अपन वाल नकर अर्ज किया तारीख
२९ जुन स

अर्जी

श्रीयुत महाराजा धिराज राजा दौलत सिंह बाहादुर के समीप मे देवी सिंह जमीदार की राम राम पहुंचे विनती यह है कि सरकारि रिसाले के सिपाहियों ने कल के रोज मेरा वीस २० वीघा खेत घोड़ों से चरवाय लिया और सारा खेत घोड़ों की टापओं के पड़ने से नाकाम होगया अब उस खेत मे कुछ भी अन्न नही पैदा होगा इस साल मे सरकारी माल गुजारी कैसे दुगां और मेरे लड़के वाले क्या खायंगे इसलिये अर्ज करता हुं के ऐसा हुकुम सरकार से हो जाय के जिससे फेर कभी ऐसा अनीतिका काम सिपाही लोग नही करें और मेरे लिये भी कुछ सहायता होय के जिस्से अपने बाल बचों को पालन कर सकुं उचित जानकर अर्ज किया तारीख १९ जुन सन १८९१ ई०

अर्जी

श्री युत महाराज राजा मानसिंह बाहादुर के समीप मे प्रजा जनों की राम राम पहुंचे बिनती यह है कि इस साल मे वर्सा कम हुई है इससे हमलोगों के खेतों मे अन्न का उपज और साल से आधो भी नहीं हुई हमलोग बहुत तंग होगये हैं लड़के वाले सब दुखी हो रहे हैं किसी भांति से निवाह खाने पीने का नहो हो सक्ता है और यैसा कोई माहाजन भो हमलोगों को नहो मिलता के जिस्से क़र्ज लेके सरकारो माल गोजारो पटादें इसलिये अर्ज करता हु के ऐसो कोई सुरत सरकार को होजाय के जिस्से हमलोगों का निवाह सो आप के राज में बना रहे उचित जान के अर्ज किया तारिख ५ जनवरी सन १८९१ ई०

श्री के समीप मे प्रजा जनों की
राम साल मे वर्सा कम हुई है
द स्पज श्रौर साल से श्राधी भी
नहि लड़के वाले सब दुखी हो रहे
हैं । नही हो सक्ता है श्रौर यैसा
को मिलता के जिस्से क़र्ज लेके
सर्ज करता हुं के ऐसो कोई
मुस लोगों का निवाह सो श्राप के
राज फ़मा तारिख ५ जनवरी सन
१८

PART IV.

TRANSLATION OF MANUSCRIPT EXERCISES.

1.—TRANSLITERATION.—*Gharīb parwar salāmat.*

Jab se fidvī yahāṇ āyā hai, hamesha bīmār rahtā hai aur koī ḥakīm is jagah nahīṇ, aur dawā bhī kuchh dastyāb *nahīṇ hotī,* lihāẓa *umedwār hūṇ ki tabdīl-ghulām kī kisī dūsrī jagah ho jāwe* warna *ghulām is jagah ẓarūr marjāwegā, wājib thā 'arẓ kiyā* faqaṭ

'Arẓī fidvī Karam Khān, jama'dar.

TRANSLATION.—*Hail, cherisher of the poor.*

Ever since your devoted one came here, he has been continually ill, and in this place there is no physician, nor is any medicine obtainable. I therefore hope that your slave's transfer to some other place may be brought about, otherwise, your slave will undoubtedly die in this place. The request is reasonable, therefore it was made.

The petition of your devoted Karam Khān, jemadar.

NOTES.—دستياب *Dastyāb*—from *dast* (hand) and *yāftan* (root *yāb*), to attain—(Persian.)

لهذا *lihāẓa*=(Arabic) particle *li*=on account of, and

هذا *hāẓa*=this.

ورنه *warna*—short for *wa-agar-na*=and if not.

فقط *faqaṭ*. This word is not translateable in its present position. It simply indicates the end of the petition. Literally it means *only*.

N.B.—The *alif* written at the head of this petition is the initial letter of *Allāh*, the name of the Deity, with which all Mahommedans begin all documentary writings.

2.—Transliteration.—*Gharīb parwar salāmat.*

Ḥasb-ul-ḥukm ḥuẓūr ke fidvī ne zilla Kānpūr jākar ek sau das ādmī qaum-i-Rājpūt se bhartī kīye haiṉ, aur ek ek rūpaya fī kas khurāk ke wāsṭe, jo ḥasbi dastūr aur ḥukm ḥuẓūr ke de dīyā. Chunānchi untīs tārīkh isī mahīne kī fidvī ma' sab ādmīyoṉ ke chhāonī meṉ ḥāẓir hogā. Lekin Agre ke rāste nahīṉ āwegā Barelī ki rāh se āwegā sunā hai ki wahāṉ bīmarī *bahut hai aur ādmī marte haiṉ.* Ittilā'an *'arẓ kīya faqaṭ. 'Arẓī fidvī Rām Parshād Hawāldar kampanī chhārum.*

Translation.—*Hail, cherisher of the poor.*

According to the order of your Honour, your devoted one having gone to the Kānpūr district, has enlisted one hundred and ten men of the Rajpūt tribe, and has given each man one rupee for sustenance, in accordance with custom and your Honour's orders. Accordingly, on the 29th instant, your devoted one, with all the men will present himself in the cantonment, but will not come by the Agra route; he will come by way of Bareli. He has heard that there is much sickness there, and men are dying.

This petition is sent by way of report.

The petition of your devoted Rām Pershād, Hawāldar of the fourth company.

NOTES.—*Notice the construction of the Agent case in the first sentence.*

في كس *fī kas*=each man. This may also be translated by *ādmī pīchhe.*

مع *ma'*=with—followed by the genitive.

بيماري *Bīmārī*=Illness—often used instead of cholera euphemistically.

اطلاعا *Iṭṭilā'an*=Arabic adverbial form from *Iṭṭilā'*—a report.

3.—TRANSLITERATION.—*Gharīb parwar salāmat.*

Aj fidvī kī ṭabī'at bahut bīmār hai, *aur ṭāqat-i-āmad o raft nahīṇ lihāza umedwār hūṇ ki rukhṣat do roz kī mil jāwe aur jo ḥuzūr rukhṣat na deṇ to 'ewazī apnā de dūṇ. Wājib thā 'arz kiyā faqaṭ.*

'Arzī fidvī Harnām, dirzī, mulāzim i ḥuzūr.

TRANSLATION.—*Hail, cherisher of the poor.*

To-day your devoted servant's health is very bad, and he has not strength to walk. I therefore hope that two days' leave may be granted, and if your Honour will not grant me leave, then I will give a substitute to take my place. The request made is a reasonable one. Enough.

The petition of the devoted Harnām, tailor, servant to your Honour.

NOTES.—*Fidvī kī ṭabī'at bahut bīmār hai.*—This idiom is one in very common use, but it is not strictly accurate, as the word *bīmār* بيمار means *ill*, and the word طبيعت means *state of health*. It should strictly be "*ṭabī'at kharāb hai* my state of health is bad; i.e., *maiṇ bīmār hūṇ* I am ill.

عوضي *'Ewazī*=a substitute, more commonly بدلي *badlī* (the men whose profession it is to write petitions for the commoner and less educated class of native servants are very fond of displaying their erudition by using high-flown words in place of the simpler words of the bazar vernacular.)

4.—TRANSLITERATION.—*Gharīb parwar salāmat.*

Kal fidvī wāsṭe lene shakkar *ke bāzār ko jātā thā jab* kotwālī *ke pās pahunchā to Nārāyan* kānstabal *ne mujhko gālī dī aur lāt* ghūṇse *se bahut mārā, tamām bāzār ke log gawāh haiṇ, lihāẓa umedwār hūṇ ki ḥuẓūr* nāmburde *ko* 'adālat *meṇ* ṭalab farmākar, *sazā deṇ, nahīṇ to sab* ra'iyat *sarkār kī* tabāh ho jāegī.

Wājib thā 'arẓ kīyā faqaṭ.

'Arẓi fidvī Hīrā Singh, baqqāl.

TRANSLATION.—*Hail, cherisher of the poor.*

Yesterday your devoted servant was going to the bāzār for the purpose of buying sugar. When I had arrived near the kotwālī, Narāyan constable abused me, and with kicks and blows severely assaulted me. All the bāzār people are witnesses. I therefore hope that your Honour having summoned the above-mentioned to the Court will punish him, otherwise all the subjects of the Government will be ruined. The petition is reasonable, therefore it is made. The petition of Hīrā Singh, greengrocer.

NOTE.—*Shakkar*—Sugar. The other words are *miṣrī, chīnī.*

Kotwālī—Police-station, where the *kotwāl* or chief police officer is.

Kānstabal—Simply our English word transliterated.

Ghūṇsā—A blow with the clenched fist; for example, "*Us ne ek ghuṇsa mārā.*" He struck him a blow with the fist.

Nāmburda—Literally he whose name (*nām*) has been taken (*burda*), the aforesaid (*Narāyan*).

'Adālat—Court. *Faujdārī 'adālat*—Criminal Court.

Dīwānī 'adālat—Civil Court.

Ṣadr 'adālat—High Court.

Ṭalab farmānā—To summon.

Ra'īyat. This is the word which the English equivalent "ryot" is intended to represent. The Hindī word is *parjā.*

Tabāh hojānā—To be ruined, destroyed, wrecked.

Baqqāl—Properly a "greengrocer," but used for the "*bunniah.*'

5.—TRANSLITERATION.—*Gharīb parwar salāmat.*

Bahut 'arṣa *hūā ki ḥuẓūr ne* zabān-i-mubārak *se farmāyā thā ki* parwarish *tumhāre beṭe kī kisī jagah waqt khālī hone* asāmī *ke hogī; ab ek* chuprās *'adālāt-i-faujdārī men khālī hūī hai lihāẓa umedwār hūn ki parwarish*-i-bandazāda *ūs asāmī par hojāwe*; *munāsib thā 'arẓ kīyā, faqaṭ.*

'Arẓī fidvī Jawāhir La'l muḥarrir-*i-'adālat.*

Muwarrakha siyum *May.*

TRANSLATION.—*Hail, cherisher of the poor.*

It is a long time ago that your Honour was graciously pleased to say "Your son's preferment shall take place to some post at the time of some vacancy occurring," so, now, a chupras has fallen vacant in the Criminal Court. Therefore, I hope that the preferment of your slave's son to that post may be brought about. The request is reasonable, therefore it is made. The petition of your devoted Jawāhir La'l, writer of the Court.

Dated the third of May.——

NOTES.—*'Arṣa*—a space of time; another word is *mī'ād.*

Zabān-i-mubārak—literally "Your auspicious mouth," &c. The equivalent English idiom is given.

Parwarish—Verbal noun from Persian *parwardan* to cherish. *Parwarda*=protégé.

Asāmī.—Arabic plural of plural, from *ism* a name; hence a list of names either of tenants of an estate or candidates for preferment. Hence used for the vacancy itself.

Chaprās.—A belt worn by certain servants as the insignia of their office. Such servants are called *chaprāsī.*

Bandazāda—Persian compound = slave's son.

Muḥarrir—Arabic word denoting a writer. The title of certain writers to the Courts of justice.

Muwarrakha—dated—passive participle. Compare *tārīkh* = date.

Sīyum—Persian ordinal. It is customary for the better class of natives to use the Persian ordinal numerals.

6.—Transliteration.—*Gharīb parwar salāmat.*

'Arṣa ek hafte kā guzrā hogā *ki musammā Rām Dyāl chaprāsī mulāzim-i-ḥuzūr sāt man dāna fidvī kī dūkān se ḥuzūr ke wāste legāyā hai aur qīmat nahīṇ de gayā. Aj fidvī ne dām nāmburde se ṭalab kīyā to gālīyāṇ dene lagā aur mārne ko* musta'idd *hūā. Ghulām ne āp ke khauf se kuchh na kahā lihāzā umedwār hūṇ ki ḥuzūr qīmat-i-dāna fidvī ko chaprāsī-i-mazkūr se* dilwāden. *Wājib thā 'arz kīyā faqaṭ. 'Arzī-i-Nand Rām baqqāl.*

Translation.—*Hail, cherisher of the poor.*

About the space of one week has passed since one Rām Dyāl, *chuprāsī*, a servant of your Honour, took seven maunds of gram from the shop of your humble servant, for your Honour's use, and did not pay the price. To-day your devoted one, demanded the price from the aforesaid (Rām Dyāl) but he began to abuse me and made preparations to beat me. Your slave, through fear of your Honour, said nothing, therefore I hope that your Honour will cause the price of the gram to be paid to your devoted one by the above-mentioned *chuprāsī*. The request is reasonable, therefore it has been made. The petition of Nand Rām baqqāl.

Notes.—*'Arṣa guzrā hogā.*—The future is used here to denote approximation to the fact stated. He is not exactly certain that it is a week.

Musta'idd.—Another example of a high-flown word. *Taiyār* would be the more simple word to use.

Dilwādena.—Doubly causal verb,—*vide* page 70, note.

7.—TRANSLITERATION.—*Gharīb parwar salāmat.*

Kal se fidvī ko tap o lārza *ā gayā hai aur tamām badan meṇ dard hai aur dambadam* qai *hotī hai harchand ki Bābū-i-shafā khāna ne dawāe dī par kuchh fāida na hūā, lihāẓā umedwār hūṇ kī rukhṣat ek hafte kī 'ināyat ho jāwe, agar rukhṣat na milegī to fidvī ẓarūr marjāegā aur yeh bhī* wāẓiḥ *ho ki fidvī ne jis roz se naukar hūā hai kabhī rukhṣat nahīṇ lī aur koī bahāna ya* ḥīla *naukarī ke waqt nahīṇ kīyā hamesha ḥukm-i-sarkār* bajā lāyā. *Wājib thā 'arẓ kīyā faqaṭ. 'Arẓī Lāl Chuprāsī.*

TRANSLATION.—*Hail, cherisher of the poor.*

Since yesterday, fever and ague have attacked your servant, and there is pain in all my body, and from time to time vomiting occurs. In spite of all the medicine that the Bābū of the dispensary has given me, no benefit has resulted; therefore I hope that a week's leave may be granted me. If leave is not obtained, then your slave will certainly die; and let this too be known, that your slave from the day on which he entered your service has never taken leave, and has never made any excuse or pretext at the time of duty, and has always carried out his master's orders.

The request was reasonable, therefore it was made.

The petition of Lal Chuprāsi.

Tap o lārza.—Hindustāni equivalent is *jārā bukhār.*

Qai.—Also *radd, ultī.* *Qai* is more elegant.

Wāẓiḥ.—Clear, evident. A usual way of commencing notifications. "*Wāẓiḥ ho ki,*" &c., &c.

Ḥīla.—Stratagem. Plural *ḥiyal, balaṭāiful ḥiyal*—artfully.

Bajā lānā.—To perform.

8.—Transliteration.—*Ghārīb parwar salāmat.*

Janāb-i-'ālī parsoṇ se fidvī bamūjib ḥukm ḥuzūr ke 'adālat meṇ ḥāẓir hai, aur gawāh bhī sab maujūd haiṇ lekin muqaddama *faiṣal nahīṇ hotā, aur kharch fidvī kā bahut hotā hai, gawāhoṇ ko khurāk detā hai, lihāẓa umedwār hūṇ kī muqaddama āj* pesh *hojāwe. Wājib thā 'arẓ kīyā faqaṭ.*

'Arẓi fidvī Kandan mudda'ī.

Translation.—*Hail, cherisher of the poor.*

My Lord—Since the day before yesterday your humble servant has been present at the Court in accordance with your Honour's order, and all witnesses too are present, but the case is not being decided, and your servant's expenses are very heavy, as the witnesses' sustenance has to be provided. Therefore I hope that the case may be called on to-day. The request is reasonable, therefore it is made. Enough.

The petition of your humble Kandan, plaintiff.

Notes.—*Muqqaddama.* This is the technical word used in the Courts, for a case.

Pesh honā.—To "be heard" to "come on" (a case).

Mudda'ī.—مدعي This is the word used to denote the plaintiff who makes the دعي plaint; the defendant is called مدعاعليه *mudda'ā 'alaihi,* or he against whom the plaint is made.

9.—Transliteration.—*Gharīb parwar salāmat.*

'Arṣa do sāl kā guẓrā ki fidvī kī beṭī kī shādī Kandan sunār ke ghar hūī thī, aur sab rusūm shādī ke bhī tamām hogaye the so ab nāmburde ne az rāh daghābāzī ke shādī dusrī jagah kardī, aur kahtā hai ki tum apnī betī kī shādī aur jagah kar lo, khudāwandā jāe inṣāf *hai, ki fidvī ne do sau rūpaya kharch karke, to shādī kī*

hai ab kahāṇ se phir itnā rūpaya lāweṇ jo shādī dusrī kare lihāẓā umedwār hūṇ ki ḥuẓūr mudda'ā ālaihi ko 'adālat meṇ ṭalab karke taḥqīqāt *farmāweṇ aur gawāh ghulām ke bahut haiṇ. Wājib thā 'arẓ kīyā faqaṭ.*

'Arẓī fidvī Behārī Sunar sākin Barelī.

Muwarrakha doyum Mai san athārah sau unāsī Isawī.

TRANSLATION.—*Hail, cherisher of the poor.*

The space of two years has elapsed since your devoted one's daughter's marriage took place at the house of Kandan, goldsmith, and all the customary observances of the marriage were duly completed, but now the aforesaid, out of craftiness, has contracted a marriage elsewhere, and says to me, "You marry your daughter in some other place." My Lord, this calls for justice, because your slave has already expended two hundred rupees in contracting this marriage. Now whence can he again obtain so large a sum as to enable him to carry out a second marriage. Therefore I hope that your Honour will summon the defendant to Court, and investigate the matter. Your slave's witnesses are many. The request, &c.

The petition of your devoted Behārī, goldsmith, living at Bareli, dated the 2nd of May, 1879 A.D.

NOTES.—*Inṣāf* انصاف Literally *equally dividing*, hence *justice—æquitas.*

Taḥqīqāt—Arriving at the truth (*ḥaqīqat*).

Isawi.—Anno Domini—opposed to هجري the year of the *Hegira.*

10.—TRANSLITERATION.—*Gharīb parwar salāmat.*

Kal fidvī ke ghar se khaṭṭ āyā hai us se daryāft hūā ki fidvī ke wālid ne is jahāṇ se intiqāl kīyā *aur ab ghar par koī sarparast jo sab bandobast gāṇw waghaira kā kare koī bāqī nahīṇ rahā. Is ḥālat meṇ fidvī kisīṭaraḥ naukarī nahīṇ karsaktā lihāẓa umedwār hūṇ ki nām fidvī kā naukarī-i-sārkār se kāṭā jāwe warna sab kār bār merā* abtar *hojāegā. Wājib thā 'arẓ kīyā faqāṭ. 'Arẓī fidvī Yār 'Alī Hawāladar number two Kompany.*

TRANSLATION.—*Hail, cherisher of the poor.*

Yesterday a letter arrived from my home; from it I learned that your servant's father has departed from this world, and now there is no responsible person who can arrange all the affairs of the village, etc., remaining. In this circumstance, your devoted servant is not able in any way to carry on his duty, therefore I hope that your slave's name may be removed from the Government service: otherwise all my business will be ruined. The request is reasonable, therefore it is made. Enough.

The petition of your devoted Yār Ali, Havildar of No. 2 Company.

انتقال کرنا *Intiqāl karnā*—To die; literally to move from one place to another.

ابتر *Abtar*—Topsy-turvy.

11.—TRANSLITERATION.—*Gharīb parwar salāmat.*

'Arṣa ek sāl kā hūā ki musammī Sardār Khān dirzī ne mablagh ek sau das rūpaya fidvī se qarẓ līye the aur tamassuk iqrārī *sāt mahīne kā likhdīyā thā. Chunānchi ab das mahīne guzr ga-e lekin nāmburda rūpaya ādā nahīṇ kartā—jo āj fidvī ne rūpaya ṭalab kīyāto kahā hamāre nām* nālish karo, *agar hamse* taqāzā *karoge to ham tumko khūb mārenge. Lihāẓa umedwār hūṇ ki nāmburde ko ḥuẓūr ṭalab karke rūpaya dilwādeṇ. Wājib thā 'arẓ kīyā.*

'Arẓī fidvī Jawāhir baqqāl.

TRANSLATION.—*Hail, cherisher of the poor.*

A year ago Sardār Khān, dirzī, borrowed the sum of one hundred and ten rupees from your humble servant, and wrote and gave a promissory note at six months. Accordingly ten months have now passed, but the aforesaid does not pay up the money. When to-day your humble servant demanded the money from him he said, Go and lodge a complaint against me; if you dun me I will beat you soundly. Therefore I hope that your Honour having summoned the aforesaid would make him pay the money. The request was reasonable, therefore it was made.

The petition of your devoted Jawāhir, grocer.

تمسک اقراري *Tamassuk iqrārī*—A promissory note.

نالش کرنا *Nālish karnā*—To lodge a complaint.

تقاضا *Taqāẓā*—Dunning.

12.—TRANSLITERATION.—*Gharīb parwar salāmat.*

'Arṣa chār mahīne kā hūā ki fidvī ne mablagh tīs *rūpaya* naqd *Rām Lāl hawāldar kampanī do ko* uske *ghar jāne ke waqt dīye the aur yeh kah dīyā thā* ki *tum yeh rūpaya hamāre bhāī Badrī Dās ko* de denā *aur* rasīd *lekar hamāre pās rawānā karnā, so kal fidvī ke makānse khaṭṭ āyā hai, us se daryaft hūā ki hawāldar*-i-mazkūr *ne wuh rūpaye nahīṇ dīye, lihāẕā umedwār hūṇ ki rūpaya ghulām kā hawāldār kī ṭalab se* dilāyā *jāwe. Faqaṭ. 'Arẕī fidvī Diyāl Sipāhī.*

TRANSLATION.—*Hail, cherisher of the poor.*

It is four months ago that your petitioner gave the sum of thirty (30) cash to Rām Lāl, Havildar of No. 2 Company, at the time of his going to his home, and said this: "You give these rupees to my brother Badrī Dās, and after taking the receipt send it off to me." So yesterday a letter arrived from your servant's home, and from it he learned that the Havildar mentioned has not given these rupees. Therefore I hope that your slave's money may be restored to him from the pay of the Havildār. Enough.

The petition of your humble Diyāl Sepoy.

مبلغ *mablagh*—a sum of money.

تیس *tīs*—30.—The character written above the word (*tīs*) is the character representing 30 in the notation called *Raqam.*

نقد *naqd*—hard cash—as opposed to نسیہ *nisiya*, credit.

اوسکے *uske.*—At the time of the Havildar's going, &c.—had the writer meant at the time of his own going he would have written اپنے *apne.* (*Vide* page 48.)

کہ *ki.*—Used to introduce the very words of the speaker cited.

دے دینا *de denā.*—Infinitive used as an imperative.

رسید *rasīd.*—Receipt. Verbal noun from *rasīdan* to arrive. This is not a corruption of the English word as might be thought

مذکور Passive participle from ذکر mentioned.

دلایا جانا Passive causal. *Vide* page 70, and note.

13.—TRANSLITERATION.—*Gharīb parwar salāmat.*

Kal Qazā-i-ilāhī *se shauhar fidvīa kā faut hogayā aur koī* shakhs *dūsrā rishtadār yā* wāris *fidvīa kā nahīn jo khabrgīrī khāne pīne kī kare aur koī* jāedād *bhī pās fidvīa ke nahīn ki jis se guzrān apnī karūn. Lihāzā umedwar hūn ki huzūr do rūpaya* mahwārī *mere khāwind kī talab se muqarrar karden ki us se* guzārā *fidvīa kā bakhūbī hojāegā aur huzūr ko du'ā karungī.* '*Arzī fidvīa* musammāt *Bilāsū* zauja *Hīra Chuprāsī* mutawaffī.

TRANSLATION.—*Hail, cherisher of the poor.*

Yesterday by the decree of God the husband of your devoted one died, and there is no other person, either relation or heir of your slave, who can look after the provision of meat and drink, and there is no property belonging to your humble one by means of which I can gain my living. Therefore I hope that your Honour would appoint to me two rupees a month from my husband's pay, because from that (sum) your servant's livelihood will be comfortable enough, and I will bless your Honour. The petition of your servant Bilāsū, wife of Hīra Chuprāsī deceased.

NOTE.—
قضاي الهي سے	*qaẓā-i-Ilāhi se.*	By the decree of God.
وارث	*wāris̤*--	heir.
جايداد	*jāedād*	property.
گذران	*guzrān* fem.	livelihood.
گذارا	*guzārā* masc.	
ماهواري	*mahwārī*	monthly pay.
مسماة	*musammāt* feminine of مسمي *musammī* named.	
زوجة	*zauja*	wife.
مُتوفى	*mutawaffī* deceased. Also expressed by the words مرحوم *marḥūm* and مغفور *maghfūr*.	

14.—TRANSLITERATION.—*Gharīb parwar salāmat.*

Jab se fidvī palṭan meṇ bhartī *hūā hai kabhī koī quṣūr nahīṇ kīyā aur naukarī se kīsī waqt* ghair ḥaẓīr *nahīṇ hūā aur apne baṛe* uhdadār *kā hameshā ḥukm mānā lekin kal ṣūbadār sāḥib ne fidvī ko* burā bhalā kahā *jāb fidvī ne kahā ki mujhe kyūṇ gālī dete ho to bole ki ham tumko fauj se nikāl deṇge. Khudāwandā fidvī ko ab naukarī manzūr nahīn. Lihāẕā umedwār hūn ki* istiʻfā *fidvī kā manzūr ho. Faqaṭ.*

ʻArẓī fidvī Hīrā Lāl Sipāhī kompanī awwal.

NOTES.— بهرتي *Bhartī*—enlisted.

غير حاضر *Ghair ḥāẓir*—absent.

عهده دار *Uhdadār*—Office-holder—Officer.

برا بهلا كهنا *Burā bhalā kahnā*—Literally to say bad and good things, to abuse.

منظور *Manẓūr*—agreed to—acceptable.

استعفا *Istiʻfā*—Literally asking for pardon or discharge; hence resignation.

TRANSLATION.—*Hail, cherisher of the poor.*

Since your humble servant was enlisted in the regiment he has never committed any fault, and never at any time has he been absent from duty, and of his own free will and accord has always obeyed the orders of his superior officer, but yesterday the Sūbadar Sāhib abused your humble servant. When your servant said "Why do you abuse me?" he said "I will turn you out of the regiment." My Lord, now no longer is service agreeable to your slave. Therefore I hope that your slave's resignation may be accepted. Enough.

The petition of your slave Hīra Lāl Sepoy, 1st Company.

15.—TRANSLITERATION.—*Gharīb parwar salāmat.*

Jab se fidvī ghar par āyā hai hamesha bīmār hai agarchi bahut ʻilāj shafā khāna waghaira kā kiyā lekin ārām nahīn hotā, tamām badan men bāi ka dard hai aur kabhi paslī men dard ho jātā hai aur ādhā sīsī kā dard *bhī hotā hai tamām badan zard hai aur hāth pāon par warm āgayā hamesha qabẓ peṭ men rahtā hai ḍartā hūn̤ ki kahīn* sarsām *nahojāwe lihāẕā umedwār hūn̤ ki rukhsat do mahīne kī mil jawe wājib thā 'arẓ kīyā. Faqaṭ. 'Arẓī fidvī Nabī Bukhsh Jam'adār.*

TRANSLATION.—*Hail, cherisher of the poor.*

Ever since your devoted servant arrived at his home he has been ill, he has undergone much treatment at the dispensary and elsewhere, but gets no relief, he has rheumatic pain in his whole body, and occasionally pain comes in his ribs, and he also suffers from migraine. His whole body is yellow, and his hands and feet have swollen. He is always constipated, and I fear that in some way or other delirium will arise, therefore I hope that I may get two months' leave. The request is reasonable, therefore it is made. Enough.

The petition of your humble Nabī Bukhsh, Jemadār.

NOTES.—*Adhā sīsī kā dard.* Hemicrania—Migraine.

Ḍartā hūn̤ ki . . . nahojāwe. Observe the construction, comparable to *vereor ne* = I fear lest, &c.

16.—TRANSLITERATION.—*Gharīb parwar salāmat.*

Zar-i-chaukidārī qadīm se fidvī ke nām par chār āna māhwārī muqarrar hai aur fidvī māh bamāh ādā kartā hai lekin kal bakhshī *ne fidvī se kahā ki tum se ham is mahīne men̤ āth āna len̤ge lihāẕa umedwār hūn̤ ki ḥuẕūr bakhshī-i-maẕkūr se daryāft farmā kar ḥukm-i-munāsib den̤, ki main̤ is ẓulm se bach jāūn̤ wājib thā 'arẓ kīyā. Faqaṭ.*

'Arẓī fidvī Narāyan darzī.

TRANSLATION.—*Hail, cherisher of the poor.*

From long time the *chaukidāri* money has been agreed upon at the rate of four annas a month to the name of your servant, and he has month by month paid it, but yesterday the paymaster said to me "I will take from you in this month eight annas;" therefore I hope that your Honour will enquire from the aforesaid paymaster, and pass a suitable order, so that I may escape from this oppression. The petition was reasonable, therefore it was made. Enough. The petition of your devoted servant Narāyan dirzī.

بخشي *Bakhshi*—paymaster.

17.—TRANSLITERATION.—*Gharīb parwar salāmat.*

Parsoṇ das baje rāt ko fidvī ke makān meṇ chorī hogāī aur āsbāb mālīyat sau rupīkā chorī gayā, jab kotwāl ṣāḥib se ittilā' kī to unhoṇ ne jawāb dīyā ki tum fareb karte ho khudāwandā jā-i ghaur hai ki fidvī kā āsbāb chorī gayā aur fidvī fareb kartā. Ḥuẓūr mauqa' *par* tashrif lāweṇ *aur gawāhoṇ se daryāft kareṇ tab fidvī kā ḥāl ḥuẓūr ko khul jāwe. Faqaṭ.*

'Arẓī fidvī Malik Chand mudda'ī.

TRANSLATION.—*Hail, cherisher of the poor.*

The day before yesterday at ten o'clock at night a robbery took place in your servant's house, and property to the amount of a hundred rupees was stolen. When I reported the matter to the Kotwāl sāhib he replied, you are cheating. My Lord, here is room for deliberation, because your humble one's property is stolen, and he himself is accused of deceit. If your Honour would visit the place and enquire of the witnesses, then your humble one's state would become known to your Honour. Enough. The petition of Malik Chand, plaintiff.

NOTES.—موقع *Mauq'*—Adverb of place, from وقع, cf. واقعه event.

تشريف لانا *Tashrif lānā*—To honour by coming. Another form of expression is قدم رنجه فرمانا *qadam ranja farmānā.*

18.—TRANSLITERATION.—*Gharīb parwar salāmat.*

Aj bhāī fidvī kā ghar se āyā hai aur irāda uskā yeh hai ki naukarī i sarkār kare aur 'umr uskī qarīb bīs baras kī hai aur likhā paṛhā *hai lihāẓa umedwār hūṇ ki ba'd mulāḥiẓa dāktar ṣāḥib ke wuh is paltan meṇ bhartī kīyā jāwe kiswāste ki fidvī ke bāp dādā qadīm se fauj meṇ* naukar rahe haiṇ *aur* fauj hī ko pasand karte haiṇ *wājib jānkar 'arẓ kīyā. Faqaṭ. 'Arẓi fidvī Kālī Charan, sipāhī.*

TRANSLATION.—*Hail, cherisher of the poor.*

To-day your devoted servant's brother came from home, and it is his wish to serve the Government. His age is about twenty years, and he can read and write. Therefore I hope that after the examination by the Doctor, he may be enlisted in this regiment, for the reason that your humble servant's ancestors for ages have served in the Army, and like no other profession. Having considered the request reasonable I have made it. Enough.

The petition of your servant Kālī Charan, sepoy.

NOTES.—*Likhā paṛhā hai.* This is a very idiomatic expression.

Naukar rahe haiṇ Have always served. This word *rahnā* (to remain) is very useful in expressing habitual action, or an action still going on.

Fauj hī ko pasand karte haiṇ. It is the Army which they like (and no other profession). All this idea is conveyed by the emphatic particle *hī*.

It should be noticed that this particle may often be used in the middle of a word: for instance, in answer to the question.

Tum Lakhnau meṇ rahte ho? We might answer, *Hāṇ Lakh hī-nau meṇ.* Yes in Lucknow itself.

19.—TRANSLITERATION.—*Gharib parwar salāmat.*

Janāb 'āli ḥasbul ḥukm ḥuẓūr ke fidvī ne do hāthī Nawāb Ṣāḥib Bahādur se lekar Kāshīpūr meṇ pahunchā dīye chār ghoṛe sarkāri *ya'ne ḥuẓūr ke maqām shafākhāne par rakhe haiṇ Jis waqt āp ko darkār hoṇ taiyār haiṇ aur Rājā Kāshīpūr bhī kahte haiṇ ki chār fīl aur shikārī ko tumko ek mahīne ke līye de sakte haiṇ agar ḥuẓūr farmāweṇ to Rājā Ṣāḥib se hāthī lekar jangal meṇ ṭaiyār rakhūṇ iṭṭilā'an 'arẓ kīyā. Faqaṭ. 'Arẓī fidvi Ināyat Khān, jama'dar.*

TRANSLATION.—*Hail, cherisher of the poor.*

Most noble Sir, in accordance with your Honour's order, your humble servant having taken two elephants from the Nawāb Sāhib Bahādur, has sent them to Kāshīpūr, and four horses belonging to Government, that is to say of your Honour's, are halted at the dispensary. Whenever they may be required by your Honour they are ready, and the Rājā of Kāshīpūr too says, "I can give you four more hunting elephants for a month." If your Honour should instruct me, then I will take the elephants from the Rājā Sahib and keep them in readiness in the jungle. The petition of your humble servant Ināyat Khān, jamadar.

NOTES.—*Sarkārī.* This is a very common word in use to express property belonging to one's master.

For instance. A master asks—*Yeh kīs kī ṭopī hai?* The bearer might answer "*Sarkār kī hai.*" It is yours, Sir.

It is also used to express the Supreme Government as "*Yeh Sarkār ka hukm hai.*" This is a Government order.

It is literally "head of affairs."

20.—TRANSLITERATION.—*Gharīb parwar salāmat.*

Fidvī ne iqbāl-i-ḥuẓūr *se āj Haryā quidī ko sāt baras kā* mi'ādi *thā giriftār kar līyā aur dusre logoṇ ki giriftārī meṇ shab o roz koshish kartā hūṇ iṭṭilā'an 'arẓ kiyā. Mukhbiron ne khabr dī hai ki tīn* ishtihāri *zilla Bijnor meṇ haiṇ so fidvī ne ek ādmī* mu'tabar *apnā rawāna kīyā hai waqt milne surāgh ka* fauran *rawāna Bijnor hūṇgā aur fidvī ko parsoṇ se tap o larza lagā bahut kamzorī hai* āftāb daulat kā tābān rahe. *Faqaṭ.*

'Arẓī fidvī Narāyan Dass, Inspector.

TRANSLATION.—*Hail, cherisher of the poor.*

Your humble servant yesterday by your Honour's good fortune arrested Haryā, the prisoner who was in for a term of six years, and is night and day striving to arrest the other men. This petition is sent by way of report. The informers have sent in word that three of the proclaimed men are in the Bijnor district, so your humble servant has sent there a trustworthy man of his own. As soon as a clue is obtained I will start for Bijnor without delay. Your humble servant has had fever and ague since the day before yesterday; there is great weakness. May the sun of wealth remain shining brightly. Enough.

The petition of Narayan Dass, Inspector.

NOTES.—*Iqbāl-i-ḥuẓūr se — Āp ke iqbāl se.* This phrase is very common, attributing any success to the good fortune of the superior.

Mi'ādī—Technical term. *Mī'ād* means a period of time.

Ishtihāri. Proclaimed—mentioned in an *Ishtihār*.

Mu'tabar. This word is vulgarly pronounced *mātabar.*

Fauran—Immediately. Hindī equivalent—*turant, jhaṭ.*

Āftāb, &c—Very common form of ending to a petition.

21.—TRANSLITERATION.—*Gharīb parwar salāmat.*

Fidvī arṣa-i-bīs sāl se pinshan pātā hai aur pahle risāla sowārān Hindūstāni meṇ naukar thā aur ab fidvī ko āriẓa fālij *kā hogayā hai, chal nahīṇ saktā—lihāẓā umedwār hūṇ ki pinshan fidvī kī fidvī ke beṭe ke nām par muqarrar ho jāwe wuh sarkār se* liyā karegā—*munāsib jānkar 'arẓ kīyā āftāb daulat kā tābān rahe. Faqaṭ.*

'Arẓī fidvī Karam Khān Sowar, pinshandār muwarrakha doyum Jūn.

TRANSLATION.—*Hail, cherisher of the poor.*

Your petitioner from the space of twenty years has drawn a pension and also served in the first Bengal Cavalry, and now paralysis has attacked your humble one, and he cannot walk; therefore I hope that your petitioner's pension may be allotted to the petitioner's son's name. He will always draw it from Government. Having considered it fitting he has made his request. May the sun of wealth remain shining. Enough.

The petition of your devoted Karam Khān Sowār, pensioner, dated the second of June.

NOTES.—*Fālij*—Hemiplegia, often associated with *laqwa* = facial palsy.

Līyā karegā—*Vide* page 70 frequentative verb.

22.—TRANSLITERATION.—*Gharīb parwar salāmat.*

Huẓūr ne farmāyā thā ki ham rūpaya tumhārā das tārīkh ko *denge, so āj das tārīkh ko fidvī ḥāẓir hūā hai lihāẓā umedwār hūn ki rūpaya fidvī kā āj mil jāwe kis wāsṭe ki fidvī ab* ghar jātā hai *munāsib thā 'arẓ kīyā. Faqaṭ.*

'Arẓi fidvī Kishan saudāgar.

TRANSLATION.—*Hail, cherisher of the poor.*

Your Honour said "I will pay you your money on the tenth," so to-day on the tenth, your servant has presented himself. I therefore hope that your servant's money may be given him to-day, because your servant is now going to his home.

It was fitting—the petition was made. Enough.

The petition of your humble Kishan, merchant.

NOTES.—*Das tārīkh ko*—On the 10th. Notice this use of particle *ko*.

Ghar jātā—Notice this idiom—not *ghar ko jātā*.

Saudāgar—Another word *Baipārī*.

23.—TRANSLITERATION.—*Gharīb parwar salāmat.*

Parson wāqi' bārahvīn māh hāzā ko musammī Kandan Singh brādar fidvi kā ba 'illat *mārpīt ke qaid hogayā hai aur pās nām burde ke* loṭā *nahīn is* bāiṣ *se bahut* taklīf *hai lihāzā umedwār hūn ki ḥukm-i-ḥuzūr wāste dilāne loṭā mazkūr ke banām* dārogha *ṣāḥib ke* ṣādir ho *jāwe ki wuh loṭā qaidī ko dilwāden. Wājib thā 'arz kīyā. Faqaṭ.*

'Arzi fidvī Jawāhir Singh, barādar-i-Kandan Singh, qaidī.

TRANSLATION.—*Hail, cherisher of the poor.*

The day before yesterday, the twelfth of this month, one Kandan Singh, the petitioner's brother, was arrested on a charge of assault, and the aforesaid (Kandan Singh) has no *loṭā*. For this reason he is greatly inconvenienced, therefore I hope that an order of your Honour's for the giving of the *loṭā* mentioned, may issue in the name of the dārogha sahib, so that he may cause to be given to the prisoner a *loṭā*. The request is reasonable, therefore it was made. Enough.

The petition of the devoted Jawāhir Singh, the brother of Kandan Singh, prisoner.

NOTES.—*'Illat*—A cause; also used to signify illness.

Bāiṣ—Syn. *wāste, līye, kāran, sabab se.*

Taklīf—Notice the gender of words of this measure (*taf'īl* is feminine (*vide* page 25).

Dārogha—This word is always mispronounced *darogha*. The long alif should be carefully remembered, to avoid confusion with the Persian word دروغ *darogh*—a lie.

Ṣādir honā—To issue. Till further orders is expressed by تاصدور حکم ثاني *ta ṣudūr i ḥukmi ṣāni*.

N. B.—*Loṭā* should be spelt لوٹا

24.—Transliteration.—*Gharīb parwar salāmat.*

Janāb 'āli fidvī dast basta mu'riẓ *hai ki ājkal* maraẓ-i chechak kā az bas zor hai *aur mere chand* ṭiflak *aise haiṇ ki jinko* ṭīkā *nahīṇ dīyā gayā aur merī* tamannā *yeh hai ki yeh kām ḥuẓūr ke dast-ī-mubārak se anjām pāwe to 'ain* khāwindī o bandanawazī *hogī jiskā* shukrīya *tamām 'umr ādā na kar sakūngā.*

'Arẓī fidvī Ināyat Khān Rāis tīswīn Januarī san Athārah sau unāsi Isawī.

Translation.—*Hail, cherisher of the poor.*

Eminent sir, your humble servant with joined hands represents that now-a-days the small-pox is very prevalent, and there are several children of mine, who have not been vaccinated. and my desire is this, that this operation should be carried out by your Honour's auspicious hand, then it will be the height of kindness and a consideration which I shall never be able to repay during my whole life.

The petition of your devoted Ināyat Khān Rāis, the 30th of January, 1879 A.D.

Notes.—*Mu'riẓ*—one who makes an *arẓ*.

Maraẓ—Disease.

Ṭiflak.—Little children—diminutive of *ṭifl*.

Ṭīkā denā or *Ṭīkā lagānā*—To inoculate—vaccinate—*Ṭīkā karnā* to mark the forehead with the *ṭikā*.

Tamannā = *Khwāhish*—desire (notice the gender, *vide* page 21).

Khāwindī.—Kindness—*Khāwind*, a lord or husband.

Bandanawāzī.—Slave-cherishing, from Persian *nawākhtan* = *parwardan*. (*gharīb parwarī*).

Shukrīya.—A thankoffering.

25.—TRANSLITERATION.—*Gharīb parwar 'ādil-i-zamān Hātim-i-waqt, Naushīrwān Janāb Lankīn Ṣāḥib Bahādur dāma iqbāluhu.*

Janāb 'ālī ḥāl yeh hai ki do qiṭa' parwāna az rāhi gharīb parwarī o banda nawāzī kī Sarkār faiz āṣār se bazaric *dāk bar makān wālid fidvī ke* marahmat *farmāyā thā pahunchā aur ḥāl parwarish fidvīkī ma'lūm hūā Khudā ḥuzūr ko aur bābā ṣāḥib ko salāmat rakhe. Ḥāl yeh hai ki jabse ḥuzūr rawāna wilāyat ko hūe fidvī ne naukarī Gheren ṣāḥib bahādur jo ki Faizābād men Ashishtant Kamishnar the wahān par mulāzim rahā 'arṣa chand roz kā hūā ki wuh marga-elihāzā fidvī kuchh tadbīr rail ke kirāya kī karke bahut jald khidmat men ḥāzir hogā. Wājib thā 'arz kīyā. Aftāb i daulat o iqbāl kā chamaktā hūjiyo.*

'Arzī fidvī khānazād Ghāsi khān khansāmān muwarrakha chahārum māh Aktobar san atharah sau ikāsī Isawī.

TRANSLATION.—*Cherisher of the poor, just one of the time, Hatim of the age, Naushīrwān of this era, &c., &c. May his prosperity continue.*

Sir, this is the state of affairs: That the two kind letters which your honour sent to the house of your servant's father, by way of favour and kindness, arrived, and the degree of favour shewn by you to your servant became known; may God preserve your honour and the young master in safety. This is the state of affairs: Since your honour set out for England, your servant entered the service of Mr. Green, Assistant Commissioner of Faizabad, and remained in his service; he died a few days ago, therefore your servant having made some arrangement for his rail-fare will very quickly present himself in your honour's service. The request was reasonable, therefore it was made. May the sun of fortune and prosperity remain shining. The petition of your house-born Ghāsi Khān khānsāmān, dated the 4th of October 1881, A.D.

26.—TRANSLITERATION.—*Gharīb parwar salāmat.*

Fidvī Ḥasan 'Alī Ṣūbadār kī 'arzī yeh hai, ki fidvī aur fidvī ke bāp dāde saikroṇ baras se Māhārājā Gwālier kā ra'īyat hai, aur das hazār bīghā zamīn lākhiraj fidvī kā maurūṣi milk hai, jis par kabhī koī kirāya muqarrar nahīn thā, aur kisī waqt meṇ kisī Mahārājā ṣāḥib ne koī khirāj ṭalab nahīn kīyā thā, aur na is waqt ke Mahārajā ṣāḥib ne kabhi kuchh kirāya na līyā. Magar in dinoṇ Mahārājā ṣāḥib ke bhāīyoṇ ne nahaqq Mahārājā ṣāḥib ke binā ḥukm kul zamīn ko ẓabt kar liyā hai, aur fidrī ki koī 'arẓ Mahārājā ṣaḥib tak pahunchnī nahīṇ dete. Is līye fidvī Mahārājā ṣaḥib ke nām kī ek 'arẓī is 'arẓī ke sath ḥuẓūr meṇ bhejtā hūṇ, aur umedwār hūṇ ki ḥuẓūr is 'arẓī ko Gwaliār ke Agent Ṣaḥib bahādur ke ḥuẓūr men bhej dījiye, tā ki wuh Mahārajā Ṣāḥib ke ḥuẓūr meṇ pesh kar deweṇ.

Almarqūm tīsrī Janwari san aṭhara sau satāsi Isawi.

TRANSLATION.—*Cherisher of the poor, Hail.*

This is the petition of your devoted Hasan Alī Subadar: That your servant and his ancestors have been for years subject of the Mahārāja of Gwalior, and ten thousand bighas of land, freehold, is the hereditary property of your petitioner. There has never been any rent assessed upon this property, nor has any Mahārāja at any time demanded any rent, nor did the former Mahārāja ever take any rent. However, nowadays the

Mahārāja's brothers, unlawfully and without the Mahārāja's orders, has confiscated the whole of the land, and do not permit my petition from your devoted servant to reach the Mahārāja. Accordingly your servants sends herewith to your honour a petition to the Mahārāja, and hopes that your honour will be good enough to send this petition to the Agent of the Gwalior State, that he may present it to the Mahārāja. Dated the 3rd of January 1887.

27.—TRANSLITERATION.—*Gharib parwar khudāwand na'mat fāiyyāẓi zamān dāma Allāhu iqbālahū.*

Janāb 'āli ṣūrat yeh hai ki jab ḥuẓūr chhāonī Sītāpūr se ṭaraf wilāyat ke tashrīf lechale yeh khānazād bhī ḥuẓūr ke hamrāh chalā shahr Kalkatte tak gayā jab ki ḥuẓūr jahāz par sawār hokar rawāna simt-i-wilāyat hue, ba'd do roz ke yeh fidvī makān rawāna hūā, lekin shab o roz yeh d'uā māngta thā ki khudā jeld ḥuẓūr ko Hindustān men lāwe jo ḥuẓūr apne risāle meṇ raunaq afroz howeṇ bande ko bahut khushi ḥāṣil howe ki Ḥaqq taāla āpko badarja 'āla ke pahunchāde roz baroz taraqqī āpkī 'umr darājī baba kī kare.

Ab fidvī umedwār hai ki kab wāsṭe is khanazad ke ḥukm ho ki fidvī khidmat guzārī āur tābi'dārī meṇ ḥazir ho. Wājib thā 'arẓ kīyā, Allāhī afṭāb iqbāl daulat kā chamaktā hujīyo. Aur yeh khānazād shahr-i-Lakhnau maḥalla Quṭabpūr muttasil-i-pul-i-āhanī lab-i-Gūmtī makān Munshī Yusuf Khān rahtā hūṇ.

Khānazād Ghāsī Khāṇ Khansāmāṇ muwarrakha tārīkh nau māh Julāī san aṭhārah sau ikāsī.

TRANSLATION.—*Cherisher of the poor, lord of favours, most generous of the age, may God prolong his fortune.*

Sir, this is the state of affairs: When your honour left the station of Sitapur for England, this houseborn slave too went with your honour, as far as the city of Calcutta. When your honour having embarked started for England, after two days your servant set out for his home, but day and night he was praying that God would quickly bring your honour back to Hindustān. If your honour should again return to your own regiment, your servant will greatly rejoice. May God promote you to great honour, and day by day increase your promotion and grant your son a long life. Now your slave is hoping and wondering when he will be summoned to serve your honour.

It was reasonable the request was made. Oh, God! may the sun of prosperity and good fortune remain shining, and this houseborn one is living in the city of Lucknow *mahalla* Qutabpur, near the iron bridge on the banks of the Gumtī, at the house of Munshī Yusuf Khan. Your servant Ghāsī Khān Khansāmān. Dated the ninth of July 1881.

28.—TRANSLITERATION.—*Janāb-i-mukarram i-mu'azzam faiyyāẓ-i-zamān Ṣāḥib Bahādur.*

Ba'd taslīm multamis hūṇ—kī chanda shafakhāne men denā ek kār-i-khair hai yeh chanda bekasān marīẓān o muḥtājān ke kām awegā aur harek zīshān o muazzaz jaise āp o nīz dīgar ṣāḥibān haiṇ ūnpar ek farẓ hai ki bechārān o māndagān ko dawā bakhsheṇ aur ḥasbul ḥukm Government-i-aliya jo ṣāḥib das rūpaya sāl se ziyādā chanda deweṇge unkā nām takhta-i-board par jo shafā khāne meṇ zarrīn harfoṇ se munaqqash hokar latkāya jāwegā mā siwā iske ḥasbi manshā-i-Government jo nafar aur ahl-i-duwal chande men sharīk hoṇge unse qīmat-i-duwāe nahīṇ lījāwegi warna qīmat-i-adwīya jo leweṇge dene paṛegī. Chūnki jānāb bhī ahl-i-duwal aur zīshān hain is līye umed-i-qawwī hai kī chanda shaṭā khāne meṇ denā manẓūr karenge. Aur takhta-i-board ab ṭaiyar ho rahā hai, aur bahut se nām likhe gaye hain.

TRANSLATION.—*Honoured and respected, Sir most generous of the age.*

After respects I beg to represent that to give a subscription to a Hospital is a good work, this subscription will be of service to unfortunate, invalid and poor people. and it is incumbent upon every honourable and noble man as you yourself and other gentlemen are, to bestow medicine upon the poor and needy, and in accordance with the orders of the Supreme Government, whatever gentleman shall contribute ten rupees a year or more, their names shall be elegantly written in letters of gold upon a board to be hung up in the Hospital.

Besides this, according to the will of Government whatever persons or wealthy men shall join the fund will not be charged for medicines, otherwise the cost of any medicines they may take will have to be paid. Inasmuch as your honour too is wealthy and honoured, therefore there is great hope that you will consent to give a subscription to the Hospital.

And the board is now being prepared, and many names have been inscribed on it.

29.—TRANSLITERATION.—*Baḥuẓūr janab Brigade Major-Ṣāḥib Chhāonī-i-Sītāpūr dām-iqbāluhū.*
Gharīb parwar Salāmat.

Janāb 'ālī fidvī Chānd Khān umedwār-i-rozgār nihāyat muddat se Saiyyid Mahomed Sādiq Ṣaḥib wakīl 'adālat ke yahāṇ rūpaya wikālat kā ujratāna wuṣūl kīyā kartā thā ab ki āmadanī wikālat kī bahut kam hai is wajh se merī guzārā nahīn hotī aur taklīf meṇ hūṇ, jo ki ḥūẓūr kī qadrdānī aur faizrasānī kā 'ām shuhra hai is līye maiṇ bhī umedwār hūṇ ki agar ḥuẓūr ke sarishte meṇ koī jagah khālī ho yā 'ewaẓī ho yā āyanda honekī umed ho to ḥuẓūr mujhko muqarrar farmā'en maiṇ apne kar-i-muta'allaqa ko musta'iddī aur hoshyārī o diyānat se anjam dūngā. Merī diyānat aur musta'iddī ke bāre men Saiyyid Mahomed Sādiq Ṣāḥib kah sakte hain wājib jānkar 'arẓ kiyā—Ziyāda hadd i adab.

Fidvī Chānd Khān, Umedwārī rozgār ma'rūza pachīs tārīkh Agast san athārah sau satatthar Isawī.

TRANSLATION.—*To the Brigade-Major of the Station of Sitapur.*

May his fortune last.

Cherisher of the poor, hail.

Sir, your servant Chānd Khān, in hope of a livelihood, for a very long time in the service of Saiyyid Mahomed Sādiq, pleader of the Court, used to receive the commission money by way of wages; now that the income of the commission is very small, for this reason I cannot exist and am in difficulties. Since your honour has a world-wide reputation for acknowledgment of worth and beneficence, I therefore also hope that, if any vacancy should occur in your honour's office, either as substitute, or if there is hope of any future vacancy, then your honour would appoint me. I will perform my allotted task with readiness, cleverness and honesty. Saiyyid Mahamed Sādiq Sāhib can speak to my honesty and energy; thinking it reasonable I made the request.

More than this exceeds the bounds of respect.

Your servant Chānd Khān, candidate for employment, written the 25th of August 1877, A. D.

30.—TRANSLITERATION.—*Byḥuẓūr faiẓ bakhsh o faiẓ-rasan Janāb Daktar G. Ranking Ṣāḥib Bahādur dāma iqbāluhū.*

Gharīb parwar salāmat.

Chūnki fidvī 'arsa chand mah se khāna nishin hai aur kār-i-taḥrīr bakhūbī saranjam de saktā hai. Ḥusn-i-ittifāq se ḥuẓūr ke daftar meṇ ek āsāmī khālī hai, agar ḥuẓūr barāh-i-khāwindī āsāmī i mazkūr par banda ko māmūr farmāweṇ to 'ain i ghurabā parwarī haī tāki fidvī apni murād-i-dilī ko pahuṇchkar ḥuẓūr kī jān o māl ko du'ā detā rahe.

Allāhī aftāb daulat kā hamesha darakhshāṇ hūjiyō 'Arẓī fidvī Amīr Khān umedwar—muwarrakha tīs January san athārah sau nawāsī Isawī.

TRANSLATION.—*To the beneficent and bountiful Doctor G. Ranking Ṣaḥib bahādur. May his prosperity continue. Cherisher of the poor, hail.*

Inasmuch as your humble servant for some months past has been sitting at home (unemployed) and is capable of performing all kinds of writing very well, by a fortunate coincidence there is a vacant post in your honour's office. If your honour will appoint your servant to the post mentioned by way of kindness, it will be the height of consideration; and your servant having attained his heart's desire will continue to bless your honour's name and property.

Oh God! May the sun of wealth always remain shining. The petition of your devoted Amīr Khān, candidate. Dated the 30th of January 1889, A.D.

31.—TRANSLITERATION.—*Ba ḥuẓūr faiẓ ganjūr janāb Daktar Ṣāḥib bahādur dāma iqbāluhu. Gharīb parwar salāmat.*

Janāb 'āli—'Arẓ fidvī kī yeh hai ki banda hafta 'ashra se ba āriẓa-i-tap-i-naubatī mubtalā hai ba bāiṣ shiddat-i garmī bukhār se az bas majbur hūṇ akṣar shab ko bawajh ḥarārat ke is darja waḥshat hotī hai ki jisse khwāb o khūrish mutlaq nahīṇ hotā, aur dauran-i-sar har dam rahtā hai jisse iḥtimāl i amrāẓ i dimāgh bhī hotā hai. 'Ilāwa az īn fidvī ko taklīf ziyāda yeh bhī hai ki is jagah koi apna hamjins nahīṇ jo kisiṭaraḥ madad pahuṇchā de Lihāza 'arẓī hāzā guzrānkar umedwār hūṇ ki āgar rukhṣat ek māh ki ḥuẓūr se 'aṭa farmāī jāwe to 'aīn khāwindī hai tā ki apnī waṭan jākar 'alāwa 'alāj muālaja ke tabdīl i āb o hawā bhī karūṇ ziyāda ḥadd i ādāb.

'Arẓī fidvī Fatḥ Khān Muḥarrir i sarā.

Untis tārīkh Janwarī san nawāsī Isawi.

TRANSLATION.—*To the storehouse of benevolence Doctor . . .*

May his fortune continue.

Cherisher of the poor, hail.

Sir, your petitioner's request is this, that your servant for the last week or ten days has been down with remittent fever. On account of the severity of the fever he is very much overcome. Most nights, by reason of feverishness, this degree of distraction occurs that sleep and food are altogether banished, and giddiness is constantly present, from which it is probable that there is disease of the brain Besides this, there is this additional distress to your servant, that in this place there is no relation who can give him any assistance.

Therefore, having presented this petition, I hope that your honour will perhaps grant me leave for one month, then it will be the height of kindness, so that I may visit my own country, and in addition to medical treatment may get a change of air. More is forbidden by respect. The petition of Fateh Khan, writer of the Sarāi. 29th January, 1889, A.D.

32.—TRANSLITERATION.—*Gharīb parwar salāmat.*

Fidvī Ḥassan Raẓā Khān Kotwāl kī 'arẓī yeh hai ki āj jo palṭan Meerath se is chhāonī meṇ pahuṇchī hai us ke chand sipāhī ne milkar aise ek gharīb lakarhāre ko mārā hai aur uskī lakrīyān chhīn lī hain wuh bechāra Kotwālī men nālishī honeko āyā. Fidvī is lakarhāre ko hamrāh lekar ṣūbadar bahādur ke pās gayā ki jin sipāhiyon ne is bechāre kī lakrīyān chhīn lī hain unki shinākht kare. Magar ṣūbadār ṣāḥib ne shinākht karne ke līye kisī sipāhī ke khīma men jāne nahīn dīyā. Islīye umedwār hūn ki ṣūbadār ṣāḥib ke nām ḥukm ho ki fidvī ko hamrāh lekar taḥqīqāt men sharīk karen—faqaṭ.

'Arẓī Hassan Raẓā Khān Kotwāl.

TRANSLATION.—*Hail, protector of the poor.*

This is the petition of Hassan Razā Khān Kotwāl that the regiment which has arrived to-day in this cantonment from Meerut, some of its sepoys having joined together, have so beaten a poor wood-cutter, and have stolen his faggots, that the unfortunate man came to complain to the kotwālī. Your servant having taken the woodman with him went to the subadar, to ask that he might identify the sepoy by whom the wood was stolen, but the subadar would not allow him to enter any sepoy's tent for the purposes of identification. Accordingly, I hope that an order may be be issued to the subadar to take your servant with him and make him assist him in the investigation. Enough. The petition of Hassan Razā Khān Kotwāl.

33.—TRANSLITERATION.—*Hindī 'arẓī.*

Srī yut Mahārāja Dhirāj Srī Chhattar Dhārī Singh Bahādur ke samīp men Senādhikārī Bhopal Singh kī rām rām pahunche. Bintī yeh hai ki āpkī āgyā anusār main ne yuddh bhūmī men apnī senā ki itnī sankhyā parmān bhejī hai ki tīn hazār (3,000) *paidal sipāhī shastardhārī aur* (2,000) *do hazār sowār aur bare bare yoddhāon ke sahit topen aur golā bārūd ādī sab yuddh kā sāmān bhī bhej chukā hūṇ. Lekin ek patr aur samar bhūmī se āyā hai likhā huā Rakhārang Singh kā, kī yahāṇ shatrūdal kā baṛā jor hai. Isse tum log andāj (5,000) pānch hazār sawār aur do topkhāna aur bhejo, to shatrū kī fauj ko haṭāe sakte haiṇ nahīṇ to shatrūoṇ kī senā hamārī sīmā meṇ āye jāegī, is se yeh bintī kar kahtā hūṇ ki jo sarkār ki āgyā howe to likhe māfik senā aur bhej dūṇ uchit jānke arj kiyā. Tārīkh aṭharah, mās Phāgun, Sudī.*

TRANSLATION.—*Petition.*

To the Possessor of Fortune, King of Kings, Srī Chattardhārī Singh, General Bhopāl Singh sends greeting. This is my petition, that in accordance with your honour's order, I sent the following number from my own army to the battle field, namely, three thousand infantry fully equipped and two thousand cavalry and with the noble heroes, guns and ammunition, *etcetera.* I have also sent all the equipment for battle. But another despatch has arrived from the battle field written by Rakhārang Singh, saying: "Here the enemy is in great force. Therefore do you send about five thousand cavalry and two more batteries of artillery, then we shall be able to defeat the enemy's army, otherwise the enemy's army will invade our territory." Therefore I make this representation that, if your honour orders, then I will send reinforcements in accordance with the despatch. Having considered it reasonable, the petition is made. Dated 18th of month Phāgun, light half.

34.—TRANSLITERATION.—*Hindī Arzi.*

Srī yut Mahārāj Rājā Mānsing Bahādur ke samīp meṇ parjā janoṇ kī rām rām pahunche. Bintī yeh hāi ki is sāl men barshā kam huī hai isse ham logoṇ ke khetoṇ meṇ ann kī upaj aur sāl se ādhī bhī nahīṇ huī. Ham log bahut tang hogaye haiṇ, larke bāle sab dukhī ho rahe haiṇ kisī bhānt se nibāh khāne pīne kā nahīṇ ho saktā hai, aur aisā koī mahājan bhī ham logoṇ ko nahīṇ miltā, ki jisse karj leke sarkārī māl gujārī patā deṇ. Is līye 'arz karte haiṇ ki aisī koī sūrat sarkār se hojāe ki jisse ham logoṇ kā nibās āpke rājya meṇ banā rahe.

Uchit jān ke 'arz kīya tārīkh, 2 *January, san athārah sau beāsī Isawi.*

TRANSLATION.—*Petition.*

Possessor of fortune, Mābārāja Mānsingh Bahadur.—May this salutation of his subjects reach his august presence. This is the petition that in this year there has been very little rain, on this account there has not been even half the produce of grain in our fields compared with other years. We are in great straits, all our children are in distress, in no way can we supply our wants for food and drink, and moreover we can find no banker from whom we may borrow and pay the Government assessment. For this reason we pray that the Government will be pleased to make some arrangement, by which we may be enabled to live in your honour's kingdom.

Having considered it right this petition is made, dated the 2nd of January, 1882, of the Christian era.

35.—TRANSLITERATION.—*Hindī Arzi.*

Srī yut Māhārājā Dhirāj Rājā Daulat Singh Bahādur ke samīp meṇ Debī Singh Jamadar kī rām rām pahunche.

Bintī yeh hai ki sarkārī risāle ke sipāhīyoṇ ne kal ke roj merā bīs (20) *bīghā khet ghoroṇ se charwāe līya aur sārā khet ghoroṇ kē tāpoṇ ke paṛne se nā kām hogaya. Ab us khet meṇ kuchh bhi ann nahīṇ paidā hogā is sāl meṇ sarkārī mālgujārī kaise dūṇga, aur mere laṛke bālē kyā khāeṇge, is līye arj kartā hūṇ ki aisā hukm Sarkār se hojāe ki jisse pher kabhī aisī anītī kā kām sīpāhī log nahīṇ kareṇ. Aur mere līye bhī kuchh sahāyetā hoe ki jisse maiṇ apne bāl bachōṇ ko pālan karsakūṇ.*

Uchit jān ke 'arẓ kiyā tārīkh unīs Jūn san athārah sau ikānawe Isawī.

TRANSLATION.—*Petition.*

Lord of fortune Maharaja Dhiraj.—Raja Daulat Singh Bahadur. May the salutation of Debi Singh, landowner, reach his presence. The petition is this, that yesterday the soldiers of the Sarkār's cavalry used a plot of land of mine of 20 bighas to graze their horses, and the whole field has become useless from the trampling by the horses' hoofs. Now no corn will grow in that field this year. How shall I pay the Government tax, and what will my children do for food? Therefore I beg that some such order may be issued by the Sarkār, which will prevent the repetition of any such oppressive action on the part of the sepoys, and also that some assistance may be granted me by which I may be enabled to provide for my family.

Having judged it reasonable I have made this request, this 19th of June, 1891, Christian era.

PART V.*
PASSAGES FOR TRANSLATION.

Colloquial Style. 1.

There was a certain Mulla in a village of Pathans. Whatever prayers for the dead they required to be performed, they used to send for him and used to get their business done. When the Shab-i-Barāt came round, from every house there was a demand for him. So one of his acquaintance asked him, saying, "Tell me, friend, how will you manage to-day all alone and in what way will you offer prayers in every house?" He said, "My brother, what have I to do with offering prayers for the dead? Whether the dead man goes to hell or to heaven I have only to look after my daily bread."†

NAQL.

Paṭhānoṇ kī kisī bastī meṇ ek Mullā thā. Jo kuchh Fātiḥa darūd kā un ko kām hotā, is ko bulā lete aur apnā kām karwā lete. Is meṇ Shab-i-Barāt jo āī to har ek ke ghar se ise bulāhaṭ hūī. Tab is ke kisī āshnā ne pūchhā ki, "kaho, dost, āj tum ikele kyā karoge, aur kistaraḥ ghar ghar Fātiḥa paṛhoge? Bolā, "Bhāi mujhe Fātiḥa paṛhne se kyā kām? Murda dozakh meṇ jāe yā bihisht meṇ, mujhe apne ḥalwe mānḍe se kām hai."

نقل .

پتھانون کي کسي بستي مين ايك ملا تها جو کچھه فاتحه درود کا اُنکو کام هوتا اسکو بلا ليتے اور اپنا کام کروا ليتے

---

* The Author's Introductory Exercises in Urdu Prose Composition published by Messrs. Thacker, Spink & Co., will be found very useful.

† Literally, sweetmeats and cakes.

اسمين شب برات جو آئي تو هر ايک کے گهر سے اسے بلاهٹ هوئي - تب اسکے کسي آشنا نے پوچها که کهو دوست آج تم اکيلے کيا کروگے اور کس طرح گهر گهر فاتحه پڑهوگے - بولا بهائي مجهے فاتحه پڑهنے سے کيا کام - مرده دوزخ مين جائے يا بهشت مين مجهے اپنے حلوے مانڈے سے کام هي -

---

Colloquial Style. 2.

A number of young nobles having driven in a peg in a certain place, and having placed a rupee upon it, were engaged in archery, and this was the condition that whoever knocked off the rupee, should take it.

By chance a devotee going to that spot asked alms of them, saying, "Sirs, make some bargain in the name of the Master."

One of them laughing said, "Shāh Ṣāhib, hit the mark and take the rupee."

The faqīr instantly taking the bow and arrow from his hand having said, "Ya, Maʻbūd!" (Oh! thou that art worshipped) shot an arrow at random, when the rupee flew off the peg. They cried Bravo! He ran and picked up the rupee, and said, "How is it, Sirs, the faqīr has got nothing."

One of them said, "Holy man, you have got the rupee, now what do you say?" He said, "Sire, this indeed I got for hitting the peg, the faqīr's alms are still to come."

Naql.

Kaī ek amīr-zāde kisī jagah ek mekh gāṛ us par rupya rakh tīr-andāzi karte the, aur shart yeh thī ki jo is rupaē ko uṛā de so le. Ittifāqan kisī āzād ne jā wahāṇ suwāl kiyā ki, "Bābā, kuchh Maulā nām kā saudā karo." Un meṇ se ek ne haṇs kar kahā ki "Shāh Ṣāḥib, nishāna māro aur rupya lo." Faqīr ne jhaṭ us ke hāth se tīr kamān le 'yā Ma'būd!' kar ke tīr aṭkal-pachchū mārā, ki wuh rupya uṛ gayā. We bole, "Wāh wāh!" Un ne dauṛ kar rupya to uṭhā liyā, aur kahā, "Kyūn bābā, faqīr ko kuchh na milā?" Un meṇ se ek ne kahā, "Sāīṇ rupya to liyā, ab kyā kahte ho?" Bolā, "Bābā, yeh to mekh mār ke liyā hai, abhī faqīr kā suwāl bāqī hai."

نقل

كئي ايک اميرزادے کسي جگه ايک ميخ گاڑ اُسپر روپيه رکهه تيراندازي کرتے تهے اور شرط يهه تهي که جو اس روپي کو اُڑادے سو لے - اتفاقاً کسي آزاد نے جا وهان سوال کيا که بابا کچهه مولا نام کا سودا کرو - انمين سے * ايک نے هنسکر کها شاه صاحب نشانه مارو اور روپيه لو - فقير نے جهٹ اُسکے هاتهه سے تير کمان لے يا معبود کرکے تير اٹکل پچو مارا - که وه روپيه اُڑ گيا - وے بولے واه واه - اُن نے دوڑ کر روپيه تو اُٹها ليا اور کها کيون بابا فقير کو کچهه نه ملا

* Note this idiom.

اُنمیں سے ایک نے کہا - سائیں روپیہ تو لیا اب کیا کہتے هو - بولا بابا یہہ تو میخ مار کے لیا هی - ابھی فقیر کا سوال باقي هی -

---

Colloquial Style. 3.

A man was a great opium-eater. In his house there was a khidmatgār lately engaged. He asked of him, saying, "My friend, you don't take any intoxicant, I suppose?" He said, "My Spiritual Guide! your slave, except opium, knows no other intoxicant." Hearing this speech, being very pleased, he took out the opium box, and himself having eaten some, gave it to him, and said, "My friend, to-day my heart desires you should cook me some sweetened rice, then we will eat. The khidmatgār said, "Very well," and began to cook it. In the meantime drowsiness came on him, and it was past twelve o'clock. The master calling out said, "Ho, my brother, is the rice cooked or not?" He said, "My Lord it is done cooking, but it wants drying now." He said, "Bring it quickly." To make a long story short, with the utmost difficulty, cooking away from early morning, he got it ready and brought it by the evening. Seeing it, his master said, "Well done! how quickly you cooked and served it!" Hearing just this much, immediately he joined his hands and said, "My Lord, your devoted one will not be able to serve your honour." He said, "How so?" He replied, "Having to hurry so will be the death of me one of these days;" and off he went.

Naql.

Ek shakhs baṛā afīmī thā. Us ke yahāṇ koī khidmatgār nayā naukar huā. Un ne us se pūchhā ki, "Miyāṇ, tū kuchh nasha to nahīṇ pītā?" Bolā, "Pīr Murshid, ghulām siwāī afīm, aur kisī nashe se āshnā nahīṇ" Yeh bāt sun bahut khush huā; afīm kī ḍibyā nikāl, un ne āp khāke de kar kahā ki, "Miyāṇ, āj hamārā jī chāhtā hai, mīṭhe chāṇwal jaldī se pakā do, khāeṇ." Khidmatgār, "Bahut achchhā," kah ke pakāne lagā. Us meṇ pīnak jo lagī, do pahar guzar gae. Āqā ne pukār ke kahā ki "Ai bhāī, chāṇwal pake yā nahīṇ?" Bolā ki, "Khudā wand, pak chuke haiṇ, par dam denā bāqī hai." Kahā, "Jaldī do." Qiṣṣa kotāh, ba-hazār kharābī fajr se pakāte pakāte, shām ko taiyār kar ke gayā. Dekh kar āqā ne kahā, "Shābāsh! kyā jaldī pakā lāyā hai!" Itnī bāt ke sunte hī, woh hāth joṛ ke bolā ki, "Fidvī se āp kī naukarī na ho sakegī." Kahā, "Kyūṇ?" Jawāb diyā, "Aisī shitābī meṇ ek roz merī jān jāti rahegī" aur chalā gayā.

نقل

ایک شخص بڑا افیمي تھا - اُسکے یہان کوئي خدمت
گار نیا نوکر ھوا - اُن نے اُس سے پوچھا کہ میان تو کچھہ نشہ
تو نہین پیتا - بولا پیر مرشد غلام سواے افیم * اور کسي
نشہ سے آشنا نہین - یہ بات سن بہت خوش ھوا - افیم کي
ڈبیا نکال اُن نے آپ کہا کے دیکر کہا کہ میان آج ھمارا
جي چاھتا ھی میٹھے چانول جلدیسے پکا دو کھائین -
خدمت گار بہت اچھا کہہ کے پکانے لگا - اُسمین پینک
جو لگي دو پھر گذر گئے آقا نے پکار کے کہا کہ اي بھائي

* Note—افیم Corrupt form of افیون opium.

چانول پکے * یا نہین بولا که خداوند پک چکے ہین * پر دم
دینا باقي هی * کہا جلدي دو - قصه کوتاه * بہزار خرابي
فجرسے پکاتے پکاتے شام کو تیار کر کے گیا دیکھکر آقا نے کہا
شاباش کیا جلدي پکا لایا هی - اتني بات کے سنتے هي
وه هاتهه جوڑ کے بولا که فدویسے آپکي نوکري نہوسکیگي *
کہا کیون - جواب دیا ایسي شتابي مین ایک روز میري جان
جاتي رهیگي * اور چلا گیا *

Colloquial Style. 4.

In a certain house five or six sepoys were sitting, bragging among themselves. One was saying "I have got four wounds." Another would say "five." In short one of them related the history of his fighting and getting wounded. An old wag was sitting near them, and said "My friend, in my youth I too fought hundreds of battles, and I too got thousands of wounds to such an extent that on my whole body there was not left room to put a grain of til. Compared with me who now will fight and who will get wounded?" Immediately on hearing this speech a young soldier among them grew angry and said, "My good Sir, take off your clothes then, let us see where you were wounded so often." He laughed and said, "My good youth that time is now no more, nor are those days now, nor does that youth remain, nor is that strength remaining, nor is even that body itself left. Now what will you see?" Saying this, he made off.

• Note this idiom.

NAQL.

Kisī makān ke bīch pāṇch sāt sipāhī baiṭhe āpas meṇ ḍīṇg mārte the. Koī kahtā, "maiṇ ne chār ghāo khāe;" aur koī kahtā thā, "Pāṇch." G͟haraẓ har ek ne apne apne laṛne aur zak͟hm khāne kā aḥwāl bayān kiyā. Ek būṛhā ṭhaṭhol un ke pās baiṭhā thā. Bolā ki, "Miyāṇ, jawānī meṇ ham bhī saikṛoṇ laṛāīyāṇ laṛe, aur ham ne bhī hazāroṇ zak͟hm khāe, aise ki kahīṇ badan par til dharne kī jagah bāqī nahīṇ rahī. Hamāre āge ab koi kyā laṛega, aur kyā koi zak͟hm khāegā?" Itnī bāt ke sunte hī un meṇ se ek jawān k͟hafā ho kar bolā, "Baṛe miyāṇ, kapṛe to utāro; dekheṇ, tum ne kahāṇ kahāṇ ghāo khāe haiṇ." Woh haṇs ke bolā, "Miyāṇ gabrū, na wuh zamāna rahā, na we din rahe, na wuh jawānī rahī, na woh taiyārī rahī, na wuh jism hī rahā. Ab kyā dekhoge?" Itnā kah, bhāg gayā.

نقل

کسي مکان کے بیچ پانچ * سات سپاهي بیٹھے آپسمین
ڈینگ مارتے تھے - کوئي کهتا تها مین نے چار گهاو کهائے
اور کوئي کهتا تها پانچ - غرض هر ایک نے اپنے اپنے لڑنے
اور زخم کهانے کا احوال بیان کیا ایک بوڑها ٹهٹهول اُنکے پاس
بیٹها تها - بولا که میان جواني مین هم بهي سیکڑون لڑائیان
لڑے * اور همنے بهي هزارون زخم کهائے - ایسے که کهین
بدنپر تل دهرنے کي جگهه باقي نهین رهي - همارے آگے
اب کوئي کیا لڑیگا اور کیا کوئي زخم کهایگا - اتني بات کے

* Note this idiom.

سنتے ہی اُنمیں سے ایک جوان خفا ہوکر بولا - بڑے میان
کپڑے تو اتارو دیکھیں تمنے کہان کہان گھاؤ کھاے ہیں
وہ ہنسکے بولا میان گبرو نہ وہ زمانہ رہا نہ وے دن رہے نہ
وہ جوانی رہی نہ وہ تیاری رہی نہ وہ جسم ہی رہا - اب
کیا دیکھوگے - اتنا کہہ بھاگ گیا

Colloquial Style. 5.

A Sipahi was a great gambler; when he use to win, from joy he used to get so careless that, if anyone had even stripped off him the clothes he wore, he would not have known it.

In expectation of this ten or a dozen* blackguards used always to stay close beside him, and when they got a chance, used to make his money fly.

One day he went to gamble in some strange assembly, and began to shove the money he won from in front of him, behind him, and the rips who were with him began to make it fly.

In the meantime, some one seeing this said to some one else, "Look! one fellow spends another man's money!" The other answered him, "Haven't you heard this proverb, that you are wondering at this?—

"The blind woman grinds (the corn) the dog eats (the flour.)
The sinner's wealth goes to nought."

NAQL.

Ek sīpāhī barā juārī thā. Jab jīttā, tab māre khushī ke aisā ghāfil ho jātā, ki koī us ke pahnne ke kapre bhī utār letā

---

* (*Lit.* ten, five).

to bhī use maʻlum na hotā. Isī umīd se das pāṇch shuhde har waqt us ke sāth lage rahte, aur jab qābū pāte to us kā māl uṛāte. Ek roz wuh kisī ghair maḥfil meṇ juā khelne ko gayā, aur lagā jīt jīt rupae apne āge se pīchhe khiskāne; aur uske sāth ke luqandre lage uṛāne. Us meṇ kisī ne dekh kar ek se kahā kī, "Dekho, kisī ki kauṛī, koī uṛāwe!" Dūsre ne jawāb diyā "Kyā yeh maṣal tum ne nahīṇ sunī jo taʻajjub karte ho? ki,

"Andhī pīse, kuttā khāe;
Pāpī kā māl akārath jāe."

نقل

ایک سپاهي بڑا جواري تها - جب جیتتا تب مارے
خوشي کے ایسا غافل هوجاتا - که کوئي اُسکے پهننے کے
کپڑے بهي اتار لیتا تو بهي اُسے معلوم نه هوتا - اسی امید
سے دس پانچ شهدے هر وقت اُسکے ساتهه لگے رهتے * اور
جب قابو پاتے تو اُسکا مال اُڑاتے * - ایک روز وه کسي
غیر محفل مین جوا کهیلنے کو گیا اور لگا جیت جیت روپئے
اپنے آگے سے پیچهے کهسکانے - اور اُسکے ساتهه کے
لقندرے لگے اُڑانے اسمین کسینے دیکهکر ایک سے کها که
دیکهو کسیکي کوڑي کوئي اُڑاوے * - دوسرے نے

* Note this idiom.

جواب دیا - کیا تمنے یهه مثل نہین سنی جو تعجب کرتے هو - کہ

اندهی پیسے کتا کهائے
پاپی کا مال اکارتهه جائے *

Colloquial Style. 6.

A certain gentleman was very fond of horses. One day he bought an Arab : upon this Munshi Badrud Din, by way of well-wishing, said :—" If a Panjabi syce is put on this horse, then it will be well cared for."

Hearing this, the gentleman called the jamadar of the syces from the stable, and ordered him to get a Panjabi syce for him, but the jamadar forgot. Twenty or five-and-twenty days afterwards, one day the gentleman recollected that matter, he had him sent for, and asked if he had got the syce or not. He said, " My Lord, your slave is searching, up to now he has not found one." Hearing this answer, the Munshi said, " What a rascal he is ! He keeps putting you off from a month past, and does not bring you a syce." The syce said :—" My lord and master, I don't mind your calling me a rascal, you are my master, whatever you feel inclined, be pleased to say—but in the presence of one's master there is no harm in speaking the truth. If I may be pardoned for saying so, this is no Maulavi or Munshi, that when you call one, a hundred should present themselves. This, Sir, is a syce, after months of searching you may possibly find one or two, or perhaps you can't even

---

* Note this idiom.

find one." Hearing this the gentleman laughed, and the candidates, Maulavis and Munshis, who were then present, were abashed, and Munshi Badrud Din held his tongue for shame.

NAQL.

Kisī ṣāḥib ko ghoṛoṇ kā bahut shauḳ thā. Ek roz ek A'rabī ghoṛā mol liyā. Is meṇ Munshī Badr-Uddīn ne az rāh-i-khair-khwāhī kahā ki, "Is ghoṛe par Panjābī Sāīs rahe to is kī khidmāt ba-khūbī ho." Yeh bāt sunke ṣāḥib ne iṣṭabal se sāīsoṇ ke jama'-dār ko bulā kar farmāyā ki, "Hameṇ ek Panjābī sāīs lā de." Lekin jama'dār bhūl gayā. Bīs pachīs din ke bā'd ek roz ṣāḥib ko woh bāt yād āī. Use bulwā ke pūchhā ki, "Sāīs milā yā nahīṇ?" Woh bolā, "Khudāwand, ghulām ḍhūṇḍhtā hai, abhī tak nahīṇ pāyā." Yeh bāt sun ke Munshī ne kahā "Kyā bad-zāt hai! Ek mahīne se ṭāl maṭāl kartā hai, aur sāīs nahīṇ lā detā hai." Bolā, "Pīr o murshid, bad-zāt ke kahne kā maiṇ burā nahīṇ māntā. Āp khudāwand haiṇ, jo mizāj meṇ āwe so kahiye. Par khudāwand ke rū-ba-rū sach bāt kahne meṇ kuchh 'aib nahīṇ. Taqṣīr mu'āf ho, yeh Maulavī, Munshī nahīṇ, jo ek ke bulāne se sau ān ḥāzir hoeṇ. Yeh to sāīs hai; mahīnoṇ kī talāsh meṇ ek ādh mil jāe to mil jāe, nahīṇ to milnā muḥāl." Yeh sun kar Ṣāḥib hanse, aur umīdwār jo Maulavī, Munshī us waqt ḥāzir the, sharminda hue, aur Munshī Badr-ud-Dīn pashīmān ho dam khā rahā.

نقل

کسي صاحب کو گھوڑون کا بہت شوق تہا - ایک روز ایک عربي گھوڑا مول لیا - اسمین منشي بدرالدین نے از راہ خیر خواهي کہا که اس گھوڑے پر پنجابي سائیس رهي تو

اسکي خدمت به خوبي هو يهه بات سنکے صاحب نے اصطبل سے سائيسون کے جمعدار کو بلاکر فرمايا که همين ايک پنجابي سائيس لادے ليکن جمعدار بهول گيا بيس پچيس دن کے بعد ايک روز صاحب کو وه بات ياد آئي - اُسے بلوا کے پوچها که سائيس ملا يا نهين وه بولا خداوند غلام ڈهونڈتا هی ابهي تک نهين پايا - يهه بات سن کے منشي نے کہا - کيا بدذات هی ايک مهينے سے ٹال مٹال * کرتا هی - اور سائيس نهين لا ديتا هی بولا پير و مرشد بدذات کے کهنے کا مين برا نهين مانتا * آپ خاوند هين جو مزاج مين آوے سو کهيئے پر خاوندو نکے روبرو سچ بات کهنے مين کچهه عيب نهين - تقصير معاف هو يهه مولوي منشي نهين جو ايک کے بلانيسے سو آن حاضر هوئين - يهه تو سائيس هی مهينون کي تلاش مين ايک آدهه * ملجائے تو ملجائے نهين تو ملنا محال يهه سن کر صاحب هنسے اور اميدوار جو مولوي منشي اُس وقت حاضر تهے شرمنده هوئے اور منشي بدرالدين پشيمان هو دم کهيا رها *

---

* Note this idiom.

Historical. 1.

Alexander learned from his spies that there was an island in the river at a distance of twenty miles; accordingly when the darkness of night came on—and when, by reason of the roaring of the wind and the violence of the rain and the thunder, it was not possible for any noise of his army to be heard—seizing his opportunity, he took with him 11,000 veterans, and in the dead of night crossed the river.

The Hindus fancied that, perhaps a small force might have crossed over; accordingly King Porus gave his son command of a few men and sent him to repel the enemy.

At the very outset King Porus's son was killed, and the army defeated; then indeed King Porus became alarmed, and became aware that Alexander himself had crossed. Without delay he took 4,000 cavalry and 30,000 infantry, with a large number of chariots and elephants, and drew up in battle array to oppose Alexander. King Porus's army evinced great bravery, but could not stand against Alexander's cavalry.

Sikandar ne apne jāsūsoṉ se daryaft kar liyā ki das kos ke fāṣile par is daryā meṉ ek jazīra hai: is līye jab ki rāt aṉdherī huī, aur hawā kā sannāṭā aur meṉh ke zor aur bādal kī garaj meṉ sipāh kā kuchh shor o ghul sunāī na de saktā thā, mauqa' pā kar gyārah hazār purāne sipāhī hamrāh lekar rāṭoṉ rāt daryā pār ho gayā. Hindūoṉ ne yeh khayāl kiyā ki thoṛe se sipahī shāyad ā nikle hoṉge, is līye Rājā Pūr ne apne beṭe ko thoṛe se ādmī de kar un ke haṭāne ke līye rawānā kiyā. Rājā Pūr kā laṛkā to jāte hī kām āyā, aur fauj ne shikast pāī. Tab to Pūr ke kān khaṛe hūe, aur samjhā ki khud Sikandar 'ubūr kar āyā hai Fauran chār hazār sawār aur tīs hazār piyāde aur bahut se rath aur hathī hamrāh lekar Sikandar ke muqābale par ṣaff-ārā huā. Rājā Pūr ke sipāh ne baṛī bahadurī dekhlāī, par Sikandar ke Sowāroṇ ke āge pesh-raft na ga'ī.

سکندر نے اپنے جاسوسون سے دریافت کر لیا که دس
کوس کے فاصله پر اس دریا مین ایک جزیره هی اسلیئے
جبکه رات اندهیري هوئي اور هوا کاسناٹا اور مینه کے زور اور
بادل کي گرج مین سپاه کا کچهه شور و غل سنائي نه دے
سکتا تها * - موقع پاکر گیاره هزار پرانے سپاهي همراه لیکر راتون
رات * دریا پار هو گیا هندوون نے یهه خیال کیا که تهوڙے سے
سپاهي شاید آ نکلے هونگے اس لیئے راجه پور نے اپنے
بیٹے کو تهوڙے سے آدمي دیکر اُنکے هٹانے کے لیئے روانه کیا
راجه پور کا لڙکا تو جاتے هي کام آیا * اور فوج نے شکست
پائي - تب تو پور کے کان کهڙے * هوئے اور سمجها
که خود سکندر عبور کر آیا هی - فوراً چار هزار سوار اور
تیس هزار پیادے اور بهت سے رتهه اور هاتهي همراه لیکر
سکندر کے مقابله پر صف آرا هوا - راجه پور کے سپاه نے
بڑي بهادري دکهلائي پر سکندر کے سوارون کے آگے پیشرفت
نه گئي *

* Note this idiom.

Historical. 2.

After the death of Isḥāq, with the exception of Subuktigin, there was no one capable of ascending the throne.

Subuktigīn by birth was a prince of the Persian dynasty, who by the vicissitudes of fortune had been sent in poverty into the service of Alaptigīn the former king of Ghaznī. Alaptigīn, seeing that he was a likely youth, had bought him, and, advancing him by degrees, had raised him to the dignity of commander-in-chief of his army. Now, having wedded the daughter of Alaptigīn, and having become the king's son-in-law, he ascended the throne, and in the very first year of his reign, that is to say, in A.D. 977, he invaded Hindustān, at that time Raja Jaipāl was Raja of Lahore.

He took Lahore and Multan, and after reducing numerous fortresses, and obtaining much plunder, he returned to his own capital, Ghazni.

Ba'd marne Isḥāq ke siwāe Subuktigīn ke koī shakhs lāiq-i-takht-nishīnī na rahā thā, Subuktigīn aṣl meṇ ek Shah-zāda Mulk-i-Īrān kā thā, jo ittifāq-i-zamāne se ḥālat-i-iflās meṇ Alaptigīn, bādshāh-i-sābiq-i-Ghaznī kī khidmat meṇ ḥāzir kiyā gayā thā. Aur Alaptigīn ne us ko honhār dekh kar kharīd liyā thā, aur darja ba-darja taraqqī de kar sipah-sālārī ke rutbe tak us ko pahuṇchā diyā thā. Ab us ne bādshāh Alaptigīn ki laṛkī se apnā nikāḥ kar ke dāmād bādshāh kā ban kar takht par julūs farmāyā. Aur apne julūs ke awwal hī sāl meṇ, ya'ne san nau sau satatthar 'Īsawī meṇ, us ne Hindustān par chaṛhāī kī. Is waqt meṇ Rājā Jāipāl Lāhor kā Rājā thā. Lāhor aur Multān us ne fatḥ kīye; aur ka'ī qil'a fatḥ kar ke, bahut sā māl lūṭ kar phir apne dār-ul-khilāfa Ghaznī ko murāja'at farmāī.

بعد مرنے اسحاق کے سواے سبکتگین کے کوئي شخص لائق تخت نشيني نرها تها - سبکتگین اصل مین ایک شہزادہ ملک ایران کا تها - جو اتفاق زمانه سے حالت افلاس مین الپتگین بادشاہ سابق غزني کے خدمت مین حاضر کیا گیا تها - الپتگین نے اُسکو هونهار * دیکهکر خرید لیا تها - اور درجه بدرجه ترقي دیکر سپه سالاري کے رتبه تک اُسکو پهونچا دیا تها - اب اوسنے بادشاہ الپتگین کي لڑکي سے اپنا نکاح * کرکے داماد بادشاہ کا بنکر تخت پر جلوس فرمایا * اور اپنے جلوس کے اول هي سال مین یعنے سنه ۹۷۷ ع مین آسنے هندوستان پر چڑهائي کي اسوقت مین راجه جیپال لاهور کا راجه تها - لاهور اور ملتان اُسنے فتح کیئے - اور کئي قلعه فتح کرکے بهت سا مال لوٹکر پهر اپنے دارالخلافه غزني کو مراجعت فرمائي -

---

Note.—ع is the initial letter of the word عیسوي *'Īsawi* or the year of our Lord, *i.e.*, the Christian Era; the Mohammedan era is denoted by the initial letter of the word هجري *Hijrī* or year of the هجرة *hijra*, or flight from Mecca (see page 81).

* Note this idiom.

Historical. 3.

With Sevajee there was a large tribal gathering of the hillmen who inhabit the southern hill-country. These people used to plunder the cities and amass wealth, so that the ruler of Beejapoor, by way of subduing them, despatched a large army, under command of Afzal Khan, to attack Sevajee. Sevajee sent word that he was willing to surrender, but that he wished for a private interview. He (Afzal Khan) agreed to this. Sevajee concealed his army in ambush, and gave orders that, on hearing the sound of the bugle, they should instantly fall upon the enemy's army. Afzal Khan, having put aside the 15,000 men whom he had brought with him, went alone to the rendezvous. Sevajee, with fear in his heart, looking cautiously on all sides, turning round at every step and looking behind him, reached the appointed place. At the instant of meeting, he embraced Afzal Khan, and instantly stabbed him in the belly with a dagger. Afzal Khan, drawing his sword, struck Sevajee a blow on the head with it, but as he had a helmet beneath his turban, he escaped unhurt, and the blow went for nothing. Sevajee struck him a second blow with a dagger and the Khan fell dead.

Sīvājī ke hamrāh pahāṛī qaum bahut thī jo junūbī kohistān meṇ rahtī haiṇ. Yeh log shahroṇ ko lūṭte aur rupya jam'a karte the, ki Bījāpūr ke ḥākim ne un ke muṭī' karne ke wāsṭe ek lashkar-i-jarrār Afẓal Khāṇ ko de kar, Sīwājī par chaṛhāī karne ko rawāna kiyā. Sīwājī ne kahlā bhejā, ki, "Mujhe iṭā'at manẓūr hai, lekin ek mulāqāt āp se tanhā karnī chāhtā hūṇ." Us ne manẓūr kiyā. Sīwājī ne apnī sipāh ghāt meṇ chhīpā dī, aur kah diyā, ki, "Jis waqt bugal kī āwāz suno, fauran dushman kī fauj par ā paṛyo. Afẓal Khāṉ, pandrah hazār ādmiyoṉ ko jin ko wuh apne sāth lāyā thā, alag kar ke tanhā maqām-i-muta'aiyan par gayā. Sīwājī bhī, dil meṉ ḍartā huā, chār ṭaraf se hoshyār ho kar, ek ek qadam par pīchhe muṛ muṛ kar dekhtā hūā, us maqām-i-mu'aiyan par pahuṉchā. Jāte hī baghal-gīr ho kar milā, aur wahīṉ Afẓal Khāṉ ke peṭ meṉ khanjar mārā. Afẓal Khāṉ ne talwār khīṉchī, aur Sīwājī ke sar par mārī; magar chūṉki us kī pagṛī ke nīche khod thā, is wāsṭe woh bach gayā, aur wār khālī gayā. Us ne dūsrā khanjar mārā, Khān-i-mazkūr kā kām tamām ho gayā.

سیواجي کے همراہ پہاڑي قوم بہت تہے جو جنوبي
کوهستان مین رهتے هین یهه لوگ شهرونکو لوٹتے اور روپیه جمع
کرتے تہے - که بیجا پور کے حاکم نے انکے مطیع کرنے کے
واسطے ایک لشکر جرار افضل خان کو دیکر - سیواجي پر چڑهائي
کرنیکو روانه کیا * سیواجي نے یهه کہلا بہیجا - که مجهے
اطاعت منظور هی * - لیکن ایک ملاقات آپسے تنها کرني
چاهتا هون * - اوسنے منظور کیا - سیواجي نے اپني سپاه گہات
مین چهپادي اور کهدیا که جسوقت بُگَل کي آواز سنو فوراً
دشمن کي فوج پر آپڑیو * افضل خان پندره هزار آدمیون کو

Note.—بُگَل This word is very frequently used. It is our English word bugle. The Hindustānī equivalent would be بوق (*m*) or تُرهي (*f*).

* Note this construction.

جنکو وہ اپنے ساتھہ لایا تھا - الگ کر کے تنہا مقام متعین پر
گیا - سیواجي بھي دلمین ڈرتا ھوا چار طرفسے ھوشیار * ھوکر
ایک ایک قدم پر پیچھے مڑ مڑ کر * دیکھتا ھوا اس مقام معین
پر پہنچا - جاتے ھي بغلگیر ھوکر ملا اور وھین افضل خان کے
پیٹ مین خنجر مارا * افضل خان نے تلوار کھینچي اور
سیواجي کے سر پر ماري مگر چونکه اسکي پگڑي کے نیچي
خود تھا اسواسطے وہ بچ گیا - اور وار خالي * گیا - اسنے دوسرا
خنجر مارا خان مذکور کا کام تمام ھوگیا *

Historical. 4.

When the news of this revolt reached General Nott, who was then in Kandahar, he despatched Colonel Maclaren to punish the mutineers. Had this force reached Kabul, it is certain that the English army would not have suffered such hardships, nor would they have lost so many soldiers.

When this force arrived near Ghazni, it was obliged to return to Kandahar, by reason of the very heavy snow which was falling. The Afghans, after taking Kabul and Ghazni, proceeded to assault Kandahar, but General Nott defeated them; the Afghans were defeated in the majority of the engagements, but many distinguished English officers fell in battle.

Jab ki is balwe kī khabar Janrail Nāṭ Ṣāḥib ko, jo Qandhār meṇ the, pahunchī, to unhoṇ ne Karnail Maklāren ko mufsidoṇ kī

---

* Note this construction.

tanbīh aur tādīb ke wāste rawāna kiyā. Agar yeh fauj Kābul meṇ pahuṇch jātī, to yaqīn thā ki fauj-i-Aṇgrezī ko is qadr taklīf na hotī, aur na is qadr sipahī tabāh hote. Yeh fauj jab Ghaznī ke qarib pahuṇchī, to ba-sabab kaṣrat bārish-i-barf ke pher Qandhār ko murāja'at kar āī. Afghānoṇ ne ba'd fatḥ karne Kābul aur Ghaznī ke pher Qandhār par ḥamla kīyā, lekin Janrail Nāt Ṣāḥib ne un ko shikast dī; akṣar laṛāiyoṇ meṇ Afghānoṇ ne shikast khāī; par kaī nāmwar Aṇgrezī 'uhda-dar laṛāiyoṇ meṇ kām ā'e.

جبکه اس بلوے کي خبر جرنيل ناٹ صاحب کو جو
قندهار مين تهے پهنچي تو انهون نے کرنيل مکلاوون کو
مفسدونکي تنبيه اور تاديب کيواسطے روانه کيا * - اگر يهه فوج
کابل مين پهنچ جاتي * تو يقين تها که فوج انگريزيکو اسقدر
تکليف نه هوتي * اور نه اسقدر سپاهي تباه هوتے * يهه فوج
جب غزني کے قريب پهنچي تو بسبب کثرت بارش برف
کے پهر قندهارکو مراجعت کرائي - افغانون نے بعد فتح
کرنے کابل اور غزني کے پهر قندهار پر حمله کيا - ليکن جنرل
ناٹ صاحب نے انکو شکست دي * - اکثر لڑائيون مين
افغانون نے شکست کهائي * پر کئي نامور انگريزي عهده دار
لڑائيونمين کام آئے *

* Note this idiom.

Historical. 5.

Sher Singh himself was a great libertine, but his Wazir used to perform all the duties of the State. One day the Maharaja Sher Singh was engaged in mustering his cavalry when Jeet Singh, under pretence of showing him a rifle, came close to Sher Singh, and killed him with the rifle. On that very day too Sher Singh's eldest son was killed. In this way great disorder again arose in the State. The Wazir, Dhiyan Singh, also fell by the hands of murderers on the same day. Accordingly his son Heera Singh went to the camp and reported the murder of Sher Singh and his own father and said to the soldiers that, if they would join him, he would increase their pay. The army, who numbered about fifty thousand men, at the very instant of hearing this suggestion, gladly and readily placed their lives at his disposal.

Accordingly Heera Singh took the army and attacked the fort of Lahore, and, after a mild engagement, took possession of the city, and having put to the sword the enemies who had murdered his father, Dhiyan Singh (the Wazir), and the Maharaja Sher Singh, had their corpses dragged through the streets.

Sher Singh khud to baṛā 'aiyāsh thā, par tamām kārobār salṭanat ke us kā wazīr kartā rahtā thā. Ek roz Mahārājā Sher Singh sawāroṇ kī maujūdāt lerahā thā ki Jait Singh, ba bahāna dekhlāne ek bandūq ke, Kūṇwar Sher Singh ke pās āyā, aur us ko us bandūq se halāk kiyā. Aur usī roz baṛā beṭā Sher Singh kā bhī mārā gayā. Is ṭaur par us Salṭanat meṇ pher be-intiẓāmī barpā huī. Wazīr Dhyān Singh bhī usī roz qātiloṇ ke hāth se maqtūl huā chunānchi isī wāsṭe us ke laṛke Hīrā Singh ne kampū meṇ jā kar Mahārājā Sher Singh aur apne bāp ke qatl kā ḥā ẓāhir kiyā; aur sipāhiyoṇ se kahā, kī "Agar tum mere sharīk hoge, to maiṇ tumhārī tankhwāh meṇ iẓāfa karūṇga." Fauj, jo kī takhmīnan pachās hazār kī thī, ba-mujarrad sunne is bāt ke khush huī, aur us ke sāth sar dene par musta'idd ho ga'ī. Chunānchi Hīrā Singh ne fauj hamrāh lekar Qil'a-i-Lāhor par ḥamlā kiyā, aur ba'd ek khafīf laṛāī ke, shahr par qābiẓ ho gayā, aur un mukhālifoṇ ko, jinhoṇ ne us ke bāp, Dhyān Singh Wazīr ko, aur Mahārājā Sher Singh ko qatl kiyā thā, tah-i-tegh kar ke un kī lāshoṇ ko kūcha ba-kūcha ghasīṭwāyā.

شیرسنگه خود بڑا عیاش * تها - پر تمام کار و بار سلطنت
کے اسکا وزیر کرتا رهتا تها * ایک روز مهاراجا شیرسنگه سوارون
کي موجودات * لے رها تها که جیت سنگه به بهانه دیکهلانے
ایک بندوق کے کنور شیر سنگهه کے پاس آیا اور اسکو اس
بندوق سے هلاک کیا اور اسي روز بڑا بیٹا شیر سنگه کا بهي
مارا گیا - اسطور پر اس سلطنت مین پهر بے انتظامي برپا هوئي
وزیر دهیان سنگه بهي اسي روز قاتلون کے هاتهه سے مقتول
هوا - چنانچه اسي واسطے اسکے لڑکے هیرا سنگه نے کمپو مین
جا کر مهاراجا شیر سنگه اور اپنے باپ کے قتل کا حال ظاهر
کیا اور سپاهیون سے کها که اگر تم میرے شریک هو گے تو
مین تمهاري تنخواه مین اضافه * کرونگا فوج جو که تخمیناً *

---

* Note this idiom.

پچاس هزار کي تهي بمُجرّد سننے * اِس بات کے خوش هوئے اور اُسکے ساتهه سر دینی * پر مستعد هوگئے چنانچه هیرا سنگه نے فوج همراه لیکر قلعه لاهور پر حمله کیا - اور بعد ایک خفیف لڑائي کے شهر پر قابض هوگیا اور ان مخالفونکو جنهون نے اسکے باپ دهیان سنگه وزیر کو اور مهاراجه شیر سنگه کو قتل کیا تها ته تیغ * کرکے انکي لاشونکو کوچه بکوچه گهستوایا -

---

Historical. 6.

On the 1st of July of the year A.D. 1848, another battle took place under the walls of Multan.

In this battle Mull Raj himself took part, but a chance ball having struck his elephant's howdah, from the force of the blow he fell from the elephant to the ground, and, mounting a horse, fled to Multan. This battle lasted six hours, and, although the Multanis fought with the utmost bravery, they could no longer withstand the English army. On the 8th of August of the above year, the English force attacked the Diwan Mulraj, and drove him from a village in which his army was encamped. The English army took possession of that village, and the enemy's force, having fled to a garden which was near the village, encamped and spent the whole

---

* Note this idiom.

day in bombarding the enemy's position; the English army being harassed, attacked the garden, the battle raged there for an hour and-a-half. English Officers, who had taken part in the former battles of the Punjab, declare that they had never seen the Sikhs fight with so great bravery, nor had their guns ever been so well served. In this battle several English Officers were killed and wounded.

Yakum Jūlāī San 1848 'Īsawī ko, Qil'a-i-Multān kī faṣīl ke nīche ek aur laṛāī huī. Us laṛāī meṇ Mul Raj ba-ẕāt-i-khud laṛtā rahā; lekin ittifāq se ek gola us ke hāthī ke haude par jo lagā, to ṣadme se wuh hāthī par se nīche gir paṛā aur ghoṛe par sawāṛ ho kar Multān ko bhāg gayā. Yeh laṛāī chhe ghante tak rahī. Agarchi Multānī kamāl shujā'at se laṛe, par Aṇgrezī-fauj ke sāmne ziyāda na ṭhahar sake. Āṭhwīṇ Agast san ṣadr ko, fauj-i-Aṇgrezī ne Dīwān Mul Rāj par ḥamla kiyā, aur ek gānw se jahāṇ us kā lashkar khīma-zan thā, us ko mār kar haṭā diyā; aur us gānw par fauj-i-Aṇgrezī qābiẓ ho ga'ī. Dushman kī fauj ek bāgh meṇ, jo ki us gānw ke qarīb thā, bhāg kar muqīm hū'ī aur wahān se din bhar gola-andazī kartī rahī. Is līye fauj-i-Aṇgrezī ne mutaḥaiyir ho kar us bāgh par ḥamla kīyā. Ḍerḥ ghanṭe tak wahāṇ laṛāī jārī rahī. 'Uhdadārān-i-Aṇgrez. jo janghā-i-sābiḳ-i-Panjāb meṇ sharīk the, yeh bayān karte haiṇ ki "Ham ne sabhoṇ ko aisī jawān-mardī se laṛte hue kabhī nahīṇ dekhā, aur na kabhī un ki topen aisī jaldī jaldī chaltī thiṇ." Us laṛai meṇ ka'ī afsarān-i-Aṇgrezī majrūḥ o maqtūl hue.

یکم جولائي سنه ۱۸۴۸ ع † کو قلعه ملتانکي فصیل
کے نیچی ایک اور لڑائي هوئي اس لڑائي مین مولراج بذات

---

† Ek hazar āṭh sau aṭhtāhs Isawī.

خون لڑتا رها لیکن اتفاق سے ایک گوله اسکے هاتهي کے هودے پر جو* لگا تو صدمے سے وه هاتهي پر سے نیچے گر پڑا اور گهوڑے پر سوار هوکر ملتان کو بهاگ گیا - یهه لڑائي چهه گهنٹے تک رهي اگرچه ملتاني لوگ کمال شجاعت سے لڑے پر انگریزي فوج کے سامنے زیاده نه ٹهر سکے آٹهوین اگست سنه صدر* کو فوج انگریزي نے دیوان مولراج پر حمله کیا اور ایک گانو سے جهان اسکا لشکر خیمه زن تها اسکو مارکر هٹا دیا اور اس گانو پر فوج انگریزي قابض هوگئي* - دشمن کي فوج ایک باغ مین جوکه اس گانو کے قریب تها بهاگ کر مقیم هوئي اور وهانسے دن بهر گوله اندازي کرتے رهے اس لئے فوج انگریزي نے متدیر* هوکر اس باغ پر حمله کیا - ڈیڑه گهنٹے تک وهان لڑائي جاري رهي* - عهده داران انگریزي جو جنگهاے سابق پنجاب مین شریک تهے یهه بیان کرتے هین که همنے سبهونکو ایسي جوانمردي سے لڑتے هوئے کبهي نهین دیکها - اور نه کبهي انکي توپین ایسي جلدي جلدي چلتي تهین اس لڑائي مین کئي افسران انگریزي مجروح و مقتول هوئے*

---

* Note this idiom.

Narrative Style. 1.

We are very pleased to hear that the rates for registration are either to be reduced from four annas to two annas or have already been reduced, but it is a matter for regret that the fares of the Punjab Northern State Railway are daily rising, and no attention is paid to the arrangements. A friend of ours says that since the officers of the railway, who, in addition to being experienced, were also energetic, have been changed, great falling off has occurred in the management of this line. He said that he was also of opinion, that in the time of Mr. Keene the line was in an excellent state, and that gentleman used to perform his duties with great energy and zeal. The Government arrangements for transport during the Afghan war were much facilitated by that gentleman's excellent arrangements. Under his regime, too, travellers experienced less trouble. The complaints against this line do not need explaining. Our correspondents from time to time have not been backward in bringing them to notice. So that to repeat them will be like always harping upon the same string.* But this demands consideration. Why does not Government direct the attention of its new officers to the arrangements?

Is bāt ke sunne se ki rusūm-i-Rejisṭirī bajāe chār āne ke do āna muqarrar hone wālī hai, yā ho gaī ham bahut khush hū'e; lekin is meṇ Panjāb Nārdarn Isṭeṭ Relwe kā kirāyā to din par din baṛhāyā jātā hai, aur intiz̤ām kī ṭaraf muṭlaq tawajjuh nahiṇ kī jātī. Ek hamāre karam-farmā farmāte haiṇ, ki afsarān-i-Relwe, jo tajriba ke 'alāwa jafā-kash bhī the, chūṇki tabdīl kiye ga'e haiṇ, is wāsṭe us lāin ke intiz̤ām meṇ farq ā gayā hai. Unhoṇ ne farmāyā, "Is se hamārā bhī ittifāq hai ki, Kīn Ṣāḥib Bahādur

---

* Note this phrase.

ke waqt meṉ lāin 'umda ḥālat meṉ thī, aur yeh Ṣāḥib nihāyat miḥnat aur sar-garmī ke sāth kām karte the. Government ko jang-i-Afghānistān meṉ sāmān-i-bār-bardārī meṉ Ṣāḥib-i-mamdūḥ kī 'khush-intiẓāmī se suhūlat hūī. Musāfiroṉ ko bhī un ke 'ahd meṉ chandāṉ taklīf na thī. Is lāin kī shikāyateṉ muḥtāj-i-bayān nahīṉ. Nāma-nigāroṉ ne waqtan fa-waqtan un ke iẓhār se kotāhi nahīṉ kī. Is liye un kā i'āda karnā misl us naghme ke hogā jis ke bār bār alāpne se lutf ḥaṣil nahīṉ hotā. Ab ghaur-ṭalab yeh amr hai, ki Government nae afsaroṉ ko intiẓām kī taraf kyūṉ tawajjuh nahīṉ dilātī.

اس بات کے سننے سے کہ رسوم رجسٹري بجاے ۴ -
آنے کے ۲ - مقرر هونیوالي هی یا هوگئي هم بہت خوش
هوئے لیکن اس مین پنجاب ناردون استیٹ ریلوے کا کرایہ
تو دن پر دن بڑهایا جاتا هے - اور انتظام کیطرف مطلق توجہ
نهین کیجاتي ایک همارے کرمفرما فرماتے هین کہ افسران
ریلوے جو تجربہ کے علاوہ جفا کش بهي تهے چونکہ تبدیل
کئے گئے هین اسواسطے اُس لاین کے انتظام مین فرق آگیا هی
اُنهون نے فرمایا اس سے همارا بهي اتفاق هی کہ کین
صاحب بهادر کے وقت مین لائین عمدہ حالت مین تهي
اور یہہ صاحب نهایت محنت اور سرگرمي کے ساتهہ کام
کرتے تهے گورنمنٹ کو جنگ افغانستان مین سامان بار برداري
مین صاحب ممدوح کي خوش انتظامي سے سهولت هوئي

مسافرون کو بھي اُنکے عہد مين چندان تکليف نہ تھي اس لائين کي شکايتين محتاج بيان نہين نامہ نگارون نے وقتاً فوقتاً انکے اظہار سے کوتاھي نہين کي اسليئي انکا اعادہ کرنا مثل اس نغمہ کے ہوگا جسکي باربار الاپني سے لطف حاصل نہين ہوتا † * اب غور طلب يہہ امر ہے کہ گورنمنٹ نئے افسرون کو انتظام کيطرف کيون توجہ نہين دلاتے *

Narrative Style. 2.

The *Indian Daily News* writes that in a few days' time a case will come on in the Police Courts in which a husband has been ill-treating his wife. The age of the wife was eleven years. The husband took her to his house; as the girl would not obey the orders of her father-in-law and mother-in-law, and would not do the work of the house he shut her up in a room, put chains on her feet and handcuffs on her hands, and for two days gave her no food; and in addition to this, she was regularly beaten.

The girl's parents informed the police; the Inspector came and saw the girl in that condition, and had the irons struck off her by a blacksmith.

Now a case is pending against the husband for unlawful imprisonment.

---

* Note this phrase.

† *Lit.* Like that strain the repeated singing of which is not a source of pleasure.

الاپنا *Alāpnā* is to tune an instrument; to "catch" a tune.

Inḍiyan Ḍelī Nīūz kahtā hai, ki chand roz ke ba'd Pūlīs Korṭ meṉ muqaddama pesh hogā, ki ek shauhar ne apnī zauja par kaisā ẓulm kiyā. Zauja kī 'umr gyārah baras kī thī. Shauhar apne ghar le gayā. Chuṉkī laṛkī ne sās susre kā kahnā na mānā, aur ghar kā kām na kartī thī, is līye us ko ek kamare meṉ band kiyā, hāth meṉ hath-kaṛī, pāṉw meṉ zanjīr ḍāl dī, do roz dāna pānī na diyā, aur 'alāwa is ke, barābar us par mār pāṛī. Laṛkī ke wālidain ne Pūlīs ko iṭṭilā' dī. Inspekṭar āyā, to laṛkī ko usī ḥālat meṉ dekhā, aur lohār se beṛiyāṉ kaṭwāīṉ. Ab shauhar par mukaddama-i-ḥabs-i-bejā qāim huā hai.

انڈین ڈیلي نیوز کہتا ہے کہ چند روز کے بعد پولیس کورٹ مین مقدمه پیش * هوگا که ایک شوهر نے اپني زوجه پر کیسا ظلم کیا زوجه کي عمر گیاره برس کي تهي شوهر اپنے گهر لیگیا چونکه لڑکي نے ساس * سسرے * کا کہنا نمانا اور گهر کا کام نکرتي تهي اسلیئے اُسکو ایک کمرے مین بند کیا هاتهه مین هتکڑي پاؤنمین زنجیر ڈالدي دو روز دانه پاني * نه دیا اور علاوه اسکے برابر اوسپر مار پڑي لڑکي کے والدین نے پولیس کو اطلاع دي انسپکٹر آیا تو لڑکي کو اوسي حالت مین دیکها اور لوهار سے بیڑیان کٹوائین * اب شوهر پر مقدمه حبس بیجا † قائم هوا هی *

---

* Note this idiom.

† See page 115

Narrative Style. 3.

The Story of the Envious and the Envied. †

Two men lived in a great city, and the door of the house of one of them was close to the door of the other. One of those two used to envy the other.

The one who was envied, by reason of the envy and annoyance of the other, wished to leave that city and remove far off, so that that envy, which he bore against him by reason of his nearness, might be removed. Although the envied one always treated the envier well, still he did not refrain himself from his envy. To such a point did this go that the envied one sold that house of his and its furniture, went to another city, and bought a suitable house at the distance of five miles from the city, in which there was a nice garden and a blind well.

That good man, after buying the house, assumed the garb of a faqir and became a dervish.

QIṢṢA ḤĀSID AUR MAḤSŪD KĀ.

Ek baṛe shahr meṇ do shakhṣ rahte the, aur darwāza ek ke ghar kā dūsre ke darwāze se muttaṣil thā. Ek shakhṣ un meṇ se dūsre shakhṣ par ḥasad kiyā kartā. Maḥsūd ne us ke ḥasad aur āzār dene se, chāhā ki us ghar ko chhoṛ ke bahut dūr jā rahe, tā ki yeh ḥasad, jo basabab nazdīk rahne ke wuh mujh se rakhtā hai, dūr ho jā'e. Bā-wajūd ki maḥsūd hamesha hāsid ke sāth sulūk kiyā kartā, lekin woh ḥasad se bāz na ātā. Yahāṇ tak ki maḥsūd ne woh ghar aur asbāb bech kar, dūsre shahr meṇ jā, ḍeṛh kos ke fāṣile par us shahr se, ek makān-i-ma'qūl mol liyā, ki jis meṇ ek bāgh-i-nafīs aur andhā kū'ā thā. Wuh nek mard, ba'd mol lene ghar ke, libās faqīrī kā pahn kar darwesh hogayā.

---

† This and the three succeeding passages are from the Arabian Nights which will be fonnd very useful to the student of Urdu.

قصه حاسد اور محسود کا

ایک بڑے شہر مین دو شخص رہتے تھے اور دروازه ایک کے گھر کا دوسرے کے دروازه سے متصل تھا ایک شخص اونمین سے دوسرے شخص پر حسد کیا کرتا محسود نے اوسکے حسد اور آزار دینے سے چاہا که اوس گھر کو چھوڑ کے بہت دور جا رہے تا که یہه حسد جو بسبب نزدیک رہنے کے ره مجھسے رکھتا هی * دور هو جاے با وجود که محسود همیشه حاسد کے ساتھه سلوک * کیا کرتا لیکن وه حسد سے باز نه آتا یہانتک که محسود نے وه گھر اور اسباب بیچکر دوسرے شہر مین جا ڈیڑه کوس کے فاصلے پر اوس شہر سے ایک مکان معقول مول لیا که جس مین ایک باغ نفیس اور اندها کنوان * تها وه نیک مرد بعد مول لینے گھر کے لباس فقیری کا پہنکر درویش هو گیا *

Narrative Style. 4.

In olden times a tailor of Kashgar, which is near the country of Tatar, used to sit in his shop and sew. He was thus sitting one day towards evening, sewing away, when suddenly a hunchbacked man with a drum came along, and sitting down

---

Note this idiom.

under his shop window began to sing. The tailor was much pleased to hear his singing, and, when it was near the time for him to go home, he said to the hunchback, "If you feel disposed come to my house which is near this, and sing and play." The hunchback agreeing, went to his house. When the tailor, having washed his hands and face, sat down, he began to say to his wife, who was pretty, and of whom he was very fond, "To-day I have brought this man, who sings and plays very well, so as to give you a chance of hearing some singing. If the dinner is ready, bring it." His wife laid the cloth and brought the dinner and placed it before him, and the lady of the house herself sat down with him, and they set to eating, and they made the hunchback too share the repast. By chance, that day, some fish had been cooked in the tailor's house, and, as he was sharing their dinner, they gave the hunchback some fish. As it was very nice the hunchback eat it so carelessly, without taking out the bones, that a bone stuck in his throat.

Agle zamāne meṇ ek darzī Kāshghar kā, jo muttaṣil Mulk-i-Tātār ke hai, apnī dūkān par baiṭh kar kapṛe siyā kartā. Chunanchi ek roz wuh baiṭhā hūā qarib shām ke sī rahā thā, ki na-gahānī ek shakhṣ kūza-pusht ṭabla le kar āyā, aur us kī dukān ke tale baiṭh kar gāne lagā. Darzī us kā gānā sun kar bahut khush hūā. Jab waqt uske ghar jāne kā qarīb pahuṇchā, us ne kubṛe se kahā, "Agar tumhārā jī chāhe, mere ghar, jo yahāṇ se qarīb hai chal kar gāo bajāo." Kubṛā rāẓī ho kar us ke ghar gayā. Jab darzī mūṇh hāth dho kar baiṭhā, apnī bībī se, ki khūb-ṣūrat thī, aur us ko nihāyat piyār kartā thā, kahne lagā, "Aj maiṇ tumhāre gānā sunāne ke wāsṭe, is shakhṣ ko, ki khūb gātā bajātā hai, lāyā hūṇ. Khānā, agar ṭaiyār ho, to lāo." Us kī bībī ne dastar khwān bichhā, khānā āge lā kar rakhā, aur miyāṇ bībī bāham baiṭh kar khāne lage, aur us kubṛe ko bhī sharīk khāne ka kīyā. Ittifāqan us roz darzī ke ghar machhlī pakī thī, aur khāne ke shumūl meṇ machhlī bhī kubṛe ko dī. Jo woh bahut laẕīẕ thī, kubṛe ne, bidūn nikālne kāṇtoṇ ke, is be iḥtiyāṭī se khāyā ki ek kāṇṭā, us ke ḥalq meṇ chubh gayā.

اگلے زمانے مین ایک درزي کاشغر کا جو متصل ملک
تاتار کے هی اپني دوکان پر بیتهکر کپڑے سیا کرتا * چنانچه
ایک روز وه بیتها هوا قریب شام کے سي رها تها * ناگهاني
ایک شخص کوزه پشت طبله لیکر آیا اور اوسکي دکان کے تلے
بیتهکر گانے لگا درزي اوسکا گانا سنکر بهت خوش هوا جب
وقت اوسکے گهر * جانے کا قریب پهنچا اوسنے کبڑے سے
کها اگر تمهارا جي چاهے * میرے گهر * جو یهان سے قریب
هی چل کر گاؤ بجاؤ کبڑا راضي هوکر اوسکے * گهر گیا جب
درزي مونهه هاتهه دهوکر بیتها اپني بي بي سے که
خوبصورت تهي اور اوسکو نهایت پیار کرتا تها کهنے لگا آج مین
تمهارے گانا سنانے کے واسطے اس شخص کو که خوب گاتا
بجاتا هی لایا هون کهانا اگر طیار هو تو لاؤ اوسکي بي بي نے

---

* Note this idiom.

Note the construction of the word گهر *ghar*, wherever it occurs in this story the postposition is omitted, see page 31.

Note.—درزي کے گهر inflected because governed by پر understood.

دسترخوان بچها کهانا آگے لاکر رکها اور میان بي بي باهم بیتهکر کهانے لگے اور اوس کبڑیکو بهي شریک کهانے کا کیا اتفاقا اوس روز درزي کے گهر مچهلي پکي تهي اور کهانے کے شمول مین مچهلي بهي کبڑے کو دي جو وه بهت لذیذ تهي کبڑے نے بدون نکالنے * کانٹون کے اس بے احتیاطي سے کهایا که ایک کانٹا اوسکے حلق مین چبهه گیا *

Narrative Style. 5.

THE DESCRIPTION OF THE FOURTH VOYAGE OF SINBAD THE SAILOR.

MY FRIENDS,—In the abundance of merrymaking all the fear and danger of all three journeys was effaced from my heart, so, having forgotten all my calamities and mishaps, the desire came upon me of amassing wealth and property and of seeing wonders. Then having made preparations for the fourth voyage, and having bought those articles of merchandise which were valued and in demand in those foreign countries to which I intended to travel, I set off for Persia. In the middle of my journey, passing by several cities, I arrived at a port, whence I again embarked; and from thence our ship sailed bound for the islands of Farma and other eastern ports. One day suddenly such a gale of wind beat upon the ship, that the captain of necessity lowered the sails of the ship and said to the sailors, "This is a hurricane, be on your guard and look out." In

---

* Note this idiom.

spite of all their care, it was of no avail; the sails of the ship being torn by the wind went to ribbons, and the ship became unmanageable (*literally*, got out of the power of the captain) to such an extent that running on the sand by reason of its weight, it was dashed to pieces. All the crew together with the freight were lost, but I and a few merchants, by the aid of planks floating along, alighted on an island which was near there. From the shore we went into the island, and by dint of living on wild fruits some degree of strength came to us.

Bayān Sindbād Jahāzī ke Chauthe Safar kā.

Ṣāḥibo, kasrat-i-'aish o'ishrat se woh sab khauf o khaṭar tīnoṇ safar ke mere dil se jāte rahe. Pher sab āfateṇ aur muṣībateṇ bhūl ke ishtiyāq jama' karne māl o āsbāb aur sair karne 'ajāibāt kā āyā, aur ṭaiyārī chauthe safar kī kar ke woh asbāb-i-tijārat jis kī khwāhish aur qadr dūr dūr mulkoṇ meṇ thī, aur unhoṇ kī ṭaraf jāne kā irāda kiyā thā, kharīd kar ke Pāras kī ṭaraf rawāna hūā. Asnā-i-rāh meṇ kitne ek shahr ṭai kartā hūā ek bandar meṇ pahuṇchā, jahāṇ se pher jahāz par sawār hūā, aur wahāṇ se jahāz hamārā jazāir-i-Farma waghaira banādir-i-sharqī kī ṭaraf jā niklā. Ek din daf'atan aisā jhoṇkā hawā kā jahāz ko lagā, ki Kaptān ne majbūr ho jahāz ke bādbān nīche kar dīye, aur khalāṣiyoṇ se kahā, "Yeh ṭūfān hai; khabardār aur hoshyār raho." Harchand ki unhoṇ ne kamāl hoshyārī kī, lekin kuchh mufīd na hūī. Jahāz kī pāleṇ bilkull ṭūfān se ṭukre ṭukre ho ga'īṇ, aur jahāz qābū se nā-khudā ke jātā rahā yahāṇ tak ki bālū par chaṛh kar, basabab bojh ke pāsh pāsh ho gayā sab jahāz ke log ma' māl o asbāb bilkull ḍūb ga'e; magar maiṇ aur chand saudāgar takhtoṇ ke sahāre se bahte hūe, ek jazīre meṇ, jo wahāṇ se qarīb thā, jā lage. Kināre se uṭh kar us jazīre meṇ ga'e, aur basabab khāne janglī phaloṇ ke fil-jumla ham meṇ ṭāqat āī.

بيان سندباد جهازي کے چوتهے سفر کا

صاحبو کثرت عيش و عشرت سے وه سب خوف و خطر تينون سفر کے ميرے دلسے جاتے رهے * پهر سب آفتين اور مصيبتين بهول کے اشتياق جمع کرنے مال و اسباب اور سير کرنے عجائبات کا آيا اور طياري چوتهے سفر کي کرکے وه اسباب تجارت جسکي خواهش اور قدر دور دور ملکون مين تهي اور اونهون کيطرف جانے کا اراده کيا تها خريد کرکے پارس کي طرف روانه هوا اثناے راه مين کتنے ايک شهر طي کرتا هوا ايک بندر مين پهنچا جهان سے پهر جهاز پر سوار هوا اور وهان سے جهاز همارا جزائر فرمه وغيره بنادر شرقي کيطرف جا نکلا * ايک دن دفعةً ايسا جهونکا هوا کا جهاز کو لگا که کپتان نے مجبور هو * جهاز کے بادبان نيچے کردئے اور خلاصيون سے کها يهه طوفان هي خبردار اور هوشيار رهو هرچند که اونهون نے کمال هوشياري کي ليکن کچهه مفيد نهوئي جهاز کي پالين بالکل طوفان سے پهتکے تکترے هوگئين اور جهاز قابو سے نا خدا کے جاتا رها * يهانتک که بالو پر چڙهکر بسبب بوجهه کے پاش پاش هوگيا سب جهاز کے لوگ مع مال و اسباب

* Note idiom.

بالکل ڈوب گئے مگر مین اور چند سوداگر تختون کے سہارے سے * بہتے ہوئے ایک جزیرے مین جو وہان سے قریب تہا جالگے * کنارے سے اوتہکر اوس جزیرے مین گئے اور بسبب کہانے جنگلي پہلون کے في الجمله * ہم مین طاقت آئي *

Narrative Style. 6.

In short, in the midst of these arrangements, King Badar's father fell sick, and his weakness increased day by day. At last, when he despaired of living, he summoned the councillors of his kingdom, and exacted from them a fresh promise of obedience to King Badar, and then departed from this transitory world. The King Badar and his Queen Gulnār were much distressed at this occurrence, and buried him with great ceremony. Badar, in accordance with the custom, remained in seclusion for a month, and held intercourse with no one; and, in sorrow for his father, wept continually. In the meantime, his mother, and Malik Ṣāliḥ, the brother of Gulnār, having arrived there with their relations, joined in the general mourning. When they had all finished the mourning ceremonies, Malik Ṣāliḥ, one day said to his sister Gulnār, "I wonder that you give no thought to the marriage of Badar; if you wish it I will seek for a princess in my dominions who shall be as beautiful as and worthy of Badar." The Queen Gulnār

---

* Note idiom.

answered, "Hitherto I had not given a thought to this matter, for this reason that I had not seen any wish nor inclination on the part of Badar in this direction, and I shall be very pleased, if some lovely princess is in your mind, inform me of her, so that I may, after enquiry, give you permission to set the matter on foot; I have great confidence, from your affection and kindness that you will seek for some such princess for him."

Alqiṣṣa, isī intiẕām meṇ, bāp Bādshāh Badr kā bīmār hūā, aur roz-ba-roz us kī 'alālat baṛhtī ga'ī. Akhir jab apnī zindagānī se māyūs hūā, wazīr aur amīr mamlakat ke jama' kīye, aur pher un se wāsṭe iṭā'at Bādshāh Badr ke mujaddadan 'ahd o paimān līye, aur is 'ālam-i-fānī se riḥlat farmāī. Is ḥādiṡe se Sulṭān Badr aur Malika Gulnār ne bahut jaza' o faza' kar ke, us ko baṛe tajammul se dafn kīyā. Badr ne, ḥasb-i-dastūr, ek mahīne tak gosha-nashīn ho ke, kisī mutanaffis se mulāqāt na kī; aur apne bāp ke gham meṇ din rāt royā kiyā. Is'arṣe meṇ, māṇ aur Malik Ṣāliḥ, bhāī Gulnār kā, apne aqribā ke sāth wahāṇ pahuṇch kar, sharīk us mātam ke hūe. Jab rusūm-i-mātam-dārī se un sab ne farāghat pāī, Malik Ṣāliḥ ne ek roz apnī hamshīra Gulnār se kahā, "Ta'ajjub hai ki tum ko abtak kuchh fikr Badr kī kat-khudāī kā nahīṇ. Agar tumhārī marẓī ho, to maiṇ koī shāh-zādī apne mulkoṇ meṇ, jo ham jamāl aur qābil Badr ke ho, talāsh karūṇ." Malika Gulnār ne jawāb dīyā ki, "Ab tak mujhe is bāt kā kuchh khayāl na thā, isī wajh se ki maiṇ ne kuchh raghbat aur khwāhish Badr kī is ṭaraf nahīṇ pāī thī; aur maiṇ bahut khush hūṇgī, agar koī shah-zadī ṣāḥib-i-jamāl tumhāre khayāl meṇ ho, to mujhe us se āgāhī karnā, tā maiṇ daryāft kar ke tumheṇ us kī silsila-jumbānī ke wāsṭe ijāzat dūṇ: aur mujh ko tumhārī maḥabbat o shafaqat se yaqīn hai, ki tum koī aisī shah-zādī us ke wāsṭe ḍhūṇḍhoge.

القصه اسي انتظام مين باپ بادشاه بدر کا بيمار هوا اور روز بروز اوسکي علالت برهتي گئي * آخر جب اپني زندگاني سے مايوس هوا وزير اور امير مملکت کے جمع کئے اور پهر اون سے واسطے اطاعت بادشاه بدر کے مجددا عهد و پيمان ليئے اور اس عالم فاني سے رحلت فرمائي * اس حادثے سے سلطان بدر اور ملکه گلنار نے بهت جزع و فزع کرکے اوسکو برے تجمل سے دفن کيا بدر نے حسب دستور ايک مهينے تک گوشه نشين هوکے کسي متنفس سے ملاقات نکي اور اپنے باپ کے غم مين دن رات رويا کيا * اس عرصے مين مان اور ملک صالح بهائي گلنار کا اپنے اقربا کے ساتهه وهان پهنچکر شريک اس ماتم کے هوئے جب رسوم ماتمداري سے اون سب نے فراغت پائي ملک صالح نے ايک روز اپني همشيره گلنار سے کها تعجب هي که تمکو ابتک کچهه فکر بدر کي کتخدائي کا نهين اگر تمهاري مرضي هو تو مين کوئي شهزادي اپنے ملکون مين جو هم جمال اور قابل بدر کے هو تلاش کرون ملکه گلنار نے جواب ديا که اب تلک مجهے اس بات کا کچهه خيال نتها اسي وجه سے که مين نے کچهه رغبت اور

* Note idiom.

خواهش بدرکي اسطرف نهين پائي تهي اور مين بهت
خوش هونگي اگر کوئي شهزادي صاحب جمال تمهارے
خيال مين هو تو مجهے اوس سے آگاهي کرنا * تا مين دريافت
کرکے تهمين اوسکي سلسله † جنباني کے واسطے اجازت دون
اور مجهکو تمهاري محبت و شفقت سے يقين هی که تم کوئي
ايسی شهزادي اوسکے واسطے ڈهونڈهوگے *

* Note idiom.

† سلسله جنباني Shaking the chain—A very common Persian idiom for starting an enterprise.

Other Works by the same Author

Crown 8vo. Cloth Rs. 5.

INTRODUCTORY EXERCISES

IN

URDU PROSE COMPOSITION

WITH

NOTES AND TRANSLATIONS.

BY

SURGEON-LIEUT.-COLONEL G. RANKING, M.A., M.D., M.R.A.S.,

Secretary to the Board of Examiners, Fort William;

Fellow of the Calcutta University.

AND

MAULAVI' MUHAMMAD YU'SUF JA'FARI,

Chief Maulavi to the Board of Examiners.

PRESS NOTICES.

"One of the best works on the Urdu language that we have yet seen . . . . the student will find in Dr. Ranking's work a really valuable aid . . . . . . The work is a thoroughly practical one, and explains all the various phrases and intricacies of a language, the acquirement of which is too often neglected by Anglo-Indians from mere prejudice.—*Indian Daily News.*

"A handy little volume of 150 pages with a few introductory remarks on construction and idiom, and a number of well selected exercises extracted for the most part from the daily papers, with the English on one page and the Urdu rendering of it on the page facing it."—*British Medical Journal.*

"This little book should prove of great service to officers and others who, from necessity or choice, study Hindustani in the Urdu character."—*Admiralty and Horse Guards Gazette.*

"Up to the present there has been no book from which a student could learn to translate from English into Urdu. To meet this pressing want is the aim of the little book before us . . . . by the aid of the work under notice the task of translating colloquial English into original Urdu is simplified to a considerable degree."—*Home News.*

Thacker, Spink and Co., Calcutta.

DIWAN-I-ATASH. Rs. 2.
KULLIYAT-I-SAUDA. Rs. 6.
URDU-I-MUALLA OF GHALIB. Rs. 3.

HINDI—HIGH PROFICIENCY.

TEXTS—Nagri Character.

RAJNITI. Official Edition. Rs. 4.
RAJNITI. Bazar Copy. As. 12.
PREM SAGAR. Edited, with Vocabulary, by EASTWICK, quarto, second-hand, about Rs. 30.
Ditto Bazar edition. Rs. 2.
RAMAYAN, Book II. Bazar edition. Re. 1-8.

TRANSLATIONS—

RAJNITI. Translated by CAPT. DOWDLER BELL. Rs. 6.
RAMAYAN, Book II. Translated with Notes by ADALUT KHAN. Rs. 4-8.
Ditto Translated by F. S. GROWSE. Rs. 3.

PERSIAN—LOWER STANDARD.

TEXT—

IQD-I-GUL. SELECTIONS from the GULISTAN. (Chapters I to IV.) Official Edition. Rs. 3-12.

TRANSLATION—

SELECTIONS from the GULISTAN. Translated by ADALUT KHAN. Rs. 3-8.

PERSIAN—HIGHER STANDARD.

TEXTS—

IQD-I-GUL; being Selections from the GULISTAN and the ANWAR-I-SUHAILI. Official Edition. Rs. 3-12.
IQD-I-MANZUM: a Selection from the BOSTAN. Official Edition. Re. 1-12.

TRANSLATIONS—

IQD-I-GUL. Translated with Notes. By ADALUT KHAN. Rs. 6-8.
IQD-I-MANZUM. Translated with Notes. By ADALUT KHAN. Rs. 5-8.

PERSIAN—HIGH PROFICIENCY AND HONOURS.

TEXTS—

GULISTAN. Official Edition. By COL. NASSAU LEES. Rs. 5-8.
Ditto Edited with complete Vocabulary. By J. T. PLATTS. 12*s.* 6*d.*

BOSTAN. Official Edition. Re. 1-8.

Ditto With Commentary in Persian. Edited by C. H. GRAF. (Vienna) half calf. Rs. 20.

Ditto Photographed from a MS. Edited by PLATTS and ROGERS. 18*s*.

MIRZA HAIRAT'S Persian translation of Malcolm's HISTORY of PERSIA. Vol. II. Rs. 10.

TRANSLATIONS—

GULISTAN. Translated by J. T. PLATTS. 12*s*. 6*d*.

Ditto Translated by E. B. EASTWICK. 10*s*. 6*d*.

Ditto Translated by JAMES ROSS. 1*s*. 6*d*.

BOSTAN. Translated into Prose. By LT.-COL. H. W. CLARK.

MALCOLM'S HISTORY of PERSIA (Modern). Edited and adapted to the Persian translation of MIRZA HAIRAT. With Notes and Dissertations. By LT.-COL. M. H. COURT. Rs. 25.

ARABIC—HIGHER STANDARD.

TEXTS—

SELECTIONS from the ALIF LAILA. Official Edition. Re. 1-10.

NAFHAT-UL-YAMAN. 1st Part. Official Edition. Rs. 2-8.

ARABIC—HIGH PROFICIENCY.

TEXTS—

SELECTIONS from the ALIF LAILA. Official Edition. Rs. 3.

NAFHAT-UL-YAMAN. Official Edition. Rs. 2-8.

PASHTU—LOWER STANDARD.

TEXTS—

GANJ-I-PUKHTO. Edited with a Glossary. By REV. T. P. HUGHES. 10*s*. 6*d*.

TRANSLATION—

GANJ-I-PUKTU. Translated. Rs. 5.

PASHTU—HIGHER STANDARD.

TEXT—

KALID-I-AFGHANI. Edited by REV. T. P. HUGHES. Second Edition. Rs. 12-8.

TRANSLATION—

KALID-I-AFGHANI. Translated into English. Rs. 17.

Calcutta, February 1901.

Thacker, Spink & Co.'s Publications.

CONTENTS:

BOOKS priced both in **Sterling and in Rupees** are published by our London firm and are subject to the same terms as all English published books; those priced in **Rupees only** are published in India, and the prices **are *net.***

THACKER, SPINK & CO., CALCUTTA.

2-1901.

SPORT AND VETERINARY WORKS.

THE ROD IN INDIA; BEING HINTS HOW TO OBTAIN SPORT, with Remarks on the Natural History of Fish and their Culture. By H. S. THOMAS, F.Z.S., &c., Author of Tank Angling in India. Third Edition, Revised. With numerous Illustrations. Demy 8vo, cloth, 15*s*. Rs. 13-2; cash, Rs. 11-4.

"A masterly treatise on the art of angling."—*Field.*

"A more complete guide to its subject than could be found elsewhere." —*Spectator.*

"His book has been for years a standard work—perhaps, without injustice to others, it may be described as *the* standard work upon Indian angling."—*Illustrated Sporting and Dramatic News.*

ANGLING ON THE KUMAON LAKES. WITH A MAP OF THE KUMAON Lake Country and Plan of each Lake. By Depy. Surgeon-General W. WALKER. Crown 8vo, cloth. Rs. 4.

"Written with all the tenderness and attention to detail which characterise the followers of the gentle art."—*Hayes' Sporting News.*

LARGE GAME SHOOTING IN THIBET, THE HIMALAYAS, NORTHERN and Central India. By Brig.-General ALEXANDER A. KINLOCH. Containing Descriptions of the Country and of the various Animals to be found; together with Extracts from a journal of several years standing. With 36 Illustrations from Photographs and a Map. Third Edition, Revised and Enlarged. Demy 4to, cloth, elegant. Rs. 25.

"This splendidly illustrated record of sport, the photogravures, especially the heads of the various antelopes, are life-like; and the letterpress is very pleasant reading."—*Graphic.*

"The book is capitally got up, the type is better than in former editions, and the excellent photogravures give an exceptional value to the work."—*Asian.*

BULLET AND SHOT, IN INDIAN FOREST, PLAIN AND HILL, with Hints to Beginners in Indian Shooting. By C. E. M. RUSSELL, late Senior Deputy Conservator of Forests, Mysore Service. Demy 8vo, cloth. 10*s*. 6*d*. Rs. 9-3; cash, Rs. 7-14.

THE SPORTSMAN'S MANUAL. IN QUEST OF GAME IN KULLU, Lahoul, and Ladak to the Tso Morari Lake, with Notes on Shooting in Spiti, Bara Bagahal, Chamba, and Kashmir, and a Detailed Description of Sport in more than 100 Nalas. With 9 Maps. By Lt.-Col. R. H. TYACKE, late H. M.'s 98th and 34th Regiments. Fcap. 8vo, cloth. Rs. 3-8.

USEFUL HINTS TO YOUNG SHIKARIS ON THE GUN AND RIFLE. By "THE LITTLE OLD BEAR." Second Edition. Crown 8vo, cloth. Rs. 2-8.

THE TOURIST AND SPORTSMAN'S GUIDE TO KASHMIR, LADAK, &c. By A. E. WARD, Bengal Staff Corps. Fourth Edition. Demy 8vo, cloth. Rs. 5.

THE GAME, SHORE, AND WATER BIRDS OF INDIA. BY COL. A. LE MESSURIER. Second Edition. Rewritten and Enlarged, with numerous Illustrations. [*In preparation.*

INDIAN WILD DUCK, AND HOW TO KNOW THEM. BY F. FINN, B.A., F.Z.S. [*In the press.*

DENIZENS OF THE JUNGLES. A SERIES OF SKETCHES OF WILD Animals, illustrating their form and natural attitude. With Letterpress Description of each Plate. By R. A. STERNDALE, F.R.G.S., F.Z.S., Author of "Natural History of the Mammalia of India," "Seonee," &c. Oblong folio, cloth. Rs. 10.

SEONEE: OR, CAMP LIFE ON THE SATPURA RANGE. A TALE OF Indian Adventure. By R. A. STERNDALE, Author of "Mammalia of India," "Denizens of the Jungles." Illustrated by the Author. With a Map and an Appendix containing a brief Topographical and Historical Account of the District of Seonee in the Central Provinces of India. Crown 8vo, cloth. 8*s*. 6*d*. Rs. 7-7; cash, Rs. 6-6.

THE SNAFFLE PAPERS. BY SNAFFLE, Author of "Gun, Rifle and Hound." Illustrated by HARRY DIXON. Large Crown 8vo. 10*s*. 6*d*. Rs. 9-3; cash, Rs. 7-14.

"Full of spirit and humour."—*Country Life.*

"'The Snaffle Papers' are well written and are extremely interesting, and the illustrations by Harry Dixon artistically executed."—*Shooting Times.*

HUNTING REMINISCENCES. By ALFRED E. PEASE, M.P., Author of "The Cleveland Hounds as a Trencher Fed Pack." With Illustrations by the late Sir FRANK LOCKWOOD, CUTHBERT BRADLEY, HEYWOOD, HARDY, and from Photographs. Crown 8vo, cloth. gilt top. 6*s*. Rs. 5-4; cash, Rs. 4-6.

RIDING FOR LADIES, WITH HINTS ON THE STABLE. A LADY'S Horse Book. By Mrs. POWER O'DONOGHUE. With 75 Illustrations by A. CHANTREY CORBOULD. Elegantly printed and bound, Imp. 16mo, gilt. 10*s*. 6*d*. Rs. 9-3; cash, Rs. 7-11.

NOTES ON STABLE MANAGEMENT. BY VETY.-CAPT. J. A. NUNN, F.R.C.V.S., C.I.E., D.S.O. Second Edition, Revised and Enlarged. With a Glossary of Hindustani Words. Crown 8vo, cloth. Re. 1-8.

"The notes are eminently practical, and give sound advice on everything pertaining to the proper care of horses, such as can be utilized by the uninitiated to the best advantage."—*Indian Daily News.*

HORSE BREEDING AND REARING IN INDIA. WITH NOTES ON Training for the Flat, and Across Country, and on Purchase, Breaking in and General Management. By Major JOHN HUMFREY, B.S.C., F.Z.S. Crown 8vo, cloth. Rs. 3-8.

INDIAN HORSE NOTES. AN EPITOME OF USEFUL INFORMATION arranged for ready reference on Emergencies, and specially adapted for Officers and Mofussil Residents. All Technical Terms explained and Simplest Remedies selected. By Major C——, Author of "Indian Notes about Dogs." Fourth Edition, Revised and considerably Enlarged. Fcap. 8vo, cloth. Rs. 2.

GUIDE TO EXAMINATION OF HORSES FOR SOUNDNESS FOR STUDENTS and Beginners. By J. MOORE, F.R.C.V.S., Army Vety. Dept., Vety. Officer, Remount Depôt, Calcutta. Fcap. 8vo, limp cloth. Re. 1.

OUR INDIAN HORSE: or a few Notes on the Animal. Compiled and Translated from the Ancient Medical and other Works of the Hindus. By RAJA SIR SOURINDRO MOHUN TAGORE, KT., C.I.E. Fcap. 8vo, sewed. As. 8.

PRACTICAL HINTS ON HORSE, HARNESS AND TRAP. By DOUGLAS WHITE. Illustrated. Crown 8vo, cloth. Rs. 2-8.

DOGS FOR HOT CLIMATES. A GUIDE FOR RESIDENTS IN TROPICAL Countries as to suitable Breeds, their Respective Uses, Management and Doctoring. By VERO SHAW and Captain M. H. HAYES. With Illustrations. Crown 8vo, cloth. 6*s*. Rs. 5-4; cash, Rs. 4-8.

"The authors of 'Dogs for Hot Climates' show in a concise practical way how to treat dogs out here, and what breeds best stand the climate. The book should be on every one's table, for sensible treatment will save the life of many a valuable and much-loved pet."—*Indian Planters' Gazette.*

INDIAN NOTES ABOUT DOGS: THEIR DISEASES AND TREATMENT. By Major C——. Sixth Edition. Fcap. 8vo, cloth. Re. 1-8.

THE MANAGEMENT AND BREEDING OF DOGS IN INDIA, and the Points to Breed for. By 'Kader,' an Associate of the English Kennel Club. Crown 8vo, cloth. Rs. 3.

HOW TO CHOOSE A DOG AND HOW TO SELECT A PUPPY, WITH Notes on the Peculiarities and Characteristics of each Breed. By VERO SHAW. Crown 8vo, sewed. 1*s*. 6*d*. Re. 1-5; cash, Re. 1-2.

A BOBBERY PACK IN INDIA: HOW TO COLLECT, TRAIN AND HUNT it: also full Instructions for laying a Drag in India. With an Appendix containing a short *Excursus* on Banting, and an Interview with Mr. Pickwick. By Captain JULIAN. Crown 8vo, sewed. Re. 1-8.

STATION POLO: THE TRAINING AND GENERAL TREATMENT OF POLO Ponies, together with Types and Traits of Players. By Lt. HUGH STEWART (LUCIFER). Crown 8vo, cloth, Rs. 2; paper, Re. 1-8.

CONTENTS:—The Polo Pony—The Raw Pony—Preliminary Training—First Introduction—Stable Management—Tricks—Injuries—Shoeing—Station Polo—How shall We Play?—The Procrastinator—The Polo Scurry—Idiosyncrasies—Types—Individual *v.* Combined Tactics—Odds and Ends.

POLO RULES. Rules of The Calcutta Polo Club and of the Indian Polo, Association, with the Article on Polo by "An Old Hand." Reprinted from *Hayes' Sporting News.* Fcap. 8vo, sewed. Re. 1.

THE POLO CALENDAR. Compiled by the Indian Polo Association. 12mo. Cloth. Contents:—Committee of Stewards, Rules for the Regulation of Tournaments, &c.—Rules of the Game—Station Polo —List of Members—List of Existing Polo Ponies, names and description, with Alphabetical List—Records of Tournaments—Previous Winners, Vol. II, 1893-94, **Re. 1-8.** Vol. III, 1894-95, **Rs. 2.** Vol. IV, 1895-96, **Rs. 2.** Vol. V, 1896-97, **Rs. 3.** Vol. VI, 1897-98, **Rs. 2.**

THE ARMS ACT (XI OF 1878). With all the Notices of the Government of India, the Bengal, North-Western Provinces and Punjab Governments, and High Court Decisions and Rulings. By W. Hawkins. Second Edition. 8vo, cloth. Rs. 7-8.

THE RACING CALENDAR, Vol. XII, from April 1899 to March 1900. Races Past. Published by the Calcutta Turf Club. Contents:—Rules of Racing, Lotteries, C. T. C., etc., Registered Colours; Licensed Trainers and Jockeys; Assumed Names: List of Horses Aged, Classed and Measured by C. T. C. and W. I. T. C.; Races Run under C. T. C. Rules: Performances of Horses; Appendix and Index. 12mo, cloth. Rs. 5.

Previous Volumes—I to VIII, Rs. 4 each: Volumes IX to XI, Rs. 5 each.

CALCUTTA RACING CALENDAR. Published every fortnight. Annual Subscription, Rs. 12.

CALCUTTA TURF CLUB RULES OF RACING, as in force on 1st April 1899. Fcap. 8vo, cloth. Rs. 2.

HISTORY, CUSTOMS, TRAVELS, RE-COLLECTIONS, Etc.

CURZON.—INDIAN SPEECHES, 1898—1900. BY HIS EXCELLENCY BARON CURZON OF KEDLESTON, P.C., G.M.S.I., G.M.I.E., Viceroy and Governor-General of India. Demy 8vo, cloth. [*In preparation.*

A SERVANT OF "JOHN COMPANY:" BEING THE RECOLLECTIONS of an Indian Official. By H. G. KEENE, C.I.E., Hon. M.A., Author of "Sketches in Indian Ink," &c. With a frontispiece Portrait of the Author, and six full-page Illustrations by W. SIMPSON, from the Author's Sketches. Demy 8vo, cloth, gilt top. 12*s.* Rs. 10-8; cash, Rs. 9.

The Volume deals with, among other subjects:—"Posting Days in England"—"Fighting Fitzgerald"—"Daniel O'Connell"—Reminiscences of the Indian Mutiny—Duelling in the Army, and the part the late Prince Consort took in the abolition of the same—Agra—Lord Canning—Sir Henry Lawrence—Anglo-Indian Society in the Days of the East India Company—Lord Dalhousie—Sir H. M. Elliot—and other well-known Indian Officials: interspersed with Original Stories and Anecdotes of the Times, with Appendix on the Present Condition of India.

THE EARLY ANNALS OF THE ENGLISH IN BENGAL: BEING THE Bengal Public Consultations for the first-half of the 18th Century, Summarised, Extracted and Edited, with Introductions and Illustrative Addenda. By C. R. WILSON, M.A. Volume I. 1704 to 1710. Royal 8vo, cloth, Rs. 12. Vol. 2. Part 1, 1711 to 1717. Royal 8vo, cloth, Rs. 12.

EARLY RECORDS OF BRITISH INDIA: a History of the English Settlements in India, as told in the Government Records, the works of old travellers, and other contemporary documents, from the earliest period down to the rise of British power in India. By J. TALBOYS WHEELER (1879). Royal 8vo, cloth. Rs. 5.

TWENTY-ONE DAYS IN INDIA: BEING THE TOUR OF SIR ALI BABA, K.C.B. By GEORGE ABERIGH-MACKAY. Sixth and Enlarged Edition. With Illustrations. Crown 8vo, cloth. 6*s.* Rs. 5-4; cash, Rs. 4-8.

A TRIP TO KASHMIR. BY JAMES ARBUTHNOT. With 64 Illustrations. Crown 4to, cloth, gilt. Rs. 8.

ECHOES FROM OLD CALCUTTA: BEING CHIEFLY REMINISCENCES of the Days of Warren Hastings, Francis and Impey. By H. E. BUSTEED. Third Edition, considerably Enlarged with additional Illustrations. Post 8vo, cloth. Rs. 6.

"The book will be read by all interested in India."—*Army & Navy Magazine.*

"Dr. Busteed's valuable and entertaining 'Echoes from Old Calcutta' revised, enlarged and illustrated with portraits and other plates rare or quaint. It is a pleasure to reiterate the warm commendation of this instructive and lively volume which its appearance called forth some years since."—*Saturday Review.*

"A series of illustrations which are highly entertaining and instructive of the life and manners of Anglo-Indian society a hundred years ago . . . The book from first to last has not a dull page in it, and it is a work of the kind of which the value will increase with years."—*Englishman.*

THE PARISH OF BENGAL, 1678 TO 1788. BY H. B. HYDE, M.A., a Senior Chaplain on H. M.'s Indian Ecclesiastical Establishment. With 19 Illustrations. Crown 8vo, sewed. Rs. 4.

"Upon every page is something of interest and of charm . . . there has seldom been a book better worth buying, better worth reading, and better worth keeping than Mr. Hyde's latest contribution to the history of old Calcutta."—*Englishman.*

THE TRIAL OF MAHARAJA NANDA KUMAR. A NARRATIVE OF A Judicial Murder. By H. BEVERIDGE, B.C.S. Demy 8vo, cloth. Rs. 5.

"Mr. Beveridge has given a great amount of thought, labour, and research to the marshalling of his facts, and he has done his utmost to put the exceedingly complicated and contradicting evidence in a clear and intelligible form."—*Home News.*

A SUMMER IN HIGH ASIA: BEING A RECORD OF SPORT AND TRAVEL in Baltistan and Ladakh. BY CAPT. F. E. S. ADAIR, Author of "Sport in Ladakh." Including a Chapter on Central Asian Trade, by Capt. S. H. GODFREY (late British Joint Commissioner at Leh). With 70 Illustrations reproduced from Drawings and Photographs by the Author; also Map of the Route. Medium 8vo, cloth. 12*s.* 6*d. net.* Rs. 12-8; cash, Rs. 10-15.

"We have read this book with great pleasure and cordially commend it to all sportsmen. There are excellent Illustrations from Sketches and Photographs and a useful Map."—*Asian.*

THACKER, SPINK & CO., CALCUTTA.

A JAUNT IN JAPAN, OR NINETY DAYS' LEAVE IN THE FAR East. By Capt. S. C. F. JACKSON, D.S.O. Royal 12mo, cloth. Rs. 3-8.

"To those in India who may be contemplating a trip to Japan, we can confidently recommend a little book by Capt. S. C. F. JACKSON . . . . . . is very readable, and moreover it contains detailed information as to steamers, places *en route*, cost of travelling and living in Japan itself, what to see, and what to avoid . . . . Capt. Jackson is a good guide. A shrewd observer of men and manners, his remarks on the transition states of the Japanese people are to the point and can be studied with advantage."—*Pioneer*.

WITH SAMPSON THROUGH THE WAR. An Account of the Naval Operations during the Spanish War of 1898. By W. A. M. GOODE. With Chapters specially contributed by Rear-Admiral SAMPSON, Captain R. D. EVANS and Commander C. C. TODD. With Portraits, Illustrations and Maps. Demy 8vo, cloth. 10*s*. 6*d*. Rs. 9-3; cash, Rs. 7-14.

THE CAVE DWELLERS OF SOUTHERN TUNISIA. Recollections of a Sojourn with the Khalifa of Matmata. Translated from the Danish by DANIEL BRUUN, by L. E. A. B., with numerous Illustrations. Demy 8vo. 12*s*. Rs. 10-8; cash, Rs. 9.

THE CONGO STATE, OR THE GROWTH OF CIVILIZATION IN Central Africa. By DEMETRIUS C. BOULGER, Author of "History of China," with 60 Illustrations. Demy 8vo. 16*s*. Rs. 14; cash, Rs. 12.

"On the whole an accurate and useful summary of the interesting enterprise on the King of the Belgians."—*Times*.

"A very full and detailed history of the growth, development, and administration of the Congo."—*Bookman*.

THE HISTORY OF CHINA. New Edition, revised and brought up-to-date, with the recent concessions to the European Powers. By DEMETRIUS C. BOULGER, Author of "Chinese Gordon." Illustrated with Portraits and Maps. 2 Vols. Demy 8vo. 24*s*. Rs. 21; cash, Rs. 18.

"Regarded as a history, pure and simple: indeed, Mr. Boulger's latest effort is all that such a work should be."—*Pall Mall Gazette*.

"One cannot read this admirable history without feeling how much Mr. Bougler's sympathies have been enlisted by the wonderful record of Chinese achievement and Chinese character which he has collected with so much charm and ability."—*Saturday Review*.

LOCKHART'S ADVANCE THROUGH TIRAH. By Captain L. J. Shadwell, p.s.c. (Suffolk Regiment), Special Correspondent of the Indian *Pioneer* and the London *Daily News*. Demy 8vo, cloth, 7*s*. 6*d*. Rs. 6-9; cash, Rs. 5-10.

THE IMAGE OF WAR; OR SERVICE IN THE CHIN HILLS. A Collection of 34 full-page Collotypes of Instantaneous Photographs and 160 interspersed in the reading. By Surgeon-Captain A. G. Newland. With Introductory Notes by J. D. Macnabb, Esq., b.c.s. 4to, cloth, gilt elegant. Rs. 16.

"It would be difficult to give a more graphic picture of an Indian Frontier Expedition."—*The Times.*

"Brings home to us the Chins themselves, their ways and homes, the nature of the country marched through, method of campaign, and daily social habits and experiences of the campaigners. The letterpress, bright and simple, is worthy of the photographs."—*Broad Arrow.*

CHIN-LUSHAI LAND. Including a Description of the various Expeditions into the Chin-Lushai Hills and the Final Annexation of the Country. By Surgn.-Lieut.-Colonel A. S. Reid, m.b., Indian Medical Service. With three Maps and eight Photo-tint Illustrations. Demy 8vo, cloth, gilt. Rs. 12.

Contains a description of the Chin-Lushai Hills and their inhabitants, from the earliest records, with an account of the various expeditions into the country, the last, *viz.*, that of 1889-90, which led to the final annexation of the wild mountainous tract which lies between India and Burma, being given in full detail.

MAYAM-MA: THE HOME OF THE BURMAN. By Tsaya (Rev. H. Powell). Crown 8vo, cloth. Rs. 2.

THE DHAMMAPADA; or, Scriptural Texts. A Book of Buddhist Precepts and Maxims. Translated from the Pali on the Basis of Burmese Manuscripts. By James Gray. Second Edition. 8vo, boards. Rs. 2

HINDU CASTES AND SECTS; AN EXPOSITION OF THE ORIGIN OF the Hindu Caste System and the bearing of the Sects towards each other and towards other Religious Systems. By Pandit JOGENDRA NATH BHATTACHARYA, M.A., D.L. Crown 8vo, cloth. Rs. 12.

CONTENTS:—The Brahmans—The Military Castes—The Scientific Castes—The Writer Castes—The Mercantile Castes—The Manufacturing and Artisan Castes—The Agricultural Castes—The Cowherds and Shepherds—Miscellaneous Castes—The Sivites—The Vishnuvites—The Semi-Vishnuvites and Guru-Worshippers—Modern Religions intended to bring about Union between Hindus and Mahomedans.

"A valuable work......... The Author has the courage of his convictions, and in setting them forth herein he states that while reverence ought by all means to be shown to persons and institutions that have a just claim to it, nothing can be more sinful than to speak respectfully of persons who are enemies of mankind and to whitewash rotten institutions by esoteric explanations and fine phrases."—*Madras Mail.*

HINDU MYTHOLOGY: VEDIC AND PURANIC. BY W. J. WILKINS, late of the London Missionary Society, Calcutta. Second Edition. Profusely Illustrated. Crown 8vo, cloth, *7s. 6d.* Rs. 6-9; cash, Rs. 5-10.

"Mr. Wilkins has done his work well, with an honest desire to state facts apart from all theological prepossession, and his volume is likely to be a useful book of reference."—*Guardian.*

MODERN HINDUISM: BEING AN ACCOUNT OF THE RELIGION AND Life of the Hindus in Northern India. By W. J. WILKINS, Author of "Hindu Mythology: Vedic and Puranic." Second Edition.

[*In preparation.*

"He writes in a liberal and comprehensive spirit."—*Saturday Review.*

THE HINDOOS AS THEY ARE. A DESCRIPTION OF THE MANNERS, Customs and Inner Life of Hindoo Society, Bengal. By SHIB CHUNDER BOSE. Second Edition, Revised. Crown 8vo, cloth. Rs. 5.

THE LIFE AND TEACHING OF KESHUB CHUNDER SEN. BY P. C. MAZUMDAR. Second and Cheaper Edition. Crown 8vo, cloth. Rs. 2.

AN INTRODUCTION TO THE STUDY OF HINDUISM. BY GURU PERSHAD SEN. Crown 8vo, cloth. Rs. 3; paper, Rs. 2.

THE ETHICS OF ISLAM. A LECTURE BY THE HON'BLE AMEER ALI, C.I.E., Author of "The Spirit of Islâm," "The Personal Law of the Mahomedans," etc. Crown 8vo, cloth gilt. Rs. 2-8.

An attempt towards the exposition of Islâmic Ethics in the English language. Besides most of the Koranic Ordinances, a number of the precepts and sayings of the Prophet, the Caliph Ali, and of 'Our Lady,' are translated and given.

THE ORIGIN OF THE MAHOMEDANS IN BENGAL. BY MOULVIE FUZL RUBBEE. Crown 8vo, cloth. Rs. 3-8.

REMINISCENCES OF BEHAR. By an old Planter. Crown 8vo, cloth. Rs. 2-8.

RURAL LIFE IN BENGAL. Illustrative of Anglo-Indian Suburban Life, more particularly in connection with the Planter and Peasantry, the varied produce of the Soil and Seasons; with copious details of the culture and manufacture of Indigo. Illustrated with 166 Engravings (1860) By COLESWORTHY GRANT. Impl. 8vo, cloth. Rs. 3.

THE FIGHTING RACES OF INDIA. BY P. D. BONARJEE, Assistant in the Military Department of the Government of India. Crown 8vo, cloth, Rs. 5.

"The author has attempted to give a brief sketch of the History, Ethnology, Customs, Characteristics, etc., of the fighting races of India so as to enable the Young British Officers to form an idea of the material of which the Native Army is composed * * * * it fills an important gap in Indian Military literature."—*Madras Mail.*

"Mr. Bonarjee's Handbook will be found most useful and complete. It is small in compass yet contains a mass of information."—*United Service Magazine.*

TALES FROM INDIAN HISTORY: BEING THE ANNALS OF INDIA re-told in Narratives. By J. TALBOYS WHEELER. Crown 8vo, cloth, 3*s.* 6*d.* Rs. 3-1; cash, Rs. 2-10. School Edition, cloth, limp. Re. 1-8.

"The history of our great dependency made extremely attractive reading. Altogether, this is a work of rare merit."—*Broad Arrow.*

"Will absorb the attention of all who delight in thrilling records of adventure and daring. It is no mere compilation, but an earnest and brightly written book."—*Daily Chronicle.*

MR. DUTT AND LAND ASSESSMENTS. (A Reply to Mr. R. C. Dutt's Book on Famines in India.) By an Indian Civilian. *Reprinted from the Calcutta "Englishman."* Demy 8vo, sewed. Re. 1-8.

A MEMOIR OF CENTRAL INDIA, INCLUDING MALWA AND ADJOINING Provinces, with the History, and copious Illustrations, of the Past and Present Condition of that Country. By Maj.-Genl. S. J. MALCOLM, G.C.B., &c. *Reprinted from Third Edition.* 2 vols. Crown 8vo, cloth. Rs. 5.

A CRITICAL EXPOSITION OF THE POPULAR "JIHAD." SHOWING that all the Wars of Mahammad were defensive, and that Aggressive War or Compulsory Conversion is not allowed in the Koran, &c. By Moulavi CHERAGH ALI, Author of "Reforms under Moslem Rule," "Hyderabad under Sir Salar Jung." Demy 8vo, cloth. Rs. 6.

BOOK OF INDIAN ERAS. WITH TABLES FOR CALCULATING INDIAN Dates. By ALEXANDER CUNNINGHAM, C.S.I., C.I.E., Major-General, Royal Engineers. Royal 8vo, cloth. Rs. 12.

THE RACES OF AFGHANISTAN: BEING A BRIEF ACCOUNT OF THE principal Nations inhabiting that Country. By Surgn.-Maj. H. W. BELLEW, C.S.I., late on Special Political Duty at Kabul. 8vo, cloth, Rs. 2.

KASHGARIA (EASTERN OR CHINESE TURKESTAN). HISTORICAL, Geographical, Military and Industrial. By Col. KUROPATKIN, Russian Army. Translated by Maj. GOWAN, H. M.'s Indian Army. 8vo, cloth. Rs. 2.

ANCIENT INDIA AS DESCRIBED BY MEGASTHENES AND ARRIAN. With Introduction, Notes and a Map of Ancient India. By J. W. McCRINDLE, M.A. Demy 8vo, cloth. Rs. 2-8.

THE COMMERCE AND NAVIGATION OF THE ERYTHRÆAN SEA; Periplus Maris Erythræi; and of Arrian's Account of the Voyage of Nearkhos. With Introduction, Commentary, Notes and Index. By J. W. McCRINDLE, M.A. Demy 8vo, cloth. Rs. 3.

ANCIENT INDIA AS DESCRIBED BY KTESIAS THE KNIDIAN. A Translation of the Abridgment of his 'Indika,' by Photios. With Introduction, Notes and Index. By J. W. McCrindle, M.A. Demy 8vo, cloth. Rs. 3.

THE SOVEREIGN PRINCES AND CHIEFS OF CENTRAL INDIA. By G. R. Aberigh-Mackay. Volume I—The House of Holkar. Imp. 8vo, cloth. Rs. 12.

SPEECHES OF LALMOHUN GHOSE. Edited by Asutosh Banerjee. Parts I and II in one Volume. Crown 8vo, sewed. Rs. 2.

DOMESTIC BOOKS.

BAKER AND COOK. A Domestic Manual for India. By Mrs. R. Temple-Wright, Author of "Flowers and Gardens." Second Edition, Revised and Enlarged. Crown 8vo, boards. Rs. 2-8.

"The outcome of long experience and many patient experiments." —*Pioneer*.

"Mrs. Temple-Wright aims at a refinement sufficiently simple to be within the reach of every householder."—*Bombay Gazette*.

"No better authority on matters relating to the Kitchen and all that pertains to *cuisine* is to be found than Mrs. Temple-Wright."—*Englishman*.

THE INDIAN COOKERY BOOK. A Practical Handbook to the Kitchen in India, adapted to the Three Presidencies. Containing Original and Approved Recipes in every department of Indian Cookery; Recipes for Summer Beverages and Home-made Liqueurs; Medicinal and other Recipes; together with a variety of things worth knowing. By a Thirty five Years' Resident. Crown 8vo, cloth. Rs. 3.

MEM-SAHIB'S COOKERY BOOK. By A. C. S. Third Edition, Revised and Enlarged. [*In the press.*

MEM-SAHIB'S BOOK OF CAKES, BISCUITS, etc. By A. C. S. With Remarks on Ovens, Hindustani Vocabulary, Weights and Measures. 18mo, cloth. Rs. 2.

EVERY-DAY MENUS FOR INDIA. By W. S. Burke. Long 12 mo. Rs. 2.

FLOWERS AND GARDENS IN INDIA. A Manual for Beginners. By Mrs. R. Temple-Wright. Fourth Edition. Post 8vo, boards. Rs. 2-8.

......"A most useful little book which we cannot too strongly recommend. We can recommend it to our readers with the utmost confidence, as being not only instructive, but extremely interesting, and written in a delightfully easy, chatty strain."—*Civil and Military Gazette.*

"Very practical throughout. There could not be better advice than this, and the way it is given shows the enthusiasm of Mrs. Temple-Wright."—*Pioneer.*

THE AMATEUR GARDENER IN THE HILLS. With a few Hints on Fowls, Pigeons and Rabbits. By An Amateur. Second Edition, Revised and Enlarged. Crown 8vo, cloth. Rs. 2-8.

FIRMINGER'S MANUAL OF GARDENING FOR INDIA. A New Edition (the Fifth) thoroughly Revised and Re-written. With many Illustrations. Imp. 16mo, cloth, gilt. [*In preparation.*

COW-KEEPING IN INDIA. A Simple and Practical Book on their care and treatment, their various Breeds, and the means of rendering them profitable. By Isa Tweed. Second Edition. With 37 Illustrations of the various Breeds, &c. Crown 8vo, cloth, gilt. Rs. 4-8.

"A most useful contribution to a very important subject, and we can strongly recommend it."—*Madras Mail.*

COWS IN INDIA AND POULTRY: their Care and Management. By Mrs. James. Second Edition. 8vo, boards. Rs. 3-4.

POULTRY-KEEPING IN INDIA. A Simple and Practical Book on their care and treatment, their various Breeds, and the means of rendering them profitable. By Isa Tweed, Author of "Cow-Keeping in India." With Illustrations. Crown 8vo, cloth, gilt. Rs. 3-8.

"A book which will be found of great use by all those who keep a poultry-yard."—*Madras Mail.*

HANDBOOK ON DUCKS, GEESE, TURKEYS, GUINEA-FOWLS Pea-Hens, Pigeons, Rabits, &c. By Isa Tweed. Illustrated.

HINTS FOR THE MANAGEMENT AND MEDICAL TREATMENT OF CHILDREN IN INDIA. By EDWARD A. BIRCH, M.D., late Principal, Medical College, Calcutta. Third Edition, Revised and Enlarged. Being the Ninth Edition of "Goodeve's Hints for the Management of Children in India." Crown 8vo, cloth. Rs. 7.

MEDICAL HINTS FOR HOT CLIMATES AND FOR THOSE OUT OF REACH OF Professional Aid. With Diagrams for Bandaging. By CHARLES HEATON, M.R.C.S. Fcap. 8vo, cloth. 3s. 6*d.* Rs. 3-1; cash, Rs. 2-10.

"We can recommend this book to those who are in the Colonies as a useful handy guide to health."—*Hospital Gazette.*

OUR INDIAN SERVANTS, and How to Treat Them: with a Sketch of the Law of Master and Servant. By Capt. ALBAN WILSON, 4th Gurkha Rifles. 18mo, sewed. Re. 1.

"Every sahib and memsahib should invest a rupee in Capt. Wilson's little book."—*Englishman.*

ENGLISH ETIQUETTE FOR INDIAN GENTLEMEN. By W. TREGO WEBB, Bengal Educational Department. Third Edition. Fcap. 8vo, cloth, Re. 1-4; paper, Re. 1.

The book comprises chapters on General Conduct, Calls, Dining-out, Levees, Balls, Garden-parties, Railway-travelling, &c. It also contains a chapter on Letter-writing, proper Modes of Address, &c., together with Hints on how to draw up Applications for Appointments, with Examples.

PERSONAL AND DOMESTIC HYGIENE FOR THE SCHOOL AND HOME: Being a Text-book on Elementary Physiology, Hygiene, Home Nursing and First Aid to the Injured; for Senior Schools and Family Reference. By Mrs. HAROLD HENDLEY, Medallist, National Health Society, England. 36 Illustrations. Ex. fcap. 8vo, cloth. Rs. 2; or cloth, gilt Rs. 2-8.

"We are decidedly of opinion that it is the most practical and useful book of its kind which has been published in India. We trust it will gain a large circulation in the schools and homes of India."—*Indian Medical Gazette.*

THACKER'S GUIDE BOOKS.

AGRA.—HANDBOOK TO AGRA AND ITS NEIGHBOURHOOD. By H. G. Keene, c.s. Sixth Edition. Revised. Maps, Plans, &c. Fcap. 8vo, cloth. Rs. 2-8.

AGRA, DELHI, ALLAHABAD, CAWNPORE, LUCKNOW, AND Benares. By H. G. Keene, c.s. With Maps and Plans. In one Fcap. 8vo volume. Rs. 5.

ALLAHABAD, LUCKNOW, CAWNPORE, AND BENARES. By H. G. Keene, c.s. Second Edition. Revised. With four Maps and a Plan. Fcap. 8vo, cloth. Rs. 2-8.

CALCUTTA.—GUIDE TO CALCUTTA. By Edmund Mitchell. Fcap. 8vo, sewed. Re. 1.

CALCUTTA ILLUSTRATED. A series of Phot Reproductions of upwards of 30 Views of the City, including the Government Offices, Public Buildings, Gardens, Native Temples, Views on the Hooghly, and other Places of Interest, with descriptive Letterpress. Oblong 4to. Paper, Rs. 4 ; cloth, Rs. 5.

DARJEELING.—GUIDE TO DARJEELING AND ITS NEIGHBOUR-hood. By Edmund Mitchell, m.a. Second Edition. By G. Hutton Taylor. With 13 Illustrations and 3 Maps. Fcap. 8vo, sewed. Rs. 2.

DELHI.—HANDBOOK TO DELHI AND ITS NEIGHBOURHOOD. By H. G. Keene, c.s. Fifth Edition. Fcap. 8vo, cloth, Rs. 2-8.

INDIA.—GUIDE TO INDIA AND INDIAN HOTELS. By G. Hutton Taylor. With 90 Half-tone Illustrations of celebrated places from Photographs. Coloured Map of India. Crown 8vo, stiff wrapper. Rs. 2.

KASHMIR.—By Joshua Duke, Surgn.-Lt.-Col., b.m.s., based on Ince's Kashmir Handbook. With Appendix containing the Jhelum Valley Road. Fifth Edition. Fcap. 8vo, cloth. [*In preparation.*

KASHMIR.—THE TOURIST AND SPORTSMAN'S GUIDE TO KASHMIR, Ladak, etc. By A. E. WARD, Bengal Staff Corps. Fourth Edition. Rs. 5.

MASURI.—GUIDE TO MASURI, LANDAUR, DEHRA DUN AND THE Hills North of Dehra, including Routes to the Snows and other places of note; with Chapter on Garhwal (Tehri), Hardwar, Rurki and Chakrata By JOHN NORTHAM. Fcap. 8vo, cloth, Rs. 2-8.

SIMLA.—GUIDE TO SIMLA AND ROUTES INTO THE INTERIOR based on Towell's Handbook and Guide to Simla. Revised with Map of Station and Index to all Houses; also Map of Hill States.

——**THACKER'S MAP OF SIMLA**. 6″=1 mile. Shewing every house. Folded in Wrapper, Re. 1.

CASHMIR EN FAMILLE. A NARRATIVE OF THE EXPERIENCES OF A Lady with Children; with useful Hints as to how the Journey and Residence there may be comfortably made. By M. C. B. With a Preface by Major E. A. BURROWS. 12mo, cloth. Rs. 2.

TOUR TO THE PINDARI GLACIER. BY MAJOR ST. JOHN GORE. With Map. Crown 8vo, sewed. Rs. 3.

FROM SIMLA TO SHIPKI IN CHINESE THIBET. AN ITINERARY OF the Roads and various minor Routes, with a few Hints to Travellers, and Sketch Map. By Major W. F. GORDON-FORBES, Rifle Brigade. Fcap. 8vo, cloth, Rs. 2.

ITINERARIES—Simla to Shipki, 'Charling' Pass, 'Sarahan to Narkunda,' Forest Road, Simla to the 'Chor,' Pooi to Dankar, Chini to Landour, and the 'Shalle.'

HILLS BEYOND SIMLA. THREE MONTHS' TOUR FROM SIMLA, through Bussahir, Kunowar, and Spiti to Lahoul. ("In the Footsteps of the Few.") By Mrs. J. C. MURRAY-AYNSLEY. Crown 8vo, cloth. Rs. 3.

ROUTES IN JAMMU AND KASHMIR. A TABULATED DESCRIPTION of over Eighty Routes, shewing Distance, Marches, Natural Characteristics, Altitudes, Nature of Supplies, Transport, etc. By Major-General MARQUIS DE BOURBEL. Royal 8vo, cloth. Rs. 10.

THE 4-ANNA RAILWAY GUIDE. For India, Burma and Ceylon. Alphabetically arranged and with Time Tables in full. With Map. Published Monthly. Annual subscription, town, Rs. 2; mofussil, Rs. 4.

A GUIDE TO THE ROYAL BOTANIC GARDEN, CALCUTTA. By Sir George King, M.B., LL.D., C.I.E., F.R.S. With a Map. 8vo, sewed. As. 8.

THE SPORTSMAN'S MANUAL. In Quest of Game in Kullu, Lahul and Ladak to the Tso Morari Lake, with Notes on Shooting in Spiti, Bara Bagahal, Chamba and Kashmir, and a Detailed Description of Sport in more than 100 Nalas. With 9 Maps. By Lt.-Col. R. H. Tyacke, late H. M.'s 98th and 34th Regiments. Fcap. 8vo, cloth. Rs. 3-8.

ROUTES TO CACHAR AND SYLHET. A Map Revised and Corrected from the Sheets of the Indian Atlas, 4 miles = 1 inch. Showing Rail, Road and Steamer Routes, Tea Gardens, &c. Four sheets, folded in Case, with a Handbook. By James Peter. Rs. 6. Mounted on Linen, in one sheet, folded in Cloth Case, Book-form, Rs. 10-8. Mounted on Linen and Rollers, Varnished, Rs. 12-8.

CALCUTTA TO LIVERPOOL, BY CHINA, JAPAN, AND AMERICA, in 1877. By Lieut.-General Sir Henry Norman. Second Edition. Fcap. 8vo, cloth. Re. 1-8.

POETRY, FICTION, Etc.

BEHIND THE BUNGALOW. By E. H. Aitken, Author of "The Tribes on My Frontier." With Illustrations by F. C. Macrae. Sixth Edition. Imp. 16mo. 6s. Rs. 5-4; cash, Rs. 4-8.

"Of this book it may conscientiously be said that it does not contain a dull page, while it contains very many which sparkle with a bright and fascinating humour, refined by the unmistakable evidences of culture."—*Home News.*

"A series of sketches of Indian servants, the humour and acute observation of which will appeal to every Anglo-Indian."—*Englishman.*

THE TRIBES ON MY FRONTIER. AN INDIAN NATURALIST'S FOREIGN Policy. By E. H. AITKEN. With 50 Illustrations by F. C. MACRAE. Uniform with "Lays of Ind." Sixth Edition. Imp. 16mo, cloth. 6*s.* Rs. 5-4; cash, Rs. 4-8.

"We have only to thank our Anglo-Indian naturalist for the delightful book which he has sent home to his countrymen in Britain. May he live to give us another such."—*Chambers' Journal.*

"A most charming series of sprightly and entertaining essays on what may be termed the fauna of the Indian Bungalow. . . . . . We have no doubt that this amusing book will find its way into every Anglo-Indian's library."—*Allen's Indian Mail.*

NATURALIST ON THE PROWL. BY E. H. AITKEN, Author of "Tribes on My Frontier," "Behind the Bungalow." Second Edition. Imp. 16mo, cloth. 6*s.* Rs. 5-4; cash, Rs. 4-8.

"Anyone who takes up this book will follow our example and not leave his chair until he has read it through. It is one of the most interesting books upon natural history that we have read for a long time."—*Daily Chronicle.*

LAYS OF IND. BY ALIPH CHEEM. COMIC, SATIRICAL, AND Descriptive Poems illustrative of Anglo-Indian Life. Tenth Edition. With 70 Illustrations. Cloth, gilt top. 6*s.* Rs. 5-4; cash Rs. 4-8.

"There is no mistaking the humour, and at times, indeed, the fun is both 'fast and furious.' One can readily imagine the merriment created round the camp fire by the recitation of 'The Two Thumpers,' which is irresistibly droll."—*Liverpool Mercury.*

"The verses are characterised by high animal spirits, great cleverness, and most excellent fooling."—*World.*

PLAIN TALES FROM THE HILLS. BY RUDYARD KIPLING. Third Edition. Crown 8vo, cloth. Rs. 2-4.

"It would be hard to find better reading."—*Saturday Review.*

DEPARTMENTAL DITTIES AND OTHER VERSES. BY RUDYARD KIPLING. Ninth Edition. With Illustrations by DUDLEY CLEAVER. Crown 8vo, cloth. Gilt top. 6*s.* Rs. 5-4; cash, Rs. 4-8. Colonial Edition. cloth, Rs. 2-4; paper, Re. 1-12.

ONOOCOOL CHUNDER MOOKERJEE. A MEMOIR OF THE LATE JUSTICE ONOOCOOL CHUNDER MOOKERJEE. By M. MOOKERJEE. Fifth Edition. 12mo, sewed. Re. 1.

"The reader is earnestly advised to procure the life of this gentleman written by his nephew, and read it."—*The Tribes on My Frontier.*

INDIA IN 1983. A REPRINT OF THE CELEBRATED PROPHECY OF Native Rule in India. Fcap. 8vo, sewed. Re. 1.

"Instructive as well as amusing."—*Indian Daily News.*

"There is not a dull page in the hundred and thirty-seven pages of which it consists."—*Times of India.*

INDO-ANGLIAN LITERATURE. BY B. A. 12mo, cloth. Re. 1.

INDIAN ENGLISH AND INDIAN CHARACTER. BY ELLIS UNDERWOOD. Fcap. 8vo, sewed. As. 12.

INDIAN LYRICS. BY W. TREGO WEBB, M.A., LATE PROFESSOR OF English Literature, Presidency College. Fcap. 8vo, cloth, Rs. 2-8; sewed, Rs. 2.

"Vivacious and clever . . . He presents the various sorts and conditions of humanity that comprise the round of life in Bengal in a series of vivid vignettes . . He writes with scholarly directness and finish."—*Saturday Review.*

LEVIORA: BEING THE RHYMES OF A SUCCESSFUL COMPETITOR. BY the late T. F. BIGNOLD, Bengal Civil Service. 8vo, sewed. Rs. 2; cloth, Rs. 2-8.

ON POSTAL AND PUBLIC SERVICE—POEMS AND SKETCHES. BY LOVELL. With Cover and Frontispiece designed by the author. 4to, sewed. Re. 1.

"To those of our readers who enjoy a laugh, we highly commend this book."—*Philatelic Journal.*

LIGHT AND SHADE. BY HERBERT SHERRING. A COLLECTION OF Tales and Poems. Crown 8vo, cloth. Rs. 3.

"Piquant and humorous—decidedly original—not unworthy of Sterne."
—*Spectator* (London).

INDIAN MELODIES. By Glyn Barlow, M.A., Professor, St. George's College, Mussoorie. Fcap. 8vo, cloth. Rs. 2.

REGIMENTAL RHYMES and other Verses. By Kentish Rag. Imp. 16mo, sewed. Re. 1; cloth, Re. 1-8.

DECADENT DITTIES, ET CETERA. By C. W. Whish, Author of "Essays," "Fin de Siècle," etc. Crown 8vo, sewed. Re. 1.

A ROMANCE OF THAKOTE and other Tales. Reprinted from *The World, Civil and Military Gazette*, and other Papers. By F. C. C. Crown 8vo, sewed. Re. 1.

THE CAPTAIN'S DAUGHTER. A Novel. By A. C. Pooshkin. Literally translated from the Russian by Stuart H. Godfrey, Captain, Bo. S.C. Crown 8vo, sewed. Rs. 2.

"Possesses the charm of giving vividly, in about an hour's reading, a conception of Russian life and manners which many persons desire to possess."—*Englishman.*

MEDICINE, HYGIENE, Etc.

HINTS FOR THE MANAGEMENT AND MEDICAL TREATMENT OF Children in India. By Edward A. Birch, M.D., late Principal, Medical College, Calcutta. Third Edition, Revised. Being the Ninth Edition of "Goodeve's Hints for the Management of Children in India." Crown 8vo. cloth. Rs. 7.

The Medical Times and Gazette, in an article upon this work and Moore's "Family Medicine for India," says:—"The two works before us are in themselves probably about the best examples of medical works written for non-professional readers. The style of each is simple, and as free as possible from technical expressions."

"It is a book which ought to be found in every household."—*Pioneer.*

THE INDIGENOUS DRUGS OF INDIA. SHORT DESCRIPTIVE NOTICES of the principal Medicinal Products met with in British India. By RAI BAHADUR KANNY LALL DEY, C.I.E. Second Edition, Revised and entirely Re-written. Demy 8vo. Rs. 12.

"It shows an immense amount of careful work upon the part of the compilers......and will be useful to students and to that very large class of people who are interested in developing the resources of the country ......above all, the work contains a really good index of 4,000 references. and a complete glossary to the vernacular names."—*Indian Daily News.*

"His work is a compendium of 40 years' experience and deserves to be widely popular and carefully studied."—*Englishman.*

THE CARLSBAD TREATMENT FOR TROPICAL AND DIGESTIVE Ailments and how to carry it out anywhere. By LOUIS TARLETON YOUNG, M.D. Second Edition, with Illustrations. Crown 8vo, cloth. 6*s.* Rs. 5-4; cash, Rs. 4-8.

"The book is of a most useful nature, and inspires confidence by the candour and fulness of its information and points of guidance."—*Irish Times.*

"The book contains the result of six years' practical experience, and should be of as much advantage to medical men as to sufferers."—*Home News.*

MATERIA MEDICA FOR INDIA. Giving the official drugs and preparations according to the British Pharmacopœia of 1898, with details of over 300 of the most important Indian Drugs, and practical statements of their Pharmacology, Therapeutics and Pharmacy. By C. F. PONDER, M.B.; and D. HOOPER, F.C.S., F.L.S. Demy 8vo, cloth. Rs. 6-0.

MEDICAL HINTS FOR HOT CLIMATES AND FOR THOSE OUT OF reach of Professional Aid. With Diagrams. By CHARLES HEATON, M.R.C.S. Fcap. 8vo, cloth. 3*s.* 6*d.* Rs. 3-1; cash, Rs. 2-10.

AIDS TO PRACTICAL HYGIENE. BY J. C. BATTERSBY, B.A., M.B., B.Ch., Univ. Dublin. Fcap. 8vo, cloth. Rs. 2.

"A valuable handbook to the layman interested in sanitation."—*Morning Post.*

"To the busy practitioner or the medical student it will serve the purposes of a correct and intelligent guide."—*Medical Record.*

PERSONAL AND DOMESTIC HYGIENE FOR THE SCHOOL AND HOME: being a Text-book on Elementary Physiology, Hygiene, Home Nursing, and First Aid to the Injured; for Senior Schools and Family Reference. By Mrs. HAROLD HENDLEY, Medallist, National Health Society, England. 36 Illustrations. Ex. fcap. 8vo, cloth, Rs. 2; or cloth, gilt, Rs. 2-8.

"We can recommend this volume without hesitation. In the absence of the doctor one might obtain hints from any page of it on Hygiene, Nursing, Accidents and Emergencies. So far as we can see nothing is omitted, and every direction is given in simple intelligible language." —*Statesman.*

MEDICAL JURISPRUDENCE FOR INDIA. By J. B. LYON, F.C.S., F.C., Brigade-Surgeon, late Professor of Medical Jurisprudence Grant Medical College, Bombay. The Legal Matter revised by J. D. Inverarity, Bar.-at-law. Third Edition, edited by Major L. A. WADDELL, I.M.S., LL.D. [*In the press.*

THE PATHOLOGY OF RELAPSING FEVER. By L. J. PISANI, F.R.C.S., Indian Medical Service Demy 8vo, 3 plates, cloth, gilt. Rs. 3-8.

THE INDIAN MEDICAL SERVICE. A GUIDE FOR INTENDED CANDIDATES for Commissions and for the Junior Officers of the Service. By WILLIAM WEBB, M.B., Surgeon, Bengal Army. (1890.) Crown 8vo, cloth. 5s. 6d. Rs. 4-13; cash, Rs. 4-2.

A SHORT TREATISE ON ANTISEPTIC SURGERY, ADAPTED TO THE special requirements of Indian Dispensaries in Romanized Hindustani (Qawaidi-Jarahat-i-Jadida). By Surgn.-Major G. M. GILES, M.B., F.R.C.S., I.M.S. Crown 8vo, boards. Re. 1.

THE LANDMARKS OF SNAKE-POISON LITERATURE: BEING A Review of the more important Researches into the Nature of Snake-Poisons. By VINCENT RICHARDS, F.R.C.S. (ED.), &c., Civil Medical Officer of Goalundo, Bengal. Crown 8vo, cloth. Rs. 2-8.

THE BUBONIC PLAGUE. By A. Mitra, L.R.C.P., L.R.C.S., F.C.S., Chief Medical Officer, Kashmir. 8vo, sewed. Re. 1.

CHOLERA EPIDEMIC IN KASHMIR, 1892. By A. Mitra, L.R.C.P., L.R.C.S., Principal Medical Officer in Kashmir. With Map and Tables. 4to, sewed. Re. 1.

AGUE; OR, INTERMITTENT FEVER. By M. D. O'Connel, M.D., 8vo, sewed. Rs. 2.

MEDICAL AND SANITARY REFORM IN INDIA. An Appeal to all whom it may concern. 8vo, sewed. Re. 1.

MALARIA; its Cause and Effects: Malaria and the Spleen: Injuries of the Spleen: An Analysis of 39 Cases. By E. G. Russell, M.B., B.Sc. Demy 8vo, cloth. Rs. 8.

THE BABY. Notes on the Feeding, Rearing and Diseases of Infants. By S. O. Moses, Licentiate of the Royal College of Physicians, Edinburgh, &c. 18mo, cloth. Rs. 2.

A RECORD OF INDIAN FEVERS. With some Hints on their Etiology, Diagnosis, and Treatment. By Major D. B. Spencer, I.M.S. With 16 Charts. Demy 8vo, cloth. 2 vols. Rs. 4.

BANTING IN INDIA. With some Remarks on Diet and Things in General. By Surgn.-Lieut.-Col. Joshua Duke. Third Edition. Fcap. 8vo, cloth. Re. 1-8.

THE INDIAN MEDICAL GAZETTE. A Monthly Record of Medicine, Surgery, Public Health, and Medical News, Indian and European. Edited by W. J. Buchanan, B.A., M.B., D.Ph., Major, I.M.S. Associate Editors, J. Maitland, M.D., Lt.-Col., I.M.S., Madras; W. K. Hatch, M.B., F.R.C.S., Lt.-Col., I.M.S., Bombay. Subscription. Rs. 12 yearly; single copy. Re. 1-4.

THACKER'S INDIAN DIRECTORIES AND MAPS.

THACKER'S MAP OF INDIA, WITH INSET MAPS, OF THE VARIOUS PRODUCTS OF INDIA AND OF THE TEA DISTRICTS, SKETCH PLANS of Calcutta, Bombay, and Madras. Edited by J. G. BARTHOLOMEW. Corrected to date. With Railways, Political Changes. Large sheets unmounted, Rs. 4; mounted on rollers and varnished, Rs. 7-8; mounted on linen in book-form with Index, Rs. 7-8.

"An excellent map."—*Glasgow Herald.*

"This is a really splendid map of India, produced with the greatest skill and care."—*Army and Navy Gazette.*

"For compactness and completeness of information few works surpassing or approaching it have been seen in cartography."—*Scotsman.*

THACKER'S INDIAN DIRECTORY. OFFICIAL, LEGAL, EDUCAtional, Professional and Commercial Directories of the whole of India: General Information; Holidays, &c.: Stamp Duties, Customs Tariff, Tonnage Schedules; Post Offices in India, forming a Gazetteer; List of Governors-General and Administrators of India from beginning of British Rule; Orders of the Star of India, Indian Empire, &c.; Warrant of Precedence, Table of Salutes, &c.; The Civil Service of India; An Army List of the Three Presidencies; A Railway Directory; A Newspaper and Periodical Directory; A Conveyance Directory; A Directory of the Chief Industries of India; Tea, Indigo, Silk, and Coffee, Cotton, Jute, Mines, Flour Mills, Rice Mills, Dairies, with details of Acreage, Management, and Trade Marks, etc.; also a separate list of Tea and Coffee Estates in Ceylon; List of Clubs in India; Alphabetical List of Residents, European and Native, and a List of British and Foreign Manufacturers with their Indian Agents. With coloured Maps. A coloured Railway Map of India, Two Maps of Calcutta, The Environs of Calcutta, Bombay, Madras; a Map of Tea Districts; and four Maps of the Products of India. Thick Royal 8vo, leather bound. Rs. 25.

A DIRECTORY OF THE CHIEF INDUSTRIES OF INDIA: Comprising the Tea and Indigo Concerns, Silk Filatures, Sugar Factories, Cinchona Concerns, Coffee Estates, Cotton, Jute, Rice and Flour Mills, Collieries, Mines, etc. With their Capital, Directors, Proprietors, Agents, Managers, Assistants, &c., and their Factory Marks, and a Directory of Estates in Ceylon. A Complete Index of names of Gardens and of Residents. With a Map of the Tea Districts and 4 Maps of the Products of India. Rs. 7-8.

MAP OF THE CIVIL DIVISIONS OF INDIA. Including Government Divisions and Districts, Political Agencies, and Native States also the Cities and Towns with 10,000 Inhabitants and upwards. Coloured. 20 in. x 36 in. Folded, Re. 1. On linen, Rs. 2.

CALCUTTA.—Plans of the Official, Business and Residence Portion, with Houses numbered, and Index of Government Offices and Houses of Business on the Map. Two Maps in pocket case. The Maps are on a large scale. Re. 1.

SCIENTIFIC AND ECONOMIC WORKS.

ON INDIGO MANUFACTURE. A Practical and Theoretical Guide to the Production of the Dye. With numerous Illustrative Experiments. By J. Bridges Lee, M.A., F.G.S. Crown 8vo, cloth. Rs. 4.

"Instructive and useful alike to planter and proprietor . . . A very clear and undoubtedly valuable treatise for the use of practical planters, and one which every planter would do well to have always at hand during his manufacturing season. For the rest, a planter has only to open the book for it to commend itself to him."—*Pioneer.*

THE CULTURE AND MANUFACTURE OF INDIGO. With a Description of a Planter's Life and Resources. By Walter Maclagan Reid. Crown 8vo, cloth. With 19 Full-page Illustrations. Rs. 5.

"It is proposed in the following Sketches of Indigo Life in Tirhoot and Lower Bengal to give those who have never witnessed the manufacture of Indigo, or seen an Indigo Factory in this country, an idea of how the finished marketable article is produced: together with other phases and incidents of an Indigo Planter's life, such as may be interesting and amusing to friends at home."—*Introduction.*

A TEA PLANTER'S LIFE IN ASSAM. BY GEORGE M. BARKER. With 75 Illustrations by the Author. Crown 8vo, cloth. Rs. 6-8.

"Cheery, well-written little book."—*Graphic.*

"A very interesting and amusing book, artistically illustrated from sketches drawn by the author."—*Mark Lane Express.*

MANUAL OF AGRICULTURE FOR INDIA. BY LIEUT. FREDERICK POGSON. Illustrated. Crown 8vo, cloth, gilt. Rs. 5.

ROXBURGH'S FLORA INDICA; OR, DESCRIPTION OF INDIAN PLANTS. Reprinted *literatim* from Cary's Edition. 8vo, cloth. Rs. 5.

COMPOSITÆ INDICÆ DESCRIPTÆ ET SECUS GENERA BENTHAMII ordinatæ. By C. B. CLARKE. 8vo, boards. Re. 1-8.

HANDBOOK TO THE FERNS OF INDIA, CEYLON, AND THE MALAY PENINSULA. By Colonel R. H. BEDDOME, Author of the "Ferns of British India." With 300 Illustrations by the Author. Imp. 16mo, cloth. Rs. 10.

"A most valuable work of reference."—*Garden.*

"It is the first special book of portable size and moderate price which has been devoted to Indian Ferns, and is in every way deserving."—*Nature.*

SUPPLEMENT TO THE FERNS OF BRITISH INDIA, CEYLON AND THE Malay Peninsula, containing Ferns which have been discovered since the publication of the "Handbook to the Ferns of British India," &c. By Col. R. H. BEDDOME, F.L.S. Crown 8vo, sewed. Rs. 2-12.

THE FUTURE OF THE DATE PALM IN INDIA (PHŒNIX DACTYliptera). By E. BONAVIA, M.D., Brigade-Surgeon, Indian Medical Department. Crown 8vo, cloth. Rs. 2-8.

A TEXT-BOOK OF INDIAN BOTANY: MORPHOLOGICAL, PHYSIOLOGIcal, and Systematic. By W. H. GREGG B.M.S., Lecturer on Botany at the Hugli Government College. Profusely Illustrated. Crown 8vo cloth. Rs. 5.

ZEMINDAREE MANUAL: A Guide to the Management of Large Estates in Bengal, with an Appendix containing all the Legislative Enactments relating to Land Revenue, with the Principal Rulings of the High Court thereon, Orders of the Board of Revenue, &c., &c. By JOGENDRA NATH BHATTACHARJEE, M.A., D.L. Royal 8vo, cloth, gilt. Rs. 16.

PEOPLE'S BANKS FOR NORTHERN INDIA. A Handbook to the Organization of Credit on a Co-operative Basis. By H. DUPERNEX, I.C.S. Demy 8vo, cloth. Rs. 4.

GOLD, COPPER, AND LEAD IN CHOTA NAGPORE. COMPILED BY W. KING, D.SC.; and T. A. POPE. With Map showing the Geological Formation and Areas taken up. Crown 8vo, cloth. Rs. 5.

A NATURAL HISTORY OF THE MAMMALIA OF INDIA, BURMAH AND CEYLON. By R. A. STERNDALE, F.R.G.S., F.Z.S., &c., Author o "Seonee," "The Denizens of the Jungle." With 170 Illustrations by the Author and others. Imp. 16mo, cloth. Rs. 10.

"The very model of what a popular natural history should be."—*Knowledge.*

"The book will, no doubt, be specially useful to the sportsman, and, indeed, has been extended so as to include all territories likely to be reached by the sportsman from India."—*Times.*

THE INLAND EMIGRATION ACT, AS AMENDED BY ACT VII OF 1893. The Health Act; Sanitation of Emigrants; The Artificer's Act; Land Rules of Assam, etc. Crown 8vo, cloth. Rs. 2.

ENGINEERING, SURVEYING, Etc.

PROJECTION OF MAPS. BY R. SINCLAIR. With Diagrams. Fcap. 8vo, boards. Rs. 2.

PERMANENT-WAY POCKET-BOOK. CONTAINING COMPLETE FORMULÆ for Laying Points, Crossings, Cross-over Roads, Through Roads Diversions, Curves, etc., suitable for any Gauge. With Illustrations. By T. W. JONES. Pocket-Book Form, cloth. Rs. 3.

RAILWAY CURVES. PRACTICAL HINT ON SETTING OUT CURVES, WITH a Table of Tangents for a 1° Curve for all angles from 2° to 135° increasing by minutes: and other useful Tables. With a Working Plan and Section of Two Miles of Railway. By A. G. WATSON, Assistant Engineer. 18mo, cloth. Rs. 4.

A HANDBOOK OF PRACTICAL SURVEYING FOR INDIA. Illustrated with Plans, Diagrams, etc. Fourth Edition, Revised. By F. W. KELLY, late of the Indian Survey. With 24 Plates. 8vo. Rs. 8.

A HANDBOOK OF PHOTOGRAPHY FOR AMATEURS IN INDIA. BY GEORGE EWING. Illustrated. 623 pages. Crown 8vo, cloth. Rs. 7.

"It is conceived on a capital scheme, and is provided with an intelligent index. All obscure points are illustrated by diagrams. A most useful and practical Handbook."—*Indian Daily News.*

"The Indian amateur is to be congratulated in having now a book that will give him all the information he is likely to require."—*Journal of the Photographic Society of India.*

EXPOSURE TABLES FOR PHOTOGRAPHERS IN INDIA AND THE EAST. By GEORGE EWING, Author of "A Handbook of Photography." 12mo, cloth. Re. 1.

LECTURES ON TELEGRAPHY, DUPLEX, QUADRUPLEX AND OTHER Circuits, Transformer and Testing. With 53 Illustrations. By BEN. J. STOW, Sub-Assistant Superintendent of Telegraphs. Fcap. 4to, cloth. Rs. 3.

COLEBROOKE'S TRANSLATION OF THE LILAVATI. WITH NOTES. By HARAN CHANDRA BANERJI, M.A., B.L. 8vo, cloth. Rs. 4.

This edition includes the Text in Sanskrit. The Lilavati is a standard work on Hindu Mathematics written by Bháskaráchárya, a celebrated mathematician of the twelfth century.

THE PRACTICE OF TRIGONOMETRY. PLANE AND SPHERICAL, with numerous Examples and Key. By WILLIAM S. HOSEASON, M.M.S.A. Crown 8vo, paper cover. [*In the press.*

MILITARY AND NAVAL WORKS.

TACTICS AS APPLIED TO SCHEMES. By Major J. Sherston, D.S.O.; and Capt. J. Shadwell, P.S.C., D.A.A.G. for Instruction; with an Appendix, Solutions to some Tactical Schemes. 7 Maps. [*Reprinting.*

Especially suitable for Majors who wish to pass an Examination in Tactical Fitness to Command and for Officers who wish to pass Promotion Examinations without attending a Garrison Class.

LOCKHART'S ADVANCE THROUGH TIRAH. By Captain L. J. Shadwell, P.S.C. (Suffolk Regiment), Special Correspondent of the Indian *Pioneer* and the London *Daily News*. Demy 8vo, cloth. 7*s.* 6*d.* Rs. 6-9; cash, Rs. 5-10.

TRANSPORT. By Major W. H. Allen, Assistant Commissary-General in India. 24mo, cloth. Re. 1-8.

THE ISSUE OF ORDERS IN THE FIELD. By Capt. Ivor Philipps, P.S.C., 5th Gurkha Rifles. Second Edition. 18mo, cloth. Rs. 2-8.

THE SEPOY OFFICER'S MANUAL. By Capt. E. G. Barrow. Third Edition, Entirely Re-written, and brought up to date. By Capt. E. H. Bingley, 7th Bengal Infantry. 12mo, cloth. Rs. 2-8.

"It seems to contain almost every thing required in one of the modern type of Civilian Soldiers . . . . In the most interesting part of the book is an account of the composition of the Bengal Army, with descriptive note on the Brahmans, Rajputs, Sikhs, Goorkhas, Pathans and other races."—*Englishman.*

"A vast amount of technical and historical data of which no Anglo-Indian Officer should be ignorant."—*Broad Arrow.*

"The notes are brief and well digested and contain all that it is necessary for a candidate to know."—*Army and Navy Gazette.*

A TEXT-BOOK OF INDIAN MILITARY LAW. Comprising the Indian Articles of War fully annotated, the Indian Penal Code and the Indian Evidence Act, and has, in the form of Appendices, all existing Regulations with regard to the Procedure of Courts-martial and Forms of Charges. With Tables shewing the Powers and Jurisdiction of different Courts-martial and the difference in Procedure and Evidence between English Military Law and Indian Military Law. By Captain E. H. Bernard, Cantonment Magistrate, Mandalay. Crown 8vo, cloth. Rs. 8.

"A well arranged and clearly printed Manual.........with ample Notes, Marginal References and Appendices........."—*Home News.*

"It is a very useful volume."—*Army and Navy Gazette.*

INDIAN ARTICLES OF WAR, revised to date. With an Appendix containing Definitions, Rules of Procedure, Forms of Charges, Statement of Objects and Reasons and an Index. By Major C. E. Poynder. Crown 8vo, cloth. Rs. 3-8.

"Possesses useful appendices together with a good Index."—*Home News.*

"The annotations are very good, and we commend the volume to all concerned in the Military Legal Procedure of India."—*Army and Navy Gazette.*

THE INDIAN FIELD MESSAGE BOOK FOR MILITARY OFFICERS. Interleaved. With Envelopes, Carbon Paper and Pencil. Re. 1-4.

NOTES ON THE COURSE OF GARRISON INSTRUCTION, Tactics, Topography, Fortifications, condensed from the Text-Books, with explanations and additional matter. With Diagrams. By Major E. Lloyd, Garrison Instructor. (1888.) Crown 8vo, cloth. Rs. 2-8.

PAPER SIGHTS FOR TARGET PRACTICE. White, Blue, Green and Red lines, or assorted colours. Packets of 100. As. 4.

NDIAN FENCING REVIEW, Quarterly Journal of the Indian Fencing Association. July 1896 to July 1898. 7 Parts. Rs. 5.

THE FIGHTING RACES OF INDIA. By P. D. Bonarjee, Assistant in the Military Department of the Government of India. Crown 8vo, cloth. Rs. 5.

CLOWE'S NAVAL POCKET BOOK. Edited by L. G. Carr Laughton. Containing full list of Battleships, Ironclads, Gunboats, Cruisers, Torpedo Boats, a list of Dry Docks and other valuable information concerning All the Navies of the World, corrected to February 1900. Fifth year of issue. 16mo, cloth. 5*s. net.* Rs. 5; cash Rs. 4-6.

"A handy volume for use anywhere and everywhere—surprisingly accurate—a marvel of cheapness."—*Naval and Military Record.*

THE IMPERIAL RUSSIAN NAVY. With 150 Illustrations from Drawings and Sketches by the Author, and from Photographs. By Fred. T. Jane. Royal 8vo, cloth, gilt. 30*s. net.* Rs. 30; cash, Rs. 26-4.

THE TORPEDO IN PEACE AND WAR, with about 30 full-page and a great many smaller Illustrations, the greater part being reproductions of sketches on board Torpedo craft by the Author. By Fred. T. Jane. Oblong folio, cloth. 10*s.* 6*d.* Rs. 9-3; cash, Rs. 7-14.

"Mr. Jane describes the social side of torpedo life as no one has ever done before. . . . . Mr. Jane's clever illustrations add greatly to the charm of this bright and fresh book."—*London Quarterly Review.*

WORKS ON HINDUSTANI.

By Lieut.-Col. RANKING, B.A., M.D.

A GUIDE TO HINDUSTANI. SPECIALLY DESIGNED FOR THE USE OF Officers and Men serving in India. Containing Colloquial Sentences in Persian and Roman Character, and in English; also a Series of Arzis in Urdu written character with their transliteration in Roman-Urdu, and English translations. By GEO. S. RANKING, B.A., M.D., Lieut.-Col., I. M. S., Secretary to the Board of Examiners, Fort William. Fourth Edition, Revised and Enlarged. Crown 8vo, cloth. Rs. 6.

"The work on the whole, we believe, will meet a want . . . . It contains an excellent list of technical military terms and idioms, and will prove especially serviceable to any one who has to act as an interpreter at courts-martial and cognate enquiries."—*Civil and Military Gazette.*

"There can be no question as to the practical utility of the book."—*Pioneer.*

"Lieut.-Col. Ranking has undoubtedly rendered good service to the many military men for whom knowledge of Hindustani is essential."—*Athenæum.*

"Has the merit of conciseness and portability, and the selections at the end of the historical and colloquial style, are well chosen."—*Saturday Review.*

A POCKET-BOOK OF COLLOQUIAL URDU. By G. S. A. RANKING, B.A., M.D., Lieut.-Col., I. M. S., Secretary to the Board of Examiners, Fort William. 16mo, cloth. Rs. 2.

INTRODUCTORY EXERCISES IN URDU PROSE COMPOSITION. A Collection of 50 Exercises with Idiomatic Phrases and Grammatical Notes, accompanied by a full Vocabulary and Translation of each passage. By G. S. A. RANKING, B.A., M.D., Lieut.-Col., I. M. S., Secretary to the Board of Examiners. Crown 8vo, cloth. Rs. 5.

"One of the best works on the Urdu language that we have yet seen . . . . the student will find in Dr. Ranking's work a really valuable aid . . . . . . The work is a thoroughly practical one, and explains all the various phrases and intricacies of a language, the acquirement of which is too often neglected by Anglo-Indians from mere prejudice."—*Indian Daily News.*

SPECIMEN PAPERS (ENGLISH AND VERNACULAR) FOR THE LOWER AND Higher Standard Examinations in Hindustani, together with a Résumé of the Regulations for these Examinations for the Guidance of Candidates. Compiled by Lt.-Col., G. S. A. RANKING, B.A., M.D. Lieut. Col., I. M. S., Secretary to the Board of Examiners, Small 4to. boards. Rs. 6.

THACKER, SPINK & CO., CALCUTTA.

HINDUSTANI, PERSIAN, Etc.

HINDUSTANI AS IT OUGHT TO BE SPOKEN. By J. TWEEDIE, BENGAL Civil Service. Third Edition, Revised. Crown 8vo, cloth. Rs. 4-8.

SUPPLEMENT containing Key to the Exercises and Translation of the Reader with Notes. Rs. 2.

The work has been thoroughly Revised and partly Re-written, and much additional matter added. The VOCABULARIES have been improved, and all words used in the book have been embodied in the GLOSSARIES, ENGLISH HINDUSTANI — HINDUSTANI-ENGLISH. A READER is also given, and a GENERAL INDEX to the whole book.

"The Young Civilian or Officer, reading for his Examination, could not do better than master this Revised Edition from cover to cover."—*Indian Daily News.*

GRAMMAR OF THE URDU OR HINDUSTANI LANGUAGE IN ITS ROMANIZED CHARACTER. By GEORGE SMALL, M.A. Crown 8vo. cloth limp. Rs. 5.

"We recommend it to those who wish to gain a more scientific knowledge of Urdu than the ordinary primers afford."—*Indian Churchman.*

"The manual altogether deserves high commendation for the lucidity with which it explains the essentials of Urdu."—*Athenæum.*

ANGLO-URDU MEDICAL HANDBOOK OR HINDUSTANI GUIDE. FOR the use of Medical Practitioners (male and female) in Northern India. By Revd. GEORGE SMALL, M.A. With the aid of Surgn.-General C. R. FRANCIS, M.B., and of Mrs. FRASER NASH, L.R.C.P. Crown 8vo, cloth limp. Rs. 5.

"This handbook should prove invaluable for use in schools and colleges where surgeons, missionaries and nurses are being trained for work in the East."—*Home News.*

"Ought to find a place on every planter's office shelf. In treating coolies and others employed on gardens it would be invaluable."—*Indian Planters' Gazette.*

GLOSSARY OF MEDICAL AND MEDICO-LEGAL TERMS INCLUDING those most frequently met with in the Law Courts. By R. F. HUTCHINSON, M.D., Surgeon-Major. Second Edition. Fcap. 8vo, cloth. Rs. 2.

A HANDBOOK TO THE KAITHI CHARACTER. By G. A. GRIERSON, C.I.E., I.C.S., PH.D. Second Edition. Quarto. Rs. 6.

TRANSLATIONS INTO PERSIAN. SELECTIONS FROM *Murray's History of India, Foliorum Centuria—Gibbon's Roman Empire—Our Faithful Ally the Nizam.* By Major Sir A. C. TALBOT. Part I, English. Part II, Persian. 2 vols. 8vo, cloth. Rs. 10.

TWO CENTURIES OF BHARTRIHARI. TRANSLATED INTO ENGLISH Verse by C. H. TAWNEY, M.A. Fcap. 8vo, cloth. Rs. 2.

PUSHTO GRAMMAR. By Genl. Sir J. L. VAUGHAN. New Edition. Revised. [*In the press.*

THE RUSSIAN CONVERSATION GRAMMAR. BY ALEX. KINLOCH, late Interpreter to H. B. M. Consulate and British Consul in the Russian Law Courts; Instructor for Official Examinations. With Key to the Exercises. Crown 8vo, cloth. 9*s*. Rs. 7-14; cash, Rs. 6-12.

This work is constructed on the excellent system of Otto in his "German Conversation Grammar," with illustrations accompanying every rule, in the form of usual phrases and idioms, thus leading the student by easy but rapid gradations to a colloquial attainment of the language.

MALAVIKAGNIMITRA. A SANSKRIT PLAY BY KALIDASA. LITERALLY translated into English Prose by C. H. TAWNEY, M.A., Principal, Presidency College, Calcutta. Second Edition. Crown 8vo, sewed. Re. 1-8.

BOOK-KEEPING AND OFFICE MANUALS.

GUIDE TO BOOK-KEEPING. By SINGLE AND DOUBLE ENTRY, including the Solution of Several Exercises of every Variety of Transactions which occur in the Course of Business. Answers to Questions in Book-Keeping set to candidates for promotion to Assistant Examiner, 1st Grade, and Accountant, 2nd Grade, from 1881 to 1898. By S. GEORGE, Late Chief Accountant of the Public Works Department, Bengal. New and Enlarged Edition. Demy 8vo, cloth. Rs. 4.

THE GOVERNMENT OFFICE MANUAL. A GUIDE TO THE DUTIES, Privileges and Responsibilities of the Government Service in all Grades By CHARLES HARDLESS. Crown 8vo, sewed. Rs. 2.

THE CLERK'S MANUAL. A COMPLETE GUIDE TO GENERAL OFFICE Routine (Government and Business). By CHARLES R. HARDLESS. Second Edition. Revised. 12mo, boards. Rs. 2.

SPENS' INDIAN READY RECKONER. CONTAINING TABLES FOR ascertaining the value of any number of articles, &c., from three pies to five rupees; also Tables of Wages from four annas to twenty-five rupees By Captain A. T. SPENS. 12mo, cloth. Re. 1-8.

PHONOGRAPHY IN BENGALI. BY DWIJENDRA NATH SHINGHAW, Professor of Phonography in Calcutta. Being a Handbook for the study of Shorthand on the principle of Pitman's System. 12mo, sewed. As. 8. With a Key. 12mo. As. 4 extra.

SIMPLEX CALCULATOR FOR THE HARDWARE TRADE OF INDIA. FOR ASCERTAINING THE VALUE OF any given numbers or weights of stores or materials from 1 to 111 in number. or from 1 lb. to 111 cwts. 3 qrs. 27 lbs. weight at varying rates per cwt. or per unit. Compiled by WALTER E. BAKER. Large 4to, cloth. Rs. 15, or bound in two volumes. Rs. 16.

EDUCATIONAL BOOKS.

THE ELEMENTS OF ARITHMETIC. By GOOROO DASS BANERJEE, M.A., D.L. Sixth Edition, Revised and Enlarged. Crown 8vo, cloth. Re. 1-8.

A COMPANION READER TO "HINTS ON THE STUDY OF ENGLISH." (Eighteenth Thousand.) Demy 8vo, sewed. Re. 1-4; Key, Rs. 2.

ENTRANCE TEST EXAMINATION QUESTIONS AND ANSWERS IN English, being the Questions appended to "Hints on the Study of English," with their Answers, together with Fifty Supplementary Questions and Answers. By W. T. WEBB, M.A. 12mo, sewed. Re. 1.

MANUAL OF DEDUCTIVE LOGIC. BY PROFESSOR M. M. CHATTERJEE. Crown 8vo. [*In the press*

THE INDIAN LETTER-WRITER. CONTAINING AN INTRODUCTION ON Letter Writing, with numerous Examples in the various styles of Correspondence. By H. ANDERSON. Crown 8vo, cloth. Re. 1.

PRINCIPAL EVENTS IN INDIAN AND BRITISH HISTORY. WITH their Dates in Suggestive Sentences. In Two Parts. By MISS ADAMS, La Martinière College for Girls, Calcutta. Second Edition. Crown 8vo, boards. Re. 1.

AN ANALYSIS OF HAMILTON'S LECTURES ON METAPHYSICS. With Dissertations and Copious Notes. By W. C. FINK. 8vo, boards. Rs. 2.

PROJECTION OF MAPS. By R. SINCLAIR. With Diagrams. Foolscap 8vo, boards. Rs. 2.

ENGLISH SELECTIONS APPOINTED BY THE SYNDICATE OF THE CALcutta University for the Entrance Examination. Crown 8vo, cloth. Re. 1-8.

THE LAWS OF WEALTH. A PRIMER ON POLITICAL ECONOMY FOR the Middle Classes in India. By HORACE BELL, C.E. Seventh Thousand. Fcap. 8vo, sewed. As. 8.

CALCUTTA UNIVERSITY CALENDAR FOR THE YEAR 1900. CONtaining Acts, Bye-Laws, Regulations, The University Rules for Examination, Text-Book Endowments, Affiliated Institutions, List of Graduates and Under-Graduates, Examination Papers, 1899. Cloth. Rs. 5.

CALENDAR for previous years. *Each* Rs. 5.

THE PRINCIPLES OF HEAT. FOR THE F. A. EXAMINATION OF THE Calcutta University. By LEONARD HALL, M.A. Crown 8vo. As. 8.

FIFTY GRADUATED PAPERS IN ARITHMETIC, ALGEBRA, AND GEOmetry for the use of Students preparing for the Entrance Examinations of the Indian Universities. With Hints on Methods of Shortening Work and on the Writing of Examination Papers. By W. H. WOOD, B.A., F.C.S., Principal, La Martinière College. Crown 8vo, sewed. Re. 1-8.

THE ENGLISH PEOPLE AND THEIR LANGUAGE. Translated from the German of Loth. By C. H. TAWNEY, M.A., Professor in the Presidency College, Calcutta. Crown 8vo, stitched. As. 8.

TALES FROM INDIAN HISTORY. BEING THE ANNALS OF INDIA re-told in Narratives. By J. TALBOYS WHEELER. School Edition. Crown 8vo, cloth Re. 1-8.

A NOTE ON THE DEVANAGARI ALPHABET FOR BENGALI Students. By GURU DAS BANERJEE, M.A., D.L. Crown 8vo, sewed. As. 4.

THE GOVERNMENT OF INDIA. A PRIMER FOR INDIAN SCHOOLS. By HORACE BELL, C.E. Third Edition. Fcap. 8vo, sewed, As. 8; in cloth, Re. 1.

Translated into Bengali. By J. N. BHATTACHARJEE. 8vo. As. 12.

AN INQUIRY INTO THE HUMAN MIND ON THE PRINCIPLES OF Common Sense. By THOMAS REID, D.D. 8vo, cloth. Re. 1-4.

ANALYSIS OF REID'S ENQUIRY INTO THE HUMAN MIND. WITH Copious Notes. By W. C. FINK. Second Edition. Re. 1-12.

NOTES ON MILL'S EXAMINATION OF HAMILTON'S PHILOSOPHY. By THOMAS EDWARDS, F.E.I.S. Fcap. sewed. Re. 1.

A TEXT-BOOK OF INDIAN BOTANY: MORPHOLOGICAL, PHYSIOLOGICAL, and Systematic. By W. H. GREGG, B.M.S., Lecturer on Botany at the Hugli Government College. Profusely Illustrated. Crown 8vo, cloth. Rs. 5.

A MORAL READING BOOK FROM ENGLISH AND ORIENTAL SOURCES. By Sir ROPER LETHBRIDGE, C.I.E., M.A. Crown 8vo, cloth. As. 14.

A PRIMER CATECHISM OF SANITATION FOR INDIAN SCHOOLS. Founded on Dr. Cunningham's Sanitary Primer. By L. A. STAPLEY. Second Edition. 18mo, sewed. As. 4.

A SHORT HISTORY OF THE ENGLISH LANGUAGE. By THOMAS EDWARDS, F.E.I.S. 18mo. Re. 1-4.

LAMB'S TALES FROM SHAKESPEARE. AN EDITION IN GOOD TYPE. 12mo. Paper cover. As. 6.

Works on Indian Law.

LAND TENURES AND LAND REVENUE.

KEDAR NATH ROY.—THE LAW OF RENT AND REVENUE OF Bengal. By KEDARNATH ROY, M.A., B.L., C.S., District and Sessions Judge of Pubna; being the Bengal Tenancy Act, Patni Laws and other Revenue Acts, with Notes, Annotations, Judicial Rulings, and Rules of the Local Government, High Court and Board of Revenue. Third Edition. With Supplement, the Bengal Tenancy Act Amendment, 1898. Royal 8vo, cloth. Rs. 10.

AZIZUDDIN AHMED.—THE N.-W. PROVINCES LAND REVENUE Act. Being Act XIX of 1873 as amended by Acts I and VIII of 1879, XII of 1881, XIII and XIV of 1882, XX of 1890, and XII of 1891. With Notes, Government Orders, Board Circulars and Decisions, and Rulings of the Allahabad High Court. By AZIZUDDIN AHMED, Deputy Collector and Magistrate. Demy 8vo, cloth. Rs. 8.

BEVERLEY.—THE LAND ACQUISITION ACTS (ACTS I OF 1894 AND XVIII of 1885, Mines). With Introduction and Notes. The whole forming a complete Manual of Law and Practice on the subject of Compensation for Lands taken for Public Purposes. Applicable to all India. By H. BEVERLEY, M.A., B.C.S. Third Edition. Demy 8vo, cloth. Rs. 6.

FORSYTH.—REVENUE SALE-LAW OF LOWER BENGAL, COMPRISING Act XI of 1859; Bengal Act VII of 1868; Bengal Act VII of 1880 (Public Demands Recovery Act), and the unrepealed Regulations and the Rules of the Board of Revenue on the subject. With Notes. Edited by WM. E. H. FORSYTH. Demy 8vo, cloth. Rs. 5.

REYNOLDS.—THE NORTH-WESTERN PROVINCES RENT ACT. With Notes, &c. By H. W. REYNOLDS, C.S. Demy 8vo. [1886.] Rs. 7.

MOOKERJEE.—THE LAW OF PERPETUITIES IN BRITISH INDIA. By the Hon. ASUTOSH MOOKERJEE, M.A., LL.D. Tagore Law Lectures, 1898. [*In the press.*

THACKER, SPINK & CO., CALCUTTA.

FIELD.—LANDHOLDING, AND THE RELATION OF LANDLORD AND Tenant in various countries of the world. By C. D. FIELD, M.A., LL.D. Second Edition. Royal 8vo, cloth. Rs. 17-12.

FIELD.—INTRODUCTION TO THE REGULATIONS OF THE BENGAL CODE. By C. D. FIELD, M.A., LL.D. Crown 8vo, cloth. Rs. 3.

CONTENTS:—(I) The Acquisition of Territorial Sovereignty by the English in the Presidency of Bengal. (II) The Tenure of Land in the Bengal Presidency. (III) The Administration of the Land Revenue. (IV) The Administration of Justice.

GRIMLEY.—MANUAL OF THE REVENUE SALE LAW AND CERTIFIcate Procedure of Lower Bengal, being Act XI of 1859; Act VII B. C. of 1868; and Act VII B. C. of 1880. The Public Demands Recovery Act, including Selections from the Rules and Circular Orders of the Board of Revenue. With Notes. By W. H. GRIMLEY, B.A., C.S. 8vo. Rs. 5-8; interleaved, Rs. 6.

PHILLIPS.—THE LAW RELATING TO THE LAND TENURES OF Lower Bengal. (Tagore Law Lectures, 1875.) By ARTHUR PHILLIPS. Royal 8vo, cloth. Rs. 8.

REGULATIONS OF THE BENGAL CODE. A SELECTION INTENDED chiefly for the use of Candidates for appointments in the Judicial and Revenue Departments. Royal 8vo, stitched. Rs. 4.

PHILLIPS.—OUR ADMINISTRATION OF INDIA: BEING A COMPLETE Account of the Revenue and Collectorate Administration in all departments, with special reference to the work and duties of a District Officer in Bengal. By H. A. D. PHILLIPS. Crown 8vo, cloth. Rs. 4-4.

"In eleven chapters Mr. Phillips gives a complete epitome of the civil, in distinction from the criminal, duties of an Indian Collector." —*London Quarterly Review.*

WHISH.—A DISTRICT OFFICE IN NORTHERN INDIA. WITH SOME Suggestions on Administration. By C. W. WHISH, B.C.S. Demy 8vo, cloth. Rs. 4.

MITRA.—THE LAND LAW OF BENGAL. By SARADA CHARAN MITRA, M.A., B.L. Being the Tagore Law Lectures for 1885. Royal 8vo, cloth. Rs. 12.

MARKBY.—LECTURES ON INDIAN LAW. By WILLIAM MARKBY, M.A. Crown 8vo, cloth. Rs. 3.

CONTENTS:—(I) Resumption of Lands held Rent-free. (II) The Revenue Sale Land of the Permanently: Settled Districts. (III) Shekust Pywust, or Alluvion and Diluvian. (IV-V) The Charge of the Person and Property of Minors. (VI) Of the Protection afforded to Purchasers and Mortgagees when their title is impeached. Appendix—The Permanent Settlement—Glossary.

HOUSE.—THE N.-W. PROVINCES RENT ACT: BEING ACT XII of 1881, as amended by subsequent Acts. Edited with Introduction, Commentary and Appendices. By H. F. HOUSE, C.S. 8vo, cloth. Rs. 10.

CIVIL LAW.

HOLMWOOD.—THE LAW AND PRACTICE OF REGISTRATION IN BENGAL: comprising the History, Statute Law, Judicial Rulings, Rules and Circular Orders of Government; Extracts and Rules under the Bengal Tenancy Act regarding Registration; The Stamp Law, with a Digest of Rulings and a List of Registration Districts and Sub-Districts. By H. HOLMWOOD, I.C.S., recently Registrar-General of Assurances, Bengal. Royal 8vo, cloth. Rs. 12.

ALEXANDER.—INDIAN CASE-LAW ON TORTS. By THE LATE R. D. ALEXANDER, C.S. Fourth Edition. Edited and brought up to date by P. L. BUCKLAND, Bar.-at-Law. Demy 8vo, cloth. Rs. 8.

MORISON.—THE INDIAN ARBITRATION ACT: BEING ACT IX OF 1899. With Explanatory Notes and Index, together with all the Statutory Provisions of a general nature in force in British India relating to the Law of Arbitration. By H. N. MORISON, Bar.-at-Law.

[*In the press.*

CHALMERS.—THE LAW RELATING TO NEGOTIABLE INSTRUMENTS IN BRITISH INDIA. By M. D. CHALMERS, M.A., Bar.-at-Law. Second Edition. By A. CASPERSZ, Bar.-at-Law. Demy 8vo, cloth. Rs. 7-8.

CHAUDHURI.—THE COOLIE ACT (XIII OF 1859.) WITH RULINGS, Circular Orders of the High Courts, Notes, Form of Labour Contract, and of a Book, Section 492, Indian Penal Code, and Settlement Rules of Assam, Fines for Payment of Arrears, List of Last Day of Payment of Revenue, and Commentaries on Section 492, I. P. C., &c. By PROKASH C. D. CHAUDHURI, Mukhtar. Third Edition. 8vo., cloth. Rs. 5.

COLLETT.—THE LAW OF SPECIFIC RELIEF IN INDIA. BEING a Commentary on Act I of 1877. By CHARLES COLLETT, late of the Madras Civil Service, of Lincoln's Inn, Bar.-at-Law, and formerly a Judge of the High Court at Madras. Third Edition, Revised and brought up to date. By H. N. MORISON, Bar.-at-Law. Demy 8vo, cloth. [*In the press.*

KELLEHER.—PRINCIPLES OF SPECIFIC PERFORMANCE AND MISTAKE. By J. KELLEHER, C.S. Demy 8vo, cloth. Rs. 8.

WOODROFFE.—THE LAW OF INJUNCTIONS AND RECEIVERS. By J. G. WOODROFFE, M.A., Bar.-at-Law, Tagore Law Lecturer, 1897.

Vol. I. Injunctions. Rs. 12.

Vol. 2. Receivers. *In preparation.*

PEACOCK.—THE LAW RELATING TO EASEMENTS IN BRITISH India. By F. PEACOCK, Bar.-at-Law, Tagore Law Lecturer, 1898-99. [*In the press.*

GHOSE.—THE LAW OF MORTGAGE IN INDIA WITH THE TRANSfer of Property Act and Notes. By the Hon'ble RASH BEHARI GHOSE, M.A., D.L. Third Edition. Re-written and Enlarged. [*In the press*

KELLEHER.—MORTGAGE IN THE CIVIL LAW: BEING AN OUTLINE of the Principles of the Law of Security, followed by the text of the Digest of Justinian, with Translation and Notes; and a Translation of the corresponding titles from the Italian Code. By J. KELLEHER, B.C.S., Author of "Possession in the Civil Law." Royal 8vo, cloth. Rs. 10.

KELLEHER.—POSSESSION IN THE CIVIL LAW. ABRIDGED FROM the Treatise of Von Savigny, to which is added the Text of the Title on Possession from the Digest. With Notes. By J. KELLEHER, C.S. Demy 8vo, cloth. Rs. 8.

CASPERSZ.—ESTOPPEL BY REPRESENTATION AND RES JUDICATA IN BRITISH INDIA. Part I—Modern or Equitable Estoppel. Part II—Estoppel by Judgment. Being the Tagore Law Lectures, 1893. By A. CASPERSZ, B.A., Bar.-at-Law. Second Edition. Royal 8vo, cloth. Rs. 12.

MITRA.—THE LAW OF JOINT PROPERTY AND PARTITION IN BRITISH INDIA. By RAM CHARAN MITRA, M.A., B.L., Vakil, High Court, Calcutta, being the Tagore Law Lectures for 1895. Royal 8vo, cloth. Rs. 12.

THE INDIAN INSOLVENCY ACT: BEING A REPRINT OF THE LAW AS to Insolvent Debtors in India, 11 and 12 Vict., Cap. 21 (June 1848). Royal 8vo, sewed. (Uniform with Acts of the Legislative Council.) Re. 1-8.

POLLOCK.—THE LAW OF FRAUD, MISREPRESENTATION AND MISTAKE IN BRITISH INDIA. By Sir FREDERICK POLLOCK, Bart., Bar.-at-Law, Professor of Jurisprudence, Oxford. Being the Tagore Law Lectures, 1894. Royal 8vo, cloth gilt. Rs. 10.

GOUR.—THE TRANSFER OF PROPERTY IN BRITISH INDIA: Being a Commentary on the Transfer of Property Act (Act IV of 1882 as amended by subsequent Acts to date). With a Chapter on Transfer by Partition, and a Collection of Precedents, a full Report of the Law Commissioners and the Legislative Council, &c. By H. S. GOUR, M.A., Barrister-at-Law. Demy 8vo. [*In the press.*

HAWKINS.—A MANUAL OF THE INDIAN ARMS ACT (Act XI of 1878). With Notes and Rules and Orders of the Imperial and Local Governments on the subject. By W. Hawkins. Second Edition. Demy 8vo, cloth. Rs. 7-8.

RIVAZ.—THE INDIAN LIMITATION ACT (Act XV of 1877) as amended to date. With Notes. By the Hon'ble H. T. Rivaz, Bar.-at-Law, Judge of the High Court of the Punjab. Fifth Edition. Edited by P. L. Buckland, Esq., Bar.-at-Law. Royal 8vo, cloth. [*In the Press.*

SUCCESSION, ADMINISTRATION, Etc.

FORSYTH.—THE PROBATE AND ADMINISTRATION ACT: Being Act V of 1881. With Notes. By W. E. H. Forsyth. Edited, with Index, by F. J. Collinson. Demy 8vo, cloth. Rs. 5.

HENDERSON.—TESTAMENTARY SUCCESSION and Administration of Intestate Estates in India. Being a Commentary on the Indian Succession Act (X of 1865), The Hindu Wills Act (XXI of 1870), The Probate and Administration Act (V of 1881), &c., with Notes and Cross References and a General Index. By Gilbert S. Henderson, M.A., Bar.-at-Law, and Advocate of the High Court at Calcutta. Second Edition, Revised. Royal 8vo, cloth. Rs. 16.

HENDERSON.—THE LAW OF TESTAMENTARY DEVISE, as Administered in India, or the Law relating to Wills in India. With an Appendix, containing:—The Indian Succession Act (X of 1865), the Hindu Wills Act (XXI of 1870), the Probate and Administration Act (V of 1881), with all amendments, the Probate and Administration Act (VI of 1889), and the Certificate of Succession Act (VII of 1889). By G. S. Henderson, M.A., Bar.-at-Law. (Tagore Law Lectures, 1887). Royal 8vo, cloth. Rs. 16.

CIVIL PROCEDURE, SMALL CAUSE COURT, etc.

MACEWEN.—**THE PRACTICE OF THE PRESIDENCY COURT OF** SMALL CAUSES OF CALCUTTA, under the Presidency Small Cause Courts Act (XV of 1882). With Notes and an Appendix. By R. S. T. MACEWEN, of Lincoln's Inn, Bar.-at-Law, one of the late Judges of the Presidency Court of Small Causes of Calcutta. Thick Demy 8vo, cloth. Rs. 10.

BROUGHTON.—**THE CODE OF CIVIL PROCEDURE:** BEING ACT X of 1877. With Notes, Appendix and Supplement, bringing it up to 1883. By L. P. DELVES BROUGHTON, of Lincoln's Inn, Bar.-at-Law. Assisted by W. F. AGNEW and G. S. HENDERSON, Bars.-at-Law. Royal 8vo, cloth. Rs. 7.

POCKET CODE OF CIVIL LAW. CONTAINING THE CIVIL PROCEDURE Code (Act XIV of 1882), The Court-Fees Act (VII of 1870), The Evidence Act (I of 1872), The Specific Relief Act (I of 1877), The Registration Act (III of 1877), The Limitation Act (XV of 1877), The Stamp Act (I of 1879). With Supplement containing the Amending Act of 1888, and a General Index. Fcap. 8vo, cloth. Rs. 4.

LOCAL SELF-GOVERNMENT.

STERNDALE.—**MUNICIPAL WORK IN INDIA;** OR, HINTS ON SANITATION, General Conservancy and Improvement in Municipalities, Towns and Villages. By R. C. STERNDALE. Crown 8vo, cloth. Rs. 3.

COLLIER.—**THE BENGAL LOCAL SELF-GOVERNMENT HANDBOOK.** Being Act III of 1885, B. C., and the General Rules framed thereunder. With Notes, Hints regarding Procedure, and References to Leading Cases, an Appendix, containing the principal Acts referred to, &c., &c. By F. R. STANLEY COLLIER, B.C.S. Fourth Edition. [*In preparation.*

COLLIER.—THE BENGAL MUNICIPAL MANUAL: BEING B. C. ACT III of 1884 as amended by B. C. Acts, III of 1886, IV of 1894 and II of 1896, and other Laws relating to Municipalities in Bengal with Rules, Circular Orders by the Local Government and Notes. By F. R. STANLEY COLLIER, C.S. Fifth Edition. [*In preparation.*

CRIMINAL LAW.

AGNEW.—THE INDIAN PENAL CODE, TO WHICH IS APPENDED THE Acts of the Governor-General in Council relating to Criminal Offences in India, with a complete Commentary and Addenda including Act IV of 1898. By W. F. AGNEW, Esq., Bar.-at-Law, Recorder of Rangoon. Royal 8vo, cloth. Rs. 14.

HAMILTON.—INDIAN PENAL CODE: WITH A COMMENTARY. By W. R. HAMILTON, Bar.-at-Law, Presidency Magistrate, Bombay. Royal 8vo, cloth. Rs. 16.

POCKET PENAL, CRIMINAL PROCEDURE AND POLICE CODES: Also the Whipping Act and the Railway Servants' Act, being Acts XIV of 1860 (with Amendments), V of 1898, V of 1861, VI of 1864, and XXXI of 1867 and XI of 1886. With a General Index. Revised 1898. Fcap. 8vo, cloth. Rs. 4.

MAXWELL.—INTRODUCTION TO THE DUTIES OF MAGISTRATES and Justices of the Peace in India. By Sir P. BENSON MAXWELL. Specially edited for India by the Hon'ble L. P. DELVES BROUGHTON. Royal 8vo, cloth. Rs. 12.

THE INDIAN CRIMINAL DIGEST. CONTAINING ALL THE IMPORTANT Criminal Rulings of the various High Courts in India, together with many English Cases which bear on the Criminal Law as Administered in India. In Four Parts: I—Indian Penal Code. II—Evidence. III—Criminal Procedure. IV—Special and Local Acts. By J. T. HUME, Solicitor, High Court, Calcutta, in charge of Government Prosecutions. Royal 8vo, cloth. Vol. I.—1862 to 1884. Rs. 7. Vol. II.—1885 to 1893. Rs. 7-8.

PHILLIPS.—COMPARATIVE CRIMINAL JURISPRUDENCE. Showing the Law, Procedure, and Case-Law of other Countries, arranged under the corresponding sections of the Indian Codes. By H. A. D. Phillips, B.C.S. Vol. I—Crimes and Punishments. Vol. II—Procedure and Police. Demy 8vo, cloth. In two volumes. Rs. 12.

TOYNBEE.—CHAUKIDARI MANUAL. Being Act VI (B. C.) of 1870, as amended by Acts I (B. C.) of 1871, 1886, and 1892. With Notes, Rules, Government Orders and Inspection Notes. By G. Toynbee, C.S., Magistrate of Hooghly. Third Edition, Revised. With additions to 1896. Crown 8vo, cloth. Re. 1-8 ; paper, Re. 1.

SWINHOE (C.)—THE CASE-NOTED PENAL CODE, and other Acts. Act XLV of 1860 as amended, with References to all Reported Cases decided under each section. By the late Charlton Swinhoe, Bar.-at-Law. Crown 8vo. cloth. Rs. 7.

SWINHOE (D.)—THE CASE-NOTED CRIMINAL PROCEDURE CODE (Act V of 1898). By Dawes Swinhoe, Bar.-at-Law, and Advocate of the High Court, Calcutta, with head Notes of all the Cases collected under each section and with Cross-references when reported under more than one section. [*In the press.*

EVIDENCE.

STEPHEN.—THE PRINCIPLES OF JUDICIAL EVIDENCE. An Introduction to the Indian Evidence Act, 1872. By Sir James Fitz-James Stephen, formerly Legislative Member of the Supreme Council of India. Crown 8vo, cloth. Rs. 3.

AMEER ALI AND WOODROFFE.—THE LAW OF EVIDENCE. Applicable to British India. By Syed Ameer Ali, M.A., C.I.E., Bar.-at-Law, Judge of the High Court of Judicature; and J. G. Woodroffe, M.A., B.C.L., Bar.-at-Law. Second Edition. Demy 8vo. cloth. [*In the press.*

MEDICAL JURISPRUDENCE.

GRIBBLE.—OUTLINES OF MEDICAL JURISPRUDENCE FOR INDIA. By J. D. B. Gribble, M.C.S. (Retired), & Patrick Hehir, M.D., F.R.C.S.E. Third Edition, Revised, Enlarged, and Annotated. Demy 8vo. Rs. 5-8.

LYON.—MEDICAL JURISPRUDENCE FOR INDIA. By J. B. Lyon F.C.S. Third edition by Major L. A. Waddell, I.M.S. [*In the press*.

DIGESTS.

MITRA.—A DIGEST OF PRIVY COUNCIL CASES, from 1825 to 1897, on appeal from the High Courts of Calcutta, Madras, Bombay, and Allahabad, The Chief Court of Punjab, The Court of the Judicial Commissioner of the Central Provinces, The Recorder of Rangoon, &c., &c. By A. C. Mitra, Bar.-at-Law. Fourth Edition. Royal 8vo. Rs. 10.

WOODMAN.—A DIGEST OF THE INDIAN LAW REPORTS and of the Reports of the cases heard in Appeal by the Privy Council with an Index of Cases. Compiled by J. V. Woodman, Bar.-at-Law. Sup. Royal 8vo.

Vol. VI, 1887—1889. Rs. 12. Vol. VII, 1890—1893. Rs. 16.
Vol. VIII, 1894—1897. Rs. 16.

HINDU AND MAHOMMEDAN LAW.

COWELL.—A SHORT TREATISE ON HINDU LAW as administered in the Courts of British India. By Herbert Cowell, Bar.-at-Law, Author of "The History and Constitution of the Courts and Legislative Authorities in India." Demy 8vo, cloth. Rs. 6.

BANERJEE.—THE HINDU LAW OF MARRIAGE AND STRIDHANA. By the Hon'ble GURUDASS BANERJEE, M.A., D.L. Second Edition, Revised. Royal 8vo, cloth. Rs. 10.

SARASWATI.-THE HINDU LAW OF ENDOWMENTS. BEING THE Tagore Law Lectures, 1892. BY PANDIT PRANNATH SARASWATI, M.A., B.L. Royal 8vo, cloth. Rs. 10.

SARVADHIKARI.—THE PRINCIPLES OF THE HINDU LAW OF Inheritance, together with I—A Description and an enquiry into the origin of the Sraddha Ceremonies; II—An account of the Historical Development of the Law of Succession, from the Vedic period to the present time; III—A Digest of the Text Law and Case Law bearing on the subject of Inheritance. By RAJ KUMAR SARVADHIKARI, B.L. (Tagore Law Lectures, 1880.) Royal 8vo, cloth. Rs. 16.

BHATTACHARJEE.—A COMMENTARY ON HINDU LAW OF IN-heritance, Succession, Partition, Adoption, Marriage, Stridhan, Endowment and Testamentary Disposition. By Pundit JOGENDRO NATH BHATTACHARJEE, M.A., B.L. Second Edition. Demy 8vo, cloth. Rs. 16.

AMEER ALI.—MAHOMMEDAN LAW, VOL. I. By THE HON'BLE SYED AMEER ALI, M.A., C.I.E., Bar.-at-Law. Containing the Law relating to Gifts, Wakfs, Wills, Pre-emption, and Bailment. According to the Hanafi, Mâliki, Shâfeï, and Shiah Schools. With an Introduction on Mahommedan Jurisprudence and Works on Law. (Being the Second Edition of Tagore Law Lectures, 1884.) Royal 8vo, cloth. Rs. 16.

AMEER ALI.—MAHOMMEDAN LAW, VOL. II. By THE HON'BLE SYED AMEER ALI, M.A., C.I.E., Bar.-at-Law. Containing the Law relating to Succession and Status, according to the Hanafi, Mâliki. Shâfeï. Shiah and Mutazala Schools, with Explanatory Notes and an Introduction on the Islâmic system of Law. Being a Second Edition of "The Personal Law of the Mahommedans." Revised. Royal 8vo, cloth. Rs. 14.

These two volumes form a complete Digest of the Mahommedan Law.

THACKER, SPINK & CO., CALCUTTA.

AMEER ALI.—THE STUDENT'S HANDBOOK OF MAHOMMEDAN LAW. By the Hon'ble SYED AMEER ALI, M.A., C.I.E., author of "The Law relating to Gifts, Trusts, &c.," "Personal Law of the Mahommedans," &c., &c. Third Edition, Revised and brought up to date, with Extra Appendices. Crown 8vo, cloth. Rs. 3.

WILSON.—INTRODUCTION TO THE STUDY OF ANGLO-MUHAMMADAN LAW. By Sir ROLAND KNYVET WILSON, Bart., M.A., L.M.M., late Reader in Indian Law to the University of Cambridge, author of "Modern English Law." Demy 8vo, cloth. *7s. 6d.* Rs. 6-9 cash, Rs. 5-10.

WILSON.—A DIGEST OF ANGLO-MUHAMMADAN LAW. SETTING forth in the form of a Code, with full references to modern and ancient authorities, the special Rules now applicable to Muhammadans as such by the Civil Court of British India. With Explanatory Notes and full reference to Modern Case-Law, as well as to the ancient authorities. By Sir ROLAND KNYVET WILSON. Demy 8vo. cloth. 15s Rs. 13-2; cash, Rs. 11-4.

SIRCAR.—MAHOMMEDAN LAW: BEING A DIGEST OF THE LAW applicable principally to the Sunnis of India. By BABU SHAMA CHURN SIRCAR. (Tagore Law Lectures, 1873.) Vol. I. Royal 8vo, cloth. Rs. 9. Vol. II. (Tagore Law Lectures, 1874.) [*Out of print.*

RUMSEY.—AL SIRAJIYYAH; OR, THE MAHOMMEDAN LAW OF INheritance, with Notes and Appendix. By ALMARIC RUMSEY, Bar.-at-Law, Professor of Indian Jurisprudence at King's College, London. Second Edition, Revised, with Additions. Crown 8vo, cloth. Rs. 4-8.

TREVELYAN.—THE LAW RELATING TO MINORS AS ADMINIStered in the Provinces subject to the High Courts of British India, together with the Practice of the Courts of Wards in Bengal, Madras, and the North-Western Provinces. By ERNEST JOHN TREVELYAN Bar.-at-Law. Second Edition, Revised and Enlarged. Royal 8vo, cloth. Rs. 16.

LAW MANUALS, Etc.

COWELL.—THE HISTORY AND CONSTITUTION OF THE COURTS AND LEGISLATIVE AUTHORITIES IN INDIA. Second Edition, Revised. By HERBERT COWELL, Bar.-at-Law. (Being Tagore Law Lectures, 1872.) Demy 8vo, cloth. Rs. 6.

HANDBOOK OF INDIAN LAW. A POPULAR AND CONCISE STATEment of the Law generally in force in British India, designed for non-legal people, on subjects relating to Person and Property. By a Barrister-at-Law and Advocate of the High Court at Calcutta. Crown 8vo. pp. xxiv, 754. Cloth gilt. Rs. 6.

"This handbook is intended primarily to present to the non-legal public and to students an abridgment of the law, criminal and civil, generally in force throughout British India. A short and excellent historical account of legislation and Courts of Law in British India from the time of the East India Company until the present day is embodied in an introduction. The Index is admirable. This book will be of great use to competition-wallahs."—*The Law Journal, December 22nd*, 1894.

"Presenting in a concise, intelligent, and popular form the law in force in British India it should meet the much-felt want of a 'ready lawyer for the office table. A clear and accurate presentment of the law is given on more than a hundred subjects arranged alphabetically, and including such subjects as most nearly concern the mercantile community."—*Capital.*

MORISON.—ADVOCACY AND THE EXAMINATION OF WITNESSES. The work treats of matters of practice such as taking instructions, speech, argument, examination-in-chief and cross-examination, and includes a résumé of the duties and liabilities of Pleaders in India. The Legal Practitioners Act, with the Rules of the High Courts relating to the admission of Pleaders and Mookhtars, appears in the form of an Appendix. By H. N. MORISON, Bar.-at-Law. Crown 8vo, cloth. Rs. 6.

"Undoubtedly juniors and, possibly, not a few seniors too, may profit by the sensible and practical hints Mr. Morison gives as to the *finesse* of Counsel, and the treatment of witnesses . . . . Mr. Morison's book is certainly one that should be bought."—*Statesman.*

UPTON.—**HANDBOOK ON THE LAW OF INTEREST ON DEBTS AND** Loans in India. By EDMUND UPTON, Solicitor and Attorney. Demy 8vo, cloth. Rs. 2-8.

CURRIE.—**THE INDIAN LAW EXAMINATION MANUAL.** By FENDALL CURRIE, of Lincoln's Inn, Bar.-at-Law. Fourth Edition, Revised. Demy 8vo. [1892.] Rs. 5.

CONTENTS:—Introduction—Hindoo Law—Mahommedan Law—Indian Penal Code—Code of Civil Procedure—Evidence Act—Limitation Act—Succession Act—Contract Act—Registration Act—Stamp and Court-Fees Acts—Mortgage—Code of Criminal Procedure—The Easements Act—The Trust Act—The Transfer of Property Act—The Negotiable Instruments Act.

GRIMLEY.—**THE SEA CUSTOMS LAW OF INDIA (ACT VIII OF** 1878) with Notes, and the Tariff Act of 1894. By W. H. GRIMLEY, I.C.S. late Secretary to the Board of Revenue, Calcutta. 8vo, cloth. Rs. 7-8.

LEGISLATIVE ACTS OF THE GOVERNOR-GENERAL OF INDIA. COUNCIL, 1899. With Table of Contents and Index. In continuation of Acts from 1834 to the present time. Royal 8vo, cloth. Rs. 5.

[*Previous Volumes available.*

DONOGH.—**THE STAMP LAW OF BRITISH INDIA.** AS CONSTITUTED by the Indian Stamp Act (II of 1899), Rulings and Circular Orders of all the High Courts, Notifications, Resolutions, Rules, and Orders of the Government of India and of the various Local Governments, together with Schedules of all the Stamp Duties chargeable on Instruments in India from the earliest times. Edited, with Notes and complete Index, by WALTER R. DONOGH, M.A., of the Inner Temple, Bar.-at-Law. Second Edition. Demy 8vo, cloth, gilt. Rs. 10.

RIDGE.—**THE INDIAN STAMP ACT, 1899.** WITH A COPIOUS INDEX, Notes, the Report of the Select Committee and Appendices, containing the Principal Notifications issued under Act II of 1899 for British India, and under Act I of 1879 for British Baluchistan of the Agency Territories regulating the Sale, &c., of Stamps, &c., &c. Compiled by G. R. RIDGE, Superintendent, Publication Branch, Legislative Department, India. Demy 8vo, cloth. Rs. 3-8.

CARNEGY.—**KACHARI TECHNICALITIES.** A GLOSSARY OF TERMS, Rural, Official and General, in daily use in the Courts of Law, and in illustration of the Tenures, Customs, Arts, and Manufactures of Hindustan. By P. CARNEGY. Second Edition. Demy 8vo, cloth. Rs. 9.

BHATTACHARJEE.—**ZEMINDAREE MANUAL**: A GUIDE TO THE Management of large Estates in Bengal, with an Appendix containing all the Legislative Enactments relating to Land Revenue with the principal Rulings of the High Court thereon, Orders of the Board of Revenue, &c., &c. By JOGENDRA NATH BHATTACHARJEE, M.A., D.L. Royal 8vo, cloth, gilt. Rs. 16.

JOURNALS

Printed and Published by Messrs. THACKER, SPINK & CO.

INDIAN MEDICAL GAZETTE.

THE JOURNAL OF THE INDIAN MEDICAL SERVICE.

A Record of Medicine, Surgery and Public Health, and of General Medical Intelligence, Indian and European, with special Attention to Diseases of Tropical Countries.

Edited by Major W. J. BUCHANAN, B.A., M.B., D.Ph., I. M. S.

Associate-Editors—Lt.-Col. J. MAITLAND, M.D., I. M. S. *Madras;* Lt.-Col. W. K. HATCH, M.B., I. M. S. *Bombay.*

Published monthly. Subscription, Rs. 12 *per annum. Single copy, Re.* 1-4.

The *Indian Medical Gazette* was founded 34 years ago. It is consequently by far the oldest Medical Journal in India, and has earned for itself a world-wide reputation by its solid contribution to Tropical Medicine and Surgery. It is in every way *the most important* representative medium for recording the work and experience of the medical profession in India, and by means of *its Exchanges* with all the leading journals in Great Britain, America and Australia, as well as by its foreign exchanges with leading French, German and Italian medical periodicals, it is enabled to diffuse information on all tropical diseases culled from an unusual variety of sources.

The Gazette is now thoroughly representative of all ranks of the profession in India. The reviews of *Current Medical Literature* are intrusted to medical officers in India with special knowledge and experience of the subject with which they deal: they consist of résumés of the most important contemporary work in the various departments of medicine and are as follows:—**(1) Tropical Medicine**; (2) **Surgery**; (3) **Obstetrics and Gynæcology**; (4) **Special Senses** (Eye, ear, etc.); (5) **Bacteriology and Pathology**; (6) **Public Health and Sanitation**; and (7) **Military Medicine and Surgery.**

"THE EMPRESS."

A Fortnightly Illustrated Magazine of Current Indian Events, Social, Political, Sporting and Dramatic.

Annual Subscription, Rs. 16. Single number, Re. 1.

Specimen copy free on Application.

THACKER, SPINK & CO., CALCUTTA.

INDEX.